FEB   2021

WITHDRAWN

MISSING
EACH
OTHER

MISSING EACH OTHER

HOW TO CULTIVATE MEANINGFUL CONNECTIONS

EDWARD BRODKIN
and ASHLEY PALLATHRA

PUBLICAFFAIRS
New York

PublicAffairs
Hachette Book Group
1290 Avenue of the Americas, New York, NY 10104
www.publicaffairsbooks.com
@Public_Affairs

Printed in the United States of America

First Edition: January 2021

Published by PublicAffairs, an imprint of Perseus Books, LLC, a subsidiary of Hachette Book Group, Inc. The PublicAffairs name and logo is a trademark of the Hachette Book Group.

The Hachette Speakers Bureau provides a wide range of authors for speaking events. To find out more, go to www.hachettespeakersbureau.com or call (866) 376-6591.

The publisher is not responsible for websites (or their content) that are not owned by the publisher.

Library of Congress Cataloging-in-Publication Data

Names: Brodkin, Edward, author. | Pallathra, Ashley, author.
Title: Missing each other: how to cultivate meaningful connections /
    Edward Brodkin and Ashley Pallathra.
Description: New York: PublicAffairs, 2021. | Includes bibliographical references
    and index.
Identifiers: LCCN 2020038457 | ISBN 9781541774018 (hardcover) |
    ISBN 9781541768383 (ebook)
Subjects: LCSH: Social interaction—Psychological aspects. | Mindfulness
    (Psychology) | Listening. | Comprehension. | Self-care, Health.
Classification: LCC HM1111 .B756 2021 | DDC 302—dc23
LC record available at https://lccn.loc.gov/2020038457

ISBNs: 978-1-5417-7401-8 (hardcover); 978-15417-6838-3 (ebook)

LSC-C

Printing 1, 2020

To Our Families

CONTENTS

A NOTE FROM THE AUTHORS

TO ILLUSTRATE THE CONCEPTS we discuss in this book, we use stories from our own lives and from our own clinical practices. To protect the confidentiality of the individuals whose stories we use, we do not use real names or any other identifying information, and many of the stories are based on composites of more than one person.

The information in this book is provided for educational and informational purposes only and is not a substitute for individualized mental health care from a clinician familiar with your specific circumstances. Accordingly, the information in this book should not be used to diagnose or treat any mental health condition, which should be undertaken only by your own health care provider.

This book contains exercises that involve physical activity. You should consult with your physician or primary health care provider before undertaking any exercise program, including the exercises described in this book. Neither the authors nor the publisher will be liable for any injuries or damages resulting from the application of any of the ideas, information, or exercises contained in this book.

A note about COVID-19: Some of the exercises provided in this book involve proximity and/or close contact with a partner. You should follow public health guidelines regarding the necessity for physical distancing during the COVID-19 pandemic, and you should not carry out the exercises involving proximity or close contact if they violate prevailing public health recommendations or the recommendations of your health care provider.

INTRODUCTION

"Only connect! That was the whole of her
sermon. Only connect the prose and the
passion, and both will be exalted, and human
love will be seen at its height. Live in fragments
no longer."

—E. M. FORSTER, *Howards End*[1]

MANY STORIES HAVE BEEN TOLD about extraordinary feats
accomplished by advanced practitioners of meditation or yoga, including the seemingly magical control they have of their own bodies and physiology. If anyone should have such powers, it would
be His Holiness the Dalai Lama, one of the great meditation masters of our time. Once, at a public talk, a close friend of the Dalai
Lama's, Professor Robert Thurman of Columbia University, was
asked very directly about this. Had Professor Thurman ever seen
the Dalai Lama perform a miracle or do something magical? He
didn't know how to answer. He'd seen some remarkable things
happen around the Dalai Lama, but perhaps His Holiness wouldn't

approve if Professor Thurman seemed to exaggerate his abilities or proselytize. As he was mulling over how to reply, Thurman's wife, Nena, also a close friend of His Holiness, spoke up and said that she'd seen him perform *plenty* of miracles. What she meant, she explained, was his ability to give his full attention and focus to each and every person he met. The gentleman, who was hoping to hear a story of some dramatic, unexplained miracle, seemed disappointed with the answer. But Nena insisted that the way His Holiness connects with people *is* miraculous.[2]

The Dalai Lama, Buddhist monk and spiritual leader to millions, is understandably a very busy person who meets with countless people at various events virtually every day. Nevertheless, many observers have described that, in every single social interaction, he engages with people by giving them his complete and total attention. No exceptions. Entering into conversation with him is a unique experience in which you feel completely seen and heard, without distraction. Professor Thurman described this by saying, "normally, when we talk to each other, we reach out to the person over there and communicate with them. With the Dalai Lama, there isn't space between us. He is over here, with us."[3] At first, it might seem inconceivable that someone's style of communication could be considered almost supernatural, a *miracle*, even if that person is the Dalai Lama. How could the ability to connect with another person ever seem outside the realm of ordinary human potential? His abilities seem virtually miraculous because so few people, despite their potential, are able to connect and communicate with people in quite that way.

This kind of connection may seem light years away from the real interactions we observe in our own lives, where we often don't pay more than cursory attention to each other. Most people move through their days chronically stressed and preoccupied with their own thoughts and worries, making them unable to really listen to others for long. With "busy" being the increasingly popular answer to questions about how someone is doing, we often seem to miss each other, like two ships passing in the night—almost touching, but not quite making contact. Even when we do meet, we somehow misunderstand each other, or we talk past one another. Genuine, lasting connections feel elusive. In an era in which technology progressively takes up time and space that had previously been devoted to live, in-person interactions, attunement—the ability to be aware of our own state of mind and body while also tuning in and connecting to another person—is perhaps the most needed, and most neglected, human capacity.

Take a moment to consider your own life and your daily interactions with others. How many work meetings have you attended that seemed to be a waste of time because people were distracted by their devices? Everyone seemed to talk over each other or past each other, and responded not to what the other person said but to what was in their own head. It was as if each participant occupied their own world and remained stuck in their own perspective. How often have you noticed yourself getting lost in those situations, unable to identify how you were feeling or how you were coming across to others? At home, how many times has your child or partner felt lectured at instead of listened to? Other times, maybe it was you who was left feeling disappointed, hurt, or alone, because even those closest to you—friends, family members, partners, children—will not, or cannot, seem to fully tune in to you, listen and understand you, respond to you. How much have you wished for someone who could?

Then there are the constant *pings* of our smartphones and tablets that have conditioned us to attend to texts, emails, social media alerts, and other notifications that seamlessly draw our attention away from each other. Often it's not until we offend our partners or friends by excessively looking at our phones when talking with them that we realize our connection was even broken. Have you ever realized that you missed everything your friend just said to you because you were lost in your own thoughts and were unable to maintain focus on even a brief conversation? You leave the interaction feeling disheartened and guilty, and you promise yourself that you'll do better next time. But when the next time comes, phones get pulled out, our attention fails, and we become distracted yet again. . . .

Maybe that's why encountering someone like the Dalai Lama can be such an emotionally powerful experience. To be seen with consistent interest and attentiveness by another person is an incredibly stimulating and empowering experience that energizes you and inspires you to invest back into the interaction, and to attend to that other person. That positive feedback loop then provides the same feeling back to the person you're interacting with. Even in brief interactions, consistent attunement to one another can leave lasting effects on any relationship. While achieving the power to connect with people like the Dalai Lama may seem beyond reach, there are concrete, progressive strategies that any one of us can implement to attain more of this ability to tune in and engage people with confidence and ease. In this book, we invite you to explore with us the science and art of attunement, and to try some strategies and exercises for developing this ability in yourself.

Our passion for this topic emerged through our work together at the University of Pennsylvania in autism research, which made us aware of the crucial role attunement plays, not just in the lives of people on the autism spectrum, but in *all* our lives. It also made us aware that the study of attunement, in psychology, psychiatry, and neuroscience is still in its infancy. It has, however, started to grow rapidly in recent years. Attunement is something we can feel subjectively in an interaction, but it can be difficult to put our finger on exactly how it works, and how we can get better at it. This realization set us on a journey to delve into the existing research and develop a framework for understanding how attunement works, a framework that is understandable and accessible to people outside of the sciences and mental health professions. In addition to understanding attunement better, we wanted to create something practical—a method for developing attunement that anyone could use. By drawing on our combined years of research and training in fields relevant to attunement—including social neuroscience, psychology, psychiatry, music, mindfulness, Tai Chi, and other martial arts/movement disciplines—we created a set of progressive exercises for developing and practicing the fundamental skills of attunement.

IN THE FALL OF 2014 at the University of Pennsylvania, we set out to explore the questions of how we connect, or fail to connect, with each other. We began from a very different place than the remarkable abilities of the Dalai Lama. We were trying to help people who were facing significant challenges in connecting with others—adults with autism spectrum disorder (ASD). The autism spectrum is part of the neurodiversity of humanity. Neurodiversity is the wide variability among human beings in brain function and behavior. Autistic individuals may be quite gifted and talented in certain areas, yet autism is largely defined by difficulties with social communication and relationships. With funding from the National Institute of Mental Health, we started to develop a novel program to provide autistic adults with support for their social functioning. Many people on the autism spectrum feel lonely and desire connections with others, but they don't know quite how to make them—especially with neurotypical people (people who are not on the spectrum)—and they don't completely understand what makes it so difficult to maintain them. As of 2014, very little work had been done in developing and testing supports and services for autistic adults.

Our challenging task, in this research study, was to determine at which points—in the intricate, complex dance of social interactions and relationships—these adults were having difficulties. We also strove to develop strategies that would help these individuals become more comfortable and capable in interacting with others. We knew that intellectual disability wasn't what was getting in the way, because the group enrolled in our study was not intellectually disabled. Many were college students, college graduates, or working professionals. Our study participants generally had difficulty "reading" social situations or navigating their way through them. For example, they might have difficulty initiating conversations or try to enter a conversation that other people were having at an awkward moment. Or they might keep talking about a topic at great length without realizing that they had monopolized the conversation and had lost the interest of the other person. While any of us might do these things from time to time, in many autistic adults, these are consistent patterns.

What makes it difficult for individuals on the spectrum to navigate typical social interactions? We already had some ideas, based on our clinical experience and previous research. We were familiar with the concept of "social cognition" (understanding other people and interactions), which has been studied at length in psychological science and has been identified as a challenging area for many autistic adults. However, as we worked with the participants in our study, we began to think more and more about an ability that includes social cognition and social skills but goes well beyond each. It's the same ability that the Dalai Lama has developed to such a remarkable degree—an ability to "make contact" with others, not only at a thought level but also at a gut and emotional level, and to stay "in tune" and "in sync" with both the feelings of others and one's own feelings, not just in a single moment of understanding or empathy but over time during the unpredictable twists and turns of an interaction. That ability—what we will call social-emotional attunement, or attunement for short—is what makes the other person feel that you have genuinely connected with them. Attunement is an elusive concept that has not gotten as much attention from researchers as it deserves, although substantial research has been done on the role of attunement in mother-infant interactions.

In more recent years, neuroscience research into "mirror neurons" has begun to suggest possible brain mechanisms of attunement.[4] Moreover, the idea of misattunement between people on the spectrum and neurotypical people is just beginning to gain traction in autism research.[5] For example, attuning with others can be challenging for autistic individuals, due to their difficulties with processing social cues or responding in ways that are considered typical by the wider society. However, it can be equally difficult for neurotypical individuals to understand and connect with people who they are unfamiliar with (e.g., people on the spectrum, strangers, bosses, and so forth), due to anxiety, fear, discomfort, or a host of other emotions, preconceived notions, and biases.

The more we considered this phenomenon of attunement, the more we began to realize that difficulties with attunement crossed all populations. We began to observe similar challenges in the lives of our colleagues, our friends, and the people we interacted with on a daily basis—as well as in ourselves. Realizing the near universality of this issue, we were inspired to explore attunement further, investigating what makes it work, how it can go awry, and how it can be developed. So we began to put together a framework that could help anyone become better attuned to another person.

WE ALL SHARE A fundamental need for human connection—something that seems increasingly neglected in our culture. In this book we emphasize and examine the research on quality connection and describe realistic ways that every one of us can work on improving the connections in our lives. We examine person-to-person connection, clearly defining attunement and exploring its components in depth, and we lay out a step-by-step, practical approach for developing it. When we refer to "connection," we are referring to a deep tuning in to each other. This tuning in is not so dependent on the amount of time you spend with someone, but has more to do with the quality of that interaction—the degree to which you and another person hear and understand each other, and the skill with which you respond to each other. The quality of the connection is determined not only by the words you say to each other but also by the skill and timing of your nonverbal communication: through the use of eye contact, facial expression, and body language.

In an age where we can use technology to communicate with anyone anywhere at the drop of a hat, the ability to remain attuned is a capacity we need more than ever before. Even though many things that humans can do are being replaced by computers and robots, true attunement is unique to living beings, particularly us humans, and is invaluable. The greater our ability to tune in and connect with others, the more effective and comfortable we will be in our personal and family relationships, and in our work. If many of us work on developing our powers of attunement, there is the potential for ripple effects that could positively impact the larger social, political, and environmental crises of our time, which are prolonged and exacerbated by poor communication across communities and governing bodies.

Developing attunement is a powerful way to improve many areas of our lives. For example, true friends are able to tune in to one another and develop mutual understanding and support. The essence of every romantic relationship is born from a feeling of connection or attunement at an intimate level. In parenting and child-rearing, secure attachment arises from a child's ability to feel, at a fundamental level, that their parents love and care about them. A child needs to trust that their parents can reliably tune in to them and can actively try to understand them. When children have this foundational feeling toward their caregivers, they become increasingly resilient and are able to thrive in a greater variety of environments. Professionally, the key to successful leadership and team building, as well as favorably engaging clients, is having the ability to connect in some way with others. If there is that feeling of connection, then motivation, communication, and cooperation within the team grows. Attunement improves communication within teams and with clients. It helps in resolving conflict and working toward a shared set of goals. In almost every workplace or profession, there are moments in which the stakes are high, anxiety peaks, and nerves are frayed, often resulting in reactive behavior that breaks communication between peers. Developing a new set of habits and skills that strengthen the capacity for attunement in your daily life allows for easier access to these skills in high stress moments, like those found at work. With regular practice, those fundamental skills of attunement become easier to tap into and use in a pinch. They empower you to focus on whomever you're working with, connect with them on a human level, and develop mutual understanding.

Missing Each Other makes an argument for reinvesting in ourselves and each other by improving the quality of our daily interactions. This book defines and explores details of what we call the four components of attunement: relaxed awareness, listening, understanding, and mutual responsiveness. Our explorations will include both the mental and physical aspects of each component, relevant research, exercises to help you develop that component, and stories that bring to life the inner workings of attunement. All four components work together, simultaneously, and they are so closely related that there is some overlap among them. Ultimately, the goal is to put all four components into action at the same time. It will take practice, but we'll show you how.

Now, about the exercises. We'll start with still meditation and mindful awareness exercises, then progress to solo movement exercises, and lastly build to partner-based movement and conversation exercises. Each exercise includes both physical and mental components. Attunement has some overlap with the concept of mindfulness—something you're probably familiar with through its wide dissemination within popular culture in recent years. The first component of attunement, relaxed awareness, is a type of mindfulness in which you are calmly aware of yourself and the person you are interacting with. But the concept of attunement goes beyond mindfulness because attunement also involves incorporating mindful strategies into dynamic social interactions. The methods for developing attunement that we present will be most helpful if you commit some time and effort to the regular practice of at least some of the exercises. The exercises are simple enough that you can do them when you don't have much time on your hands or when you just want to reorient yourself to the components of attunement.

A major, recurring theme of *Missing Each Other* is balance. Developing attunement involves balancing the physical and mental aspects of the exercises, balancing physical alignment and muscle relaxation, balancing awareness and calmness, and balancing awareness of oneself and awareness of the other person.[6] But the goal is not to reach a static, motionless balance point that one could call a final state of perfect attunement. Our interactions with others are always evolving and changing, so attunement is a dynamic process that ebbs and flows around a balance point. Attunement is always a work in progress. Much like a dance, attunement involves alternating between leading and following, connecting and taking some space.

Developing attunement ultimately involves developing attention and timing, developing the ability to be in sync and connected during the twists and turns of a changing interaction, and developing the ability to respond flexibly and appropriately according to what the particular moment of the interaction calls for. Whether it is two people having a conversation in which they feel mutually heard and understood, two dancers moving smoothly together, two basketball teammates moving down the court in a well-coordinated fast break, or two musicians improvising together, the elements of relaxed awareness, listening, understanding, and mutual responsiveness are involved. Attunement is a kind of power worth developing, because it can widen and deepen our perceptions of ourselves and other people, which in turn can lead to remarkable improvements in our effectiveness, in our ability to manage conflict, and in the quality of our interactions in many different contexts and many types of relationships.

Our work as researchers and clinicians is in the tradition of scientist-practitioners, and we bring this balanced approach to the way that we have structured the book. *Missing Each Other* is devoted not only to developing a more detailed understanding of the elements of attunement but also to showing you how to develop these elements and how to put them into practice in your day-to-day life. By the end, this book should bring you greater awareness of your own connections with others and the knowledge and skills necessary to grow, deepen, and strengthen these bonds further. Let's get started.

CHAPTER ONE

WHAT IS ATTUNEMENT, AND WHY IS IT IMPORTANT?

"Only through our connectedness to others can we really know and enhance the self. And only through working on the self can we begin to enhance our connectedness to others."

—HARRIET GOLDHOR LERNER[1]

WE ARE WIRED FOR HUMAN CONNECTION. Our drive to connect with others is evident from the earliest moments of our lives. Infants recognize and demonstrate a preference for human faces, suggesting that we have an innate interest and curiosity about others.[2] As infants continue to develop in a safe, nurturing environment, they develop the ability to form emotional and physical attachment bonds to their parent or caregiver, something that provides them with the sense of security necessary to explore, take chances, and develop their own sense of self. Over time, as children begin to acquire language, they quickly learn the monumental value of connecting their minds with others through verbal and nonverbal communication. Kids learn, over time, to engage in complex interactions that allow for the exchange of ideas or experiences. We have an intrinsic interest in and capability of learning about someone else's experience, and an interest in determining how their experience may connect to ours.[3] There are, without a doubt, individual differences in how much motivation we have to engage with others, or in how interesting and pleasurable social interactions are to us. Rarely do we want to be connected to someone all the time. But overall, whether you consider yourself an introvert or an extrovert, you are generally compelled to generate some degree of a physical, emotional, and/or intellectual connection to those around you.

We know that humans have an inherent need for social bonds, and we also know what happens when we're deprived of them, especially early in life. Early deprivation of social contact (e.g., being embraced, rocked, hugged) has been linked to alterations in brain development and consequent disruption of a child's ability to develop positive attachments to others. Over time, this early lack of social engagement with caretakers can lead to trouble regulating emotions, low self-esteem, behavioral issues, and impaired cognitive development. Social isolation is costly to our well-being in adulthood as well, and it has negative effects on overall health and longevity that are comparable to the negative effects of other well established risk factors, such as obesity.[4] Having a low number of social bonds is also associated with declines in physical and mental health outcomes.[5] The poorer health you have, the less likely you are to socially engage with others, perpetuating the cycle.

Evolutionary psychologists tell us that there were adaptive reasons for humans' tendency to connect with each other, that social cooperation was driven by our need to survive and reproduce. We need others in order to gain information and resources, to protect ourselves and our offspring from danger, and to find help in solving problems. So you might think that we need connection purely for utilitarian reasons, such as survival and reproduction. But selfless acts of kindness for strangers provide examples of how social connection is not necessarily motivated by kinship and functionality. From childhood, we learn to identify shared goals with others and make connections based on our similarities. As we get older, we grow the capacity to accept and love one another despite stark differences. These experiences serve as reminders of how powerful and nearly universal the desires are to connect with each other and develop deep, emotional bonds, both platonic and romantic. That fundamental skill of connecting to each other is attunement.

WHAT ATTUNEMENT LOOKS AND FEELS LIKE

Attunement is the ability to be aware of your own state of mind and body while also tuning in and connecting to another person. It is *the* fundamental social skill and the foundation of human relationships, without which we are isolated from others and cut off from our own inner life. Attunement relies not only on spoken language, but also on the communication of feeling states through unspoken signals that we exchange, such as facial expressions, tone of voice, and body language. Reciprocal communication is a dance between attention and gesture that flows most effectively when people are in tune with one another.[6] The nonverbal components of communication start to develop almost as soon as we are born, and they are nurtured in our interactions with our parents or caregivers. We continue to develop them over the course of a lifetime. In relationships and interactions of any depth, attunement plays an important role.

Attunement helps us to feel aware of ourselves and connected to another person, and it helps that other person feel just as connected to us. Attunement is a whole-body experience, both kinesthetic and emotional, in which you can sense someone's rhythm, affect, and experience by essentially feeling like you're in their skin. Attunement goes one step past empathy by creating a two-person experience of feeling connected, which is accomplished through reciprocal, dynamic responding to one another's emotional states, needs, and desires.[7]

Attunement should not be viewed as simply fostering a touchy-feely emotional connection with others, but as a unique power—a power that enables us to perceive communications from others, to connect and have our message understood, and to manage conflict. Rather than an abstract, intangible concept, attunement is based on a specific set of skills which, research suggests, can be developed with time and practice. True social-emotional attunement can most easily be identified as those moments in which your attention is completely engrossed in a social interaction with someone, whether that someone is your closest confidante or a recent acquaintance. You can have a quality interaction with someone that includes elements like mindfulness, presence of mind, active listening, empathy, and cognitive understanding, but any one of these skills on their own is not attunement. True attunement is born from all of these elements working in conjunction, which allows you to be in sync and in tune with someone's expression of their experience.

Think of a time when you've comforted someone close to you who is grieving. This is a moment that calls for enhanced empathy and awareness of both your own emotions and those of the other person. A major loss, like a death in the family, can be so shocking that it stops us in our tracks, puts all of our usual distractions on hold, and reminds us of the importance of human-to-human connection. As you provide comfort, you pay greater attention to what the grieving person is saying and the body language they use. This focus helps you try to anticipate their needs, whether it be for a tissue, an embrace, or just being present as you sit and listen. As a result, you become in tune with one another, causing a positive feedback loop in which the grieving person feels connected to you and you feel connected to their experience. While you can't bring back the deceased person, your presence and the connection between you is deeply comforting. Attuned connection between you and another person has great power to foster emotional healing.

An important characteristic of attunement is that it has both inner and outer aspects. In other words, attunement involves paying attention inwardly to our own emotional state, thoughts, and feelings, as well as paying attention outwardly to the cues from the person we're interacting with. When you comfort a person who is sad, it's helpful to be somewhat aware of (but not completely overwhelmed by) your own feelings, as you attend to theirs. Maybe when you're comforting someone who has just lost a parent, it brings up emotions within you because you're currently caring for an elderly parent yourself. An interaction like that might make you feel anxious, stressed out, or sad, because you are reminded of your own family situation. While that is completely normal and understandable, it takes a certain level of conscious awareness to identify those emotions within yourself. That awareness allows you to regulate your emotions while you maintain a mindful connection with the other person's experience. Without an awareness that the other person's loss is stirring up your own feelings about your family situation, you may unknowingly get distracted by your own emotions and experience during the conversation. As a result, you may lose focus on the emotions of the grieving person. So, ironically, some degree of self-awareness can help you to stay aware of the other person. Awareness of both our own state and the other person's state makes room for the connection between both parties to deepen.

Attunement can be attained in joyful situations as well. It can occur between two people who are deeply in love with one other; between two old friends who know and understand each other inside and out; between a parent and their new baby laughing and cuddling; or among musicians, dancers, or team athletes who perform in close physical, mental, and emotional coordination with each other. These kinds of interactions carry with them a beauty.

And people who are highly connected with each other in that way often have a feeling of euphoria during their moments of attuned interaction, which they may miss when the interaction is over. For people in love with each other, for parents with their new babies, or for musicians, dancers, and athletes, those periods of connection are often the moments that they live for and can't wait to get back to.

The conscious and unconscious utilization of attunement skills starts in early childhood and continues to be cultivated across the lifespan. These skills are frequently observed in mother-infant interactions in particular. Nora Johnson and her three-month-old infant daughter Taylor, clients at a child development workshop we attended, were a dyad that perfectly demonstrated the fluid give and take required of strong attunement, and they did so without ever realizing it. As they played, they connected by making eye contact with one another, and by exchanging facial expressions that were imitated by one another. They shared smiles, laughs, and coos. Nora and Taylor's interactions showed how primal and fundamental attunement is in our lives, even before a baby starts to speak in words. While they clearly shared a bond and special closeness, Nora was quick to notice Taylor's need for breaks and space, something that Taylor would demonstrate through micro moments in which she might look away or disengage momentarily. Attunement between a parent and child can occur not only in behavior, as evidenced between Nora and her baby, but even at the physiological level of hormone fluctuations and heart rate variability. As you attune to each other behaviorally, your body follows suit and your physiology can become in tune with someone else's.[8]

If you've ever enjoyed playing with a baby, you know it can be tempting to do anything you can to keep their attention and shower them with constant affection. But those of you with kids, or who have spent extended time with young ones, know that pleading for their nonstop attention usually doesn't play out well. Nora didn't insist on keeping Taylor's attention at every moment.

Rather, Nora's responses to Taylor highlight how attunement isn't about being continuously close to the other person and in constant communication—it involves sensing when the other person needs some time away and granting them that space.

The more you learn about attunement, the more you'll start to notice the diversity and versatility of these skills in your life and in the lives of others. Attunement can be useful in different ways, depending on the situation and type of relationship. Some examples may even surprise you. For instance, attunement plays a strong role in a lot of creative fields, like music, comedy, and sports. As fans of jazz will tell you, it is fairly easy to notice how musical improvisation involves attunement. The quality of the connection among musicians enhances the music that they make together. Trumpeter Kenny Wheeler and pianist John Taylor had a multi-decade musical collaboration that resulted in their ability to create a high level of attunement, expressed through improvisation. When improvising together, each person needs to be aware of themselves and what they are doing, as well as aware of the other person and the interaction in real time. By definition, musical improvisation is unpredictable, which means each person has to remain open to what is happening in the flow of the music. Improvisational music is an ever-changing, flowing process, not a final, static destination or state that is reached. Attunement, like Wheeler and Taylor's improvisation skills, involves not a merger or simple mirroring of each other. Rather, it requires a kind of turn-taking, push-pull type of interaction, with an alternation of leading and following. In an NPR review of their posthumous album *On the Way to Two*, reviewer Kevin Whitehead describes how the two musicians shared a "subtle . . . but not ambiguous" sense of harmony. "Each player heard where the other was going, and they were always in alignment. The pianist knew how to keep the trumpeter moving, when to let him stretch the time and when to pull him back. . . . The players' mutual understanding and close listening also animate . . . cohesive free improvisations."[9] Finding the balance of knowing when to push or pull, and when to follow, can sometimes be the most challenging element of attunement.

Comedians are another example of those who use a high level of attunement to produce great art. Stand-up comedy performances are challenging and can seem magical due to the nature of a live show. These performers must live in the moment and be constantly attuned to themselves and their specific audience in order to make adjustments at the drop of a hat. Successfully performing in front of a crowd, spotlights glaring, beads of sweat sliding down their forehead, is a feat in and of itself. Many comics have spoken about the need to stay cool and aware (what we will describe as "relaxed awareness") to be ready for anything, whether it be a crowd that doesn't jibe with their rhythm and material, or a ruthless heckler who's ready to cause a scene. Their attunement skills are stretched even further during improvisation that occurs when working with other comedians.

The great performer Jerry Lewis once said that his straight man, Dean Martin, was "the best that had ever lived," and what made him so good was his power to tune in to Lewis and know how to respond at just the right time. Lewis described how Martin "knew when I was doing something that I wasn't really having fun at, and he watched me until he jumped in and saved me from a place I didn't want to be. How did he know that? I mean, I'm talking about the second or third night that we ever performed together, he knew when I was going to take a breath. It was an incredible relationship based on, my God—a comic seeing someone else understand his beats and his rhythms."[10] It was not about whether Martin and Lewis agreed or disagreed with each other's perspectives. Rather, it was about how they could sense each other and feed off each other to keep the dialogue flowing smoothly.

Attunement in this context is grounded in a shared goal that requires many elements, some of which include close listening, full attention, setting aside egos, equal participation, and the potential for failure. All these components can be found across music, comedy, or just regular conversation. In fact, during our time working together we've experienced moments of attunement ourselves. For example, in the early stages of developing our autism treatment program at the University of Pennsylvania, we were attuned while brainstorming different components of the program and piecing together the necessary logistics. At certain times we felt wholly in sync, finishing each other's thoughts and feeding off each other's ideas in a way that felt like we were riding the same wavelength with ease. Those moments can feel like magic, full of warmth and satisfaction from knowing that you are experiencing pure connection and clear communication. But then there were times when our attunement seemed to break down, temporarily, as time crunches or the stress of managing lots of personalities on one team caused anxiety, tension, and frustration. Regardless of whether our frustration was with ourselves or the other person, the threshold for getting out of sync was immediately lowered. During those times, it was much easier to misinterpret the other person's ideas or intentions and lose our cool and our ability to stay calm and listen. It's great when attunement forms naturally. But learning to be mindful and to identify distractors is the first step to staying calm and focusing your attention so that you can stay in that zone of attunement for longer.

Close relationships are the classic situations in which attunement comes into play, but attunement can also play an important role in enhancing our ability to function in less intimate interactions, such as with acquaintances or even people who we've just encountered for the first time. Generating some degree of attunement with others does not require knowing them well, nor does it require having lengthy, deep, meaningful conversations. An attuned interaction is born from the experience of being present and connected with someone, for however long or short that connection may last. In less intimate situations, attunement skills enhance your ability to stay calm, and to keep your eyes and ears open to perceive the other person clearly and accurately. By maintaining some awareness of your own reactions (e.g., becoming overwhelmed, distracted, emotional), you're often better able to handle anything that arises between you and the other person, and to do so much more skillfully.

Although it can enhance your sense of closeness, attunement does *not* mean becoming so close to another person that you give up your independence of thought and action. Only two individuals who have a clear sense of themselves as separate individuals can be truly attuned to each other (with the exception of infants, who have not developed much sense of self yet). When you give up your sense of individuality and autonomy for someone else—or another person gives up their individuality and autonomy for you—this is merging, or it could mean that one person dominates and controls the other, which is very different from attunement. Attunement involves two or more individuals finding a balance of connection with personal space and freedom, depending on the particular relationship and the context.

Attunement is even helpful for navigating our way through conflicts that seem to inevitably arise between people. Say you are in a high-stress meeting with your boss in which they are giving you critical performance feedback. Both of you are experiencing rising tensions. Your boss is trying to straddle the line between being constructive and critical, and you are stressed about how well you are doing at your job. Either, or both, of you may feel so consumed by your own feelings, reactions, and defenses that you have trouble accurately perceiving the other person, yourselves, and the situation. As a result, either of you may do or say things that you later regret. While attunement certainly doesn't quell emotions, heightened attunement skills allow individuals to engage calmly and not get overwhelmed by emotional reactivity. This perspective allows people to hear and understand each other more clearly. It enables each person to respond to what the other person actually did or said, rather than to misperceptions of what was done or said. While it may seem paradoxical, when we're in conflict with someone, we're actually much more effective in navigating that conflictual situation if we stay connected with that other person—when we can actually hear and understand that person clearly, and respond to what was really said and meant. If you lose your connection to the other person, your ability to assert yourself in the conflict or situation is diminished. If your responses to your boss are not really responding to what your boss is actually saying or means, then your responses will seem irrelevant and will be more easily dismissed or deflected. To make a convincing argument or case to the other person, it is crucial that you stay cool, that you listen to and understand what is being said, that you know where the other person is coming from, and that you then construct your argument in such a way that the other person will be able to hear it.

It's not easy to connect with someone who has very different views from your own. When you fundamentally disagree with someone, how can you expect to connect with them? Most people have been hit by a moment in which they realize, or are surprised to learn, that not everyone is interpreting the world the way they are. It can be a tough pill to swallow when we interact with someone who has a different perspective on the same situation, especially when those interactions relate to hot-button topics like racism, religion, politics, or parenting. There can be an almost automatic urge to either react or disengage, either of which usually leads to ineffective communication. But attunement with others does not require agreeing with them, nor does it mean having the same perspective on life that they have. It does require that you keep yourself calm enough to be aware, that you sincerely listen and understand, and that you stay in touch with your own reactions and those of the other person, so that the whole interaction can go more smoothly and productively. Attunement offers up the chance to take the path less traveled, the counterintuitive path—using connection to navigate conflict—even in moments where throwing up your hands and walking away feels like the easier choice. It's no magic pill, but the exercises that we offer to develop each component of attunement will allow you to take mindful practices off of your couch at home and turn them into practical strategies that you can bring into your everyday interactions.

DISCONNECTION IN THE AGE OF CONNECTION

You might wonder why we would be concerned about social connection in this age of technology and social networking, in which we have constant access to online socialization. In our high-tech times, it would seem we are in no danger of losing social connections. While unlimited connections are seemingly at the tips of our index fingers and thumbs, the depth and quality of those connections, as well as our capacity to wholly and mindfully tune in to another person, are at risk of being compromised. We may be wired for social connection, but that doesn't always translate to being "good" at sustaining attunement and relationships with others. And the research is clear: low-quality social connections can have startlingly negative consequences on our social, emotional, and even physical health.

Previously we used the example of connecting with someone who was grieving, and the ways in which attunement is built during those moments of deep emotional closeness. While beautiful, that kind of intense connection takes time, effort, and energy, all things that can feel like luxuries in our busy daily lives. It is a challenge to stay present or mindful in the countless interactions we have on a daily basis. In the rush of life, it can be easy to get lost in the "go go go" mentality of modern society, making it difficult to even identify when your attention and energy are being drawn away from social interactions. Attunement can be broken in the blink of an eye. First, distractors like technology and social media divert our attention and energy away from being present with people, causing us to lose our ability to listen, hear, and internalize what someone else is saying to us. Second, our own thoughts, emotions, and anxieties can have meaningful influences on our ability to connect with someone.

It can sometimes feel like a Herculean effort to listen to your child or partner talk about their day, especially if you're mentally running through an endless to-do list, wondering when you're going to have time to grocery shop, pay bills, reply to work emails, and pick up that gift you need for your nephew's birthday party on Saturday. The energy it takes to balance everything going on inside your head and around you can quickly sweep you up and away, preventing you from being in tune with the person in front of you.

Moments of misattunement happen all the time. They can come in the form of something as trivial as forgetting a new acquaintance's name as soon as they introduce themselves, or not hearing someone's reply to a question as you looked away to respond to an email. But those quick moments don't have much of a lasting impact. The problem arises when we fall out of tune with people on a more regular basis or for longer periods of time. When those small moments of being unaligned and out of sync stack up, they can quietly become a problem. They start to wear away at your relationships, silently at first, until one day you begin to realize that the quality of a relationship has plummeted, making it difficult to know how to get it back on track.

SOCIAL CONNECTION HAS EVOLVED to take on different forms, especially through the explosive growth of the internet and social media. Our social networks have grown exponentially compared to past generations. You can keep in touch with almost anyone you come in contact with, from high school classmates to the couple you met on your last summer holiday. With chatting now a feature on most apps, you can be balancing conversations with one person on multiple different platforms at the same time. We can send you a book recommendation via text, direct message an announcement about a new meditation group on Instagram, and forward a funny video via WhatsApp, all within a few seconds. Most of these "conversations" come in the form of sharing photos, videos, and/or memes, instead of substantive exchanges. Phone calls to catch up seem almost burdensome in comparison to the short, quick messages you can send instead. On the plus side, the speed and efficiency of these forms of technology allow us to connect with more people, more often. Communities around the world were reminded of this when video chatting became an even more heavily relied on tool during the 2020 COVID-19 pandemic. But what is the quality of social connection produced from these types of interactions? If there is a distinct difference between online connections and in-person interactions, are we learning or utilizing the same attunement skills in both forms of communication?

In the last decade or two, in which more and more of our communication is done through screens and devices, our ability to tune in to ourselves and tune in to others seems to be changing, flattening, and perhaps withering.[11] This alienates us from both our own inner life and from others. The more time we invest in our online conversations, the less effort we put into prioritizing in-person conversations with other people, and the fewer opportunities we have to develop the confidence and skill needed in having those types of interactions. As a result, many of us start to feel alone in the virtual crowd, isolated and disconnected.[12] To assuage our loneliness, we turn to more technology, leading to a vicious cycle.[13]

Many writers have noted an association among the pervasive use of social media, distraction from face-to-face interaction, and feelings of isolation and alienation.[14] Revered neurologist and writer Oliver Sacks compared the ubiquity of smartphones to the 1909 story "The Machine Stops" by E. M. Forster, in which people live in isolated cells underground, communicating only through devices. Sacks noted how, in the story, humankind is subsumed by the "Machine," which caters to every need or desire one could want "except the need for human contact."[15] In a lot of ways, Dr. Sacks was right: sometimes the "Machine" or online social connection can be deceiving. It's easily possible to go an entire day without physically coming in contact with anyone, yet you could have multiple conversations with people over your phone. In some ways, that represents a phenomenal feat of technology, something to be celebrated. Family members separated across different countries can let each other know they're okay. It allows for a person confined to their hospital bed a chance to talk to their loved ones. During the COVID-19 pandemic, video chat technology provided a crucial lifeline between patients and family members, and was the only way that patients hospitalized with COVID-19 could see their loved ones. But for everyday life, when we are not in the midst of a pandemic, this technology might inadvertently reduce the social and emotional benefits of physical human contact. Researchers who investigate the impact of technology on our social well-being suggest there is an urgent need for our culture to reinvest in face-to-face conversations, because it is those conversations that lead to true empathy, deeper friendship, love, and productivity.[16]

Dating apps are another avenue in which shallow connections have grown exponentially. Don't get us wrong—the increasing number of wedding invitations from people who've met online is evidence of its success in bringing people together. But dating apps have become so popular, ubiquitous, and heavily marketed that some might have the misimpression that we've successfully hacked relationships with this technology alone. The first step, striking up a conversation on an app, is relatively easy. However, on average, these conversations tend to fizzle, or one suitor will ghost the other before they even get a chance to meet in person. While the app can connect you, it's the follow-up and accompanying ability to tune in to each other that are necessary for the birth of a lasting, genuine connection. Compared to merely swiping right or left on a dating app, these attunement skills are a lot more complex, nuanced, and intricate, and they involve a set of abilities that need to be practiced. And sometimes it feels as though both our opportunities to practice these skills and the motivation of newer generations to put them into action are decreasing at a steady rate.

Although the growth of technological "connection" through smartphones and social media likely contributes to a sense of disconnection, technology alone is not the full explanation. Rather, technology is only one of a complex set of cultural, social, economic, and political factors that is contributing to loneliness. Dr. Cornel West, professor of the practice of public philosophy at Harvard University, has argued that the dark side of our profit-focused society—in which everything and everyone can feel like a commodity—includes lack of community, failed intimacy, loneliness, or what playwright Arthur Miller called the American disease of unrelatedness.[17] The dark side of an individualistic society lies in the "every man for himself" mentality that aims to promote individual success at the expense of the advantages that come with valuing community bonds. Many social trends indicate an increase in atomization and isolation in the United States, even in highly populated cities. Levels of trust in other people, time spent with neighbors, and overall "social capital" (people's network of relationships and shared experiences) have decreased over the last several decades, despite the growth of online communities.[18] In 1985, 36 percent of American adults reported having no close friends, and by 2004 it was 53.4 percent.[19]

Loneliness is not defined by isolation or solitude, but rather by how satisfied you are with your connectedness to people or by how socially isolated you perceive yourself to be.[20] Research on loneliness clearly identifies that the quantity of relationships—the number of people you know—is far less important than the quality of those relationships.[21] Many people know what it's like to sometimes feel lonely in a room full of people. True social satisfaction comes not from the measure of the number of people we know, but from knowing you have people on whom you can depend and who can depend on you in return.[22] Even having just one person who is available and tuned in to you has been shown to yield much lower rates of depression and relationship difficulties, even in the presence of adverse life experiences.[23]

Unfortunately, globally, we are experiencing decreasing levels of empathy and trust and increasing cases of loneliness, social isolation, and anxiety/depression at both the individual and community level.[24] In twenty-first-century America, a surprisingly high percentage of people lack relationships with others who know them really well, who they can connect with easily. In a 2018 survey conducted by the health insurance company Cigna, more than twenty thousand American adults were asked to fill out the UCLA Loneliness Scale questionnaire. Fifty-four percent of adults surveyed said that they sometimes or always feel that no one really knows them well; 39 percent said they sometimes or always feel that they are no longer close to anyone; and 27 percent rarely or never feel as though there are people who really understand them. Levels of loneliness were found to be highest in young adults, with 68 percent of Generation Z'ers (those who are now ages 18–22) feeling that no one really knows them well.[25] As we are writing this book during the first months of the COVID-19 pandemic, we are seeing additional spikes in loneliness due to "social distancing" (i.e. physical distancing between people to prevent spread of the coronavirus), which became an urgent public health requirement. Many media commentaries during the pandemic focused on the terrible aloneness that was being felt all over the world.

As social beings who inherently crave depth of connection in order to thrive, we're facing an array of societal factors that drive down the quality of our social connections and offer us endless opportunities for shallow connections. This leaves us feeling increasingly lonely and dissatisfied with our relationships. Yet, despite our loneliness, we often feel too busy to spend much time with people close to us. We've all had moments when we pushed off a coffee date with a friend because "things are just too crazy right now." Or sometimes those catch-up conversations at home with your partner or your kids get shortened or get less attention because things just "need to get done." So what gives? Why is it so hard to just slow down and really invest in our live (in-person) interactions and relationships? For one thing, many Americans need to work multiple jobs in order to support themselves and their families, which leaves them little time to invest in their relationships. More economically privileged Americans may feel many societal pressures to "keep it moving" and to always be "producing," in both their personal and professional lives. And a constant stream of electronic messages feeds into this pressure with unceasing demands for their attention. Another part of the answer may lie in the vicious cycle that many of us get into where we respond to disconnection with greater disconnection.

GETTING YOUR ATTUNEMENT SKILLS INTO SHAPE

Maybe you are going through a significant bout of loneliness, isolation, or disengagement and you want to find ways of nurturing greater connection in your life. Or maybe you are someone who has existing, positive relationships with a partner, family, or friends but hopes that these bonds and connections can be strengthened. Maybe you are looking for better ways to manage conflict or become more effective in interacting with clients or coworkers. No matter who you are, developing greater attunement skills can be applicable and helpful at all those moments on your journey through life. To understand more about where you are on the spectrum of attunement, or where you may be having difficulty with attunement, take the Attunement Quiz in the Appendix of the book. You might notice that you have strengths in some areas of attunement and lower scores in other areas, which will be important information that informs your practice as you work on these skills.

The good news is, our capacity for connection is far from immutable at any point in life. Our ability to connect on a deeper level with others is a set of malleable skills that can be developed—growth and change are possible. Of course, the exercises that we introduce in this book to develop attunement won't solve the many social and economic issues that seem to be contributing to loneliness and disconnection. To address the large scope of loneliness in our society, broader social and cultural changes are needed. Nevertheless, to the extent that you have the time and space to read on and try these exercises, you can do a great deal to enhance your own attunement, which in turn can go a long way toward helping you deepen your relationships and connections with others. Think of attunement like a muscle that can grow with training and consistent practice. Nourishing and growing your attunement skills takes commitment and focus, but the greater the effort you make to incorporate this practice into your daily life, the stronger this muscle becomes and the easier it gets to start connecting more effectively with those around you.

Building attunement not only deepens close relationships but also can help you decide if you want to engage in a relationship with someone at all. For example, when meeting a person on a first date, or in another situation, something about the interaction may feel "off." By developing your capacity to tune in and listen carefully, not only to the other person but also to your own internal reactions, you can make better-informed decisions for yourself about whether to get involved with someone. By gaining skill in attunement, you should become less likely to be manipulated, because you will be better able to recognize the difference between attempts to manipulate you versus genuine efforts to connect.

BREAKING DOWN ATTUNEMENT INTO PARTS

We think of attunement as being made of four main parts: relaxed awareness, listening, understanding, and mutual responsiveness. The first component of attunement is *relaxed awareness*, which is the ability to be aware of yourself—your own body, feelings, and thoughts—as well as the ability to be aware of what is going on around you, while remaining calm. To get a sense of relaxed awareness, take a moment to imagine an interaction you've had in which you felt truly connected when conversing with someone. What was that experience like? Did you feel present? Did you feel anxious and tense, or did you feel more relaxed? Our bet is you were at ease, which allowed you to feel open to the interaction. Feeling free from physical and emotional tension gave you a greater capacity to be aware of everything the person in front of you was contributing to the conversation, and you were also aware of how they were impacting you during the interaction. Relaxed awareness is this ability to be aware of yourself, your environment, and the other person while staying relaxed and open, even when under some stress, or even when feelings and emotions arise during an interaction. Through practice, you can enhance your ability to be aware and composed, even when strong emotions are pulling you toward disengagement. Being mindful of your experience, and that of the person in front of you, creates the conditions needed for attunement to grow.

As a psychiatrist and a therapist, we are consistently using all the components of attunement, including relaxed awareness, when working with patients in the therapy room. In a therapeutic relationship, attunement is essential to the connection between patient and clinician, and is necessary for therapy to be effective. The "therapeutic alliance" between the patient and clinician is consistently one of the best predictors of how positively impactful therapy can be. Mind you, we probably don't practice attunement to such a high degree in our relationships outside of the therapy room, but this type of therapeutic relationship—in which we put aside the many distractions and demands of daily life to focus on the patient and our interactions with the patient—is an unusually "concentrated" example of attunement, and so it is helpful for illustrating the essential components of attunement. When we are sitting across from a patient, as they begin to open up about their primary concern, we do our best to put aside any worries or tensions from the day. We do this by relaxing the body and mind, and by sitting in an aligned but relaxed way that is physically oriented toward the patient. We do these things in order to focus on what the patient is saying. Even when our attention lapses momentarily—which is inevitable—we'll use a combination of strategies to return our attention back to the patient and our own physical posture and breath. It's a dynamic process that requires sufficient attention to balance the awareness of our own state with active openness and curiosity about what the patient is communicating.

Let us take you into the therapy room for a minute. Caleb was one of Ashley's patients. He was a young adult who came into therapy to talk about some interpersonal issues he was having. Similar to many patients who come into therapy for the first time, Caleb was very polite and kind, but understandably it took him time to warm up and become more open and vulnerable. Especially in a case like this, when the patient has little experience with therapy and may be unsure of what's expected or hesitant about how to engage, it was important for Ashley, as his therapist, to model relaxed awareness for him. In the first session, Caleb began by describing a falling-out that he recently had with a close friend. As he recounted their history as friends, it was important for Ashley to be aware of her body alignment and her relaxed breaths, while also dynamically moving her focus among the different verbal and nonverbal cues that he provided. Modeling relaxed awareness for patients can be helpful, especially for those patients who may not even realize how physically tense they are. Even though a first session usually focuses on giving the patient space to talk, a therapist can also introduce a patient to muscle relaxation or mindfulness exercises (which we'll describe at the end of Chapter 2) to help build rapport and develop a foundation for relaxed awareness.

Relaxed awareness is the foundation for the second component of attunement, *listening*. When you are able to stay relaxed while being aware, you're in a much better position to "listen," in the broadest sense of that term—to pay careful attention to what you see and hear from the other person, and to pay attention to your own reactions. (To listen can involve a heavier emphasis on either hearing or seeing, depending on the context or on impairments in either of those senses.) Listening, in that broad sense, involves focusing on the other person's verbal and nonverbal communication—including facial expression, body language, and tone of voice—over the course of the interaction, and it also involves noticing your own reactions and emotions that are elicited by the other person. Beyond just paying attention to the other person, listening involves an active, but unconscious, process by which our brains "resonate with" and "mirror" the sounds, sights, and emotions of the other person. We explain this more fully in Chapter 3.

When working with Caleb, employing good listening skills meant paying attention to the emotional quality of the language he used. It was important to "listen" to what he conveyed with his facial expressions and body language as well. During the first session with Caleb, his hunched shoulders, interlocked and tense hands, and lack of eye contact spoke just as loudly as the words he vocalized. As clinicians, we collect information purposefully, as a means to understand and help our patients to the best of our abilities. But even if this situation were just one of us listening to a friend in need, rather than a patient, we would be doing the same thing. By *listening* to all that he is conveying, Ashley's capacity to *hear* him in a more comprehensive way is increased, which in turn can have a powerful and far-reaching impact on how seen and heard he feels.

In addition to the raw sensory information about the other person and yourself that you attend to while listening, attunement requires an ability to *understand* or interpret this information, to decipher the other person's cues and put them in perspective. Understanding the interaction includes being able to appreciate the point of view and intentions that both you and the other person have in order to recognize what is happening between the two of you. While *listening* involves perceiving and sensing the other person and yourself at a basic "gut" level, *understanding* involves more cognitive processing of those raw perceptions and feelings, more thinking and reflection, in order to understand the other person and yourself.

Ashley used *understanding* skills during sessions with Caleb, which helped her to process his verbal and nonverbal cues in the context of the discussion. For example, as he elaborated on the falling-out with his friend, Ashley noted how strongly he wound his hands together. There were brief moments in which his jaw locked and his knee started to bounce with agitation. By "listening" to all these cues, Ashley developed a deeper understanding of Caleb's emotions about his friendship. These details helped illustrate how significantly impacted Caleb was by the loss of this relationship. Ashley balanced both broad listening and understanding of the information Caleb communicated, which made it easier for her to ask targeted questions that made Caleb feel heard. This, in turn, enabled Caleb to slowly open up about how this person had been his best friend since childhood, and about how the loss of this friendship prompted him to question his ability to trust others. There's a spiraling effect as we put these skills of relaxed awareness, listening, and understanding into practice. The better we get at using them, the more other people feel comfortable opening up, and the more they feel attuned to you—ultimately, positively reinforcing the cycle of connection.

Finally, in addition to *relaxed awareness*, *listening*, and *understanding*, attunement involves an active interchange, a back-and-forth *mutual responsiveness*, which includes an ability to maintain the connection during the twists and turns of a conversation, and to keep pace with the timing of the interaction. You can think about this as the quality of a conversation that makes it feel "natural." The ability to maintain a feeling of mutual connection during a conversation seems to come easily to some people, but it is much more difficult for others, and is actually a remarkably challenging feat. Imagine for a second that you were trying to teach someone the rules of conversation. This would include helping to prepare them for how to respond to any type of topic, whether it be congratulating someone on a success, providing sympathy for their grief, or giving support for their frustration. The combinations of examples are endless, and it would probably feel like a monumental challenge to try to prepare someone for every possible situation, and to teach them how to respond to the other person in a way that feels graceful and well-timed. Some of our patients on the autism spectrum know the socially "appropriate" thing to say or not say in certain situations, but the way they interact is still sometimes out of tune with the other person because of the difficulties of handling the complex skill of mutual responsiveness.

Simulating mutual responsiveness has become an area of interest for technology companies. Scientists are working hard to create artificial intelligence (AI) programs that can engage more skillfully in conversation than the ones currently available, like Amazon Alexa, Siri by Apple, or Google Assistant. These programs are all probably pretty good at answering your questions. But if you were to have a back-and-forth conversation with a live version of any of these AIs, there would be a stilted, awkward quality to the conversational dynamic, one that does not match the quality of a well-attuned human being.

One last time, let's go back to the therapy room with Caleb. During the second or third session, Caleb was finishing up a description of an important moment in the evolution of his friendship when it became difficult for Ashley to avoid getting lost in her own train of thought, which was triggered by Caleb's description. As her focus on Caleb's words decreased and drifted toward a related topic, Ashley lost focus on practicing relaxed awareness, ultimately leading her to cross her legs, tense her shoulders, and briefly interrupt her eye contact with him. That momentary break in attunement, something that all of you have probably experienced, led to an awkward pause. Ashley squirmed slightly and stuttered in order to buy time and try to remember what he just said, until she finally realized it was necessary to simply ask Caleb to repeat his last thought. These types of small breaks in attunement are very common and inevitable, and if handled well, almost certainly would not irreparably break a connection. While small breaks like these don't feel great, we usually are able to repeat what was said, listen better, and restart mutual responsiveness. There is no such thing as continuously perfect attunement in any relationship, no matter how good it is. Small breaks and then repairs of attunement are what happen in real relationships. However, over time, the addition of many small moments like this one, one on top of another—without enough effort spent in repairing and restoring the attunement—can start to silently erode connection and weaken the relationship.

All four components of attunement are highly interrelated to each other, and the earlier ones (relaxed awareness, listening) form the foundation for the later ones (understanding, mutual responsiveness). Separating them out from each other is somewhat artificial, but we do that in this book to try to help you better understand the inner workings of attunement, and to develop a series of exercises that will help you build your attunement skills from the fundamentals on upward. It's a bit like learning basketball by doing separate drills for dribbling, passing, shooting, and rebounding. Ultimately, all these skills will need to work smoothly together, but for the sake of building skills and understanding the principles of the game, it can be helpful to separate them out at first. But as you can see even from these initial examples, if the boundaries between these four components of attunement start to seem fuzzy, or if you find it a bit difficult to tell where one component ends and the other one starts, don't worry! You're correctly perceiving the close interactions among these components.

STRENGTHENING ATTUNEMENT IN YOUR DAILY LIFE

Let's take another example of how these skills, or lapses in these skills, can snowball. Imagine you're in a work meeting and someone just spoke up and made a point that you strongly disagree with, so much so that you think this idea would derail your momentum and progress as a team and distract you from your ultimate goals. As you listen to this coworker speak, and you start to feel worried and mad, you begin to think about all the ways in which you want to respond, and your shoulders begin to tighten. As all those reactions are occurring in rapid succession, you have already stopped truly listening to what that coworker is saying. Can you picture how this story plays out? You react and reply out of anger and territoriality, focusing on your own perspective, but not in a way that connects with the other person. The coworker replies similarly, and then maybe someone else jumps in to take sides. Soon enough, you're all in a conversation in which everyone is talking but no one is saying anything that is being heard by the rest of the group. The connection has been broken and emotional reactivity has taken the reins.

We don't mean to suggest that attunement skills will completely prevent these situations or make your office dynamics all sunshine and daisies. But attunement skills can serve as tools that help reduce the amount of time spent in those endless cycles of talking *at* people instead of *with* them. In especially heated moments, it can seem difficult to pause and implement attunement skills. That's because it is. It takes a good amount of energy and effort to catch yourself and draw on these strategies. That's why we lay them out in a progressive series of exercises that can be gradually practiced, over time, so you can grow new habits that become second nature, such that they can kick in naturally during difficult situations. Similar to the office meeting example, try to keep in mind moments in your own life that are important to you—moments in which you can start to identify breaks in connection—so that you can direct your practice toward engaging those moments as you progress through the book. As busy people leading busy lives, most of us have had little time to practice and strengthen the attunement "muscles" that breed social connection. We can sit and read about mindfulness all day, but unless we put these skills into action in practical ways and develop new habits, we will find it difficult to really incorporate these concepts into our daily lives.

EXERCISES TO BUILD ATTUNEMENT

In the upcoming chapters on each of the four components of attunement, we will go over some exercises to build skills related to each component. Many of these exercises are derived from both mindfulness and meditation practices, as well as from Tai Chi. Mindfulness and meditation practices derived from various Eastern religions (especially Buddhism) have exploded in popularity in recent years, gracing magazine covers and making headlines. Invariably, the story is about the innumerable benefits these practices can bring to our physical, emotional, and spiritual lives. However, as they've been modified to become accessible to a Western audience, the intention of the practices has gotten lost. The moment the words "meditation" or "mindfulness" come up, many people in the West think of "escape" or about pausing their daily life and ignoring everything around them so as to take in the present moment. This pause might involve sitting on a cushion in a dimly lit, quiet room, where you take five to ten minutes to enter into a trancelike state and clear your mind. You might be surprised to learn that true mindfulness is not about escape, rather it's about awareness. Mindful awareness is the ability to notice, without judgement, whatever is going on in your mind and body, and allowing your thoughts and feelings to come and go, without getting attached to them. Positive, negative, or neutral thoughts and emotions pass through your mind constantly, and they often can pass through you without your conscious awareness. Mindfulness strengthens your ability to become better in tune with how you're feeling at any given time. The goal is not to clear your head of all thoughts and feelings, but to allow yourself to notice them and direct some acceptance toward them.

While quiet, reflective, meditation can be powerful, our goal is to help you take these practices off the cushion and carry them into your daily life. We want these skills to be practical enough to take into the kitchen as the family rushes to get ready for the day, into the next big work presentation, into a difficult conversation with your partner, or into a first date that fills you with countless emotions. Whatever moment you face, we'll show you how you can build upon these progressive exercises in a way that will make them easier to apply in any context.

You may be wondering what Tai Chi is and why we choose to include some exercises from this discipline in order to develop attunement. Tai Chi—the full name is Tai Chi Chuan—is a Chinese martial art that is at least several hundred years old. Tai Chi includes a remarkably systematic, step-by-step curriculum for cultivating the essential elements of attunement using a type of nonverbal communication of body language and movement. Tai Chi is not the only discipline that is useful for learning and practicing elements of attunement, of course. Meditation, yoga, music, dance, the Alexander technique, and even improvisational theater or stand-up comedy can be very useful for focusing on one or two elements of attunement. But, in our view, Tai Chi contains within it one of the most complete curricula for developing the essential elements of attunement. Tai Chi training develops these elements in a progressive, step-by-step manner that enables you ultimately to integrate the elements and put attunement into practice.

Tai Chi Chuan was developed in the 1600s in Chen Village, a small town in the countryside of Henan province, China. Members of that village developed Tai Chi by synthesizing elements of existing Chinese martial arts together with principles of Chinese health, breathing, and meditation practices, as well as the yin-yang theory about the balance and interplay of opposites. These elements of Tai Chi are even older, reportedly dating back more than one thousand years. From the very beginning of its development, Tai Chi included both individual and interactive practices. Tai Chi only really reached the West, including America, in the twentieth century.[26] In this book, we present a few of the very basic, foundational individual and partner exercises in Tai Chi. These exercises represent only a very small fraction of the system of Tai Chi, but are foundational exercises that we consider to be very useful basic training in the elements of attunement. These basic exercises are fairly simple, but they are very effective and should be accessible to most people. They don't require any special talent, background, prior training, or equipment. Many can be done on your own, virtually anywhere, and some involve one other person as a training partner. Our goal here is not to teach you a martial art, but to extract from this martial art a few of its essential elements that are useful for developing attunement.

BEFORE WE JUMP INTO the rest of the book, take a few minutes to complete the Attunement Quiz located in the Appendix. Reflect on some of these self-assessment questions to see how attunement skills may already play a strong role in your life. The questions may also prime you to start thinking about how misattunement—with yourself or with people you interact with—may be impacting your life. Some of the questions are about attunement in general, and some are about each of the four components of attunement. The quiz may be helpful in clarifying your overall relationship with attunement and misattunement, and it may also help you determine which components contribute most to any issues you have. You can also use these questions to think about the strengths or challenges that other people in your life have with attunement—just make the questions about that other person, rather than yourself. We hope this will ground you in a general understanding of what attunement looks like in your life and how you can move forward and use this book in the most effective way possible.

CHAPTER TWO

RELAXED AWARENESS

"Breathing in, I am aware of the waves in my life.
Breathing out, I find my peaceful center amidst
the challenges of the moment."

—THICH NHAT HANH[1]

WHAT IS RELAXED AWARENESS?

"Relaxed awareness" means being aware of yourself and your environment, including other people, while staying calm and relaxed, and letting go of tension. This state of mind and body is the foundation of attunement, on which all the other components of attunement are built. To develop a state of relaxed awareness, you start with your physical state and work your way to your mental state, as we'll show you, which eventually gives you an overall feeling of calm alertness. This calm alertness, in turn, lays the groundwork for being able to listen, understand, and more intimately connect with your environment and the people around you.

The importance of awareness and relaxation for attunement becomes fairly obvious if you consider extreme examples. To be attuned and connected with yourself and another person, you have to be **aware**—you can't have your senses dulled or impaired, nor can you be in a panic. If you're drifting off to sleep at the end of a long day, then clearly you can't really be tuned in to your partner's work woes or your child's story about art class. If you're the opposite of relaxed—in a complete panic or freaking out about something—you're going to tend to lose touch with those around you, and you can even lose touch with what you're feeling or thinking at that moment.

What may be less obvious is how difficult it is to be really relaxed *and* aware in our typical daily interactions, and how fragile and tenuous our relaxed awareness seems to be. For example, if you're high on that third cup of coffee and mentally running through a mile-long to-do list as you catch up with a friend (we've all done it), then the details of the encounter aren't likely to stay with you, and your friend will more than likely sense your distracted headspace. Even when we're trying to have an intimate conversation with someone, and really focus on what they're saying, distractions crop up. Our mind drifts elsewhere; our attention lapses; we hear the ping of a text on our smartphone; the temptation to scroll through Facebook or Instagram becomes too great to resist. Also, in the midst of the conversation, we may suddenly get anxious about something, which causes our mind to go elsewhere. Stress and tension are such common background states for many of us that we barely notice them and how they impact us. Many of us are just aware enough and just relaxed enough that we can roughly follow what our conversation partner is saying over short periods of time, but our relaxation and awareness don't have much depth or stability—any relatively minor stress or source of distraction that pops up can disrupt our ability to pay attention to the other person or ourselves.

What's more, the idea of balancing awareness with relaxation really well—maintaining both at the same time over sustained periods—may seem counterintuitive. How can you stay alert and actively attentive to your own feelings, the surrounding environment, and other people, which all often cause us stress, while also remaining calm and relaxed? Awareness and relaxation may seem almost like opposites—as if trying hard at one will mess up the other. We tend to associate a high level of awareness with tension—with an eager or anxious focus; a tense, alert watchfulness or vigilance; a state of being overwhelmed with stressful things and events coming at us. Really trying to pay attention, over time, to the person we're talking with can be difficult, a strain on us, and what they do or say may make us anxious or tense. On the other hand, we often associate relaxation with becoming less attentive—relaxation comes to mean distracting ourselves from something stressful, such as what that other person is saying; or it means spacing out, watching TV, surfing the internet, texting, drinking alcohol, or sleeping.

But developing a balance of awareness with relaxation *is* possible. People vary in their natural aptitude for it. But with practice, you can learn to become progressively more relaxed, even while maintaining awareness of yourself and what is happening around you. To give you more of an idea of what we're talking about, let's look at some outliers—people who've developed extraordinary abilities of relaxed awareness.

WHAT DO MICHAEL JORDAN AND THE DALAI LAMA HAVE IN COMMON?

Many elite athletes have outstanding strength, speed, and physical coordination. But when you consider legendary, once-in-a-generation champions, one of the qualities that sets them apart, in addition to their athleticism, is their unique ability to remain deeply relaxed and aware. Not unlike the comedy greats we mentioned in Chapter 1, these champions retain a unique state of relaxed awareness even while under tremendous strain and pressure. Celebrated basketball coach Phil Jackson described an unusually strong capacity for relaxed awareness in Michael Jordan, a quality that was one secret of his success: "the most serene person I've ever seen is Michael. He has a great sense of awareness. He loves the feeling of being calm in the midst of a storm of activity. He'd like to have that feeling every waking hour."[2] In this state of relaxed awareness, in the midst of the game's storm of activity, Jordan was "in the zone," or what psychologist Mihaly Csikszentmihalyi has called a flow state.[3] Jordan was acutely, but calmly, aware of the movements of himself and his teammates all around him, often perfectly coordinating his own movements with theirs. Because he was not physically tense, his movements could flow unimpeded. Moreover, he was able to achieve a remarkably calm state of mind under the pressure of overwhelming commotion, ear-splitting noise, and what were, for him and his teammates, the highest of personal and professional stakes.

This ability to relax deeply while maintaining awareness, even during intensely high pressure situations, is also characteristic of the gold-medal-winning, world-record-setting Olympic swimmers Michael Phelps and Katie Ledecky. When a top exercise physiologist, Dr. Michael Joyner, watched them swim, what stood out to him was the extraordinary degree to which they could remain relaxed and aware during intense competition. In particular, Dr. Joyner was captivated by watching Phelps swim in the 2008 Summer Olympics. Unlike global audiences who were focused on Phelps's world records and increasing medal count, Dr. Joyner, a competitive swimmer himself, found Phelps's presence in the pool to be most notable. "'I have never seen anyone so relaxed in the water,' he said. . . . And relaxation can be taught. . . . People like Michael Phelps . . . are masters of relaxation, able to get into a rhythm and stay there even with the intense pressure of Olympic competition."[4]

Leading up to the 2016 Olympics, Dr. Joyner's impression of the then eighteen-year-old, world-record-setting champion Katie Ledecky was remarkably similar. He noted that she was gifted with an ability to push herself to the max, which can be physically very painful, yet maintain a maximal level of relaxation at the same time.[5]

This combination of pushing the body to its physical limits while maintaining a sense of calm is something common among endurance athletes. An exceptional example is Eliud Kipchoge, who in 2019 became the first person to run a marathon in under two hours. Despite the tremendous pain of running at a pace of just under four minutes thirty-five seconds per mile for over twenty-six miles, he was able to stay mentally calm and physically relaxed, his stride smooth and flowing. He's been described as someone who is very strong mentally, has a Zen-like character, and can achieve a meditation-like state while running.[6]

The exceptional relaxation ability that Michael Jordan shows in the midst of a high-stakes game, that Michael Phelps and Katie Ledecky show in Olympic competition, and that Eliud Kipchoge shows in a marathon, isn't a dulled and distracted relaxation, of course. On the contrary, it's a state of mind and body that is lively, energetic, vigorous, fully aware, and engaged in what's happening, yet it is relaxed in the sense of being free of tension, flexible, supple, and ready for action. The actor and martial artist Bruce Lee described it this way: "Do not be tense. Just be ready, not thinking but not dreaming, not being set but being flexible. It is being 'wholly' and quietly alive, aware and alert, ready for whatever may come."[7] Because it isn't a dulled and distracted relaxation, it's not an unemotional state—Jordan, Ledecky, and Kipchoge can experience their own emotions, but their emotions don't cause them to constrict or tense up to the extent that they would in most people. These athletes and their coaches realized, whether consciously or intuitively, that there is great power in balancing and integrating the seeming opposites of awareness and relaxation. If you can be aware of yourself, your environment, and other people in a way that is relaxed and open, then you will be able to more fully engage in what is happening moment by moment and use your full abilities to meet any situation, flexibly, as it arises.

Relaxation isn't an all-or-nothing phenomenon—it occurs in degrees. Most of us carry around much more mental and physical tension than we're even aware of. Dr. Joyner noticed that many elite swimmers could relax to some extent in the water, even to a great extent, but Phelps and Ledecky went beyond that to a truly noteworthy depth of relaxation, even while dealing with intense mental pressure or physical pain. Similarly, Phil Jackson certainly saw basketball players who could stay cool and calm during games, but Jordan was the most serene player that he'd seen. And it was this remarkable relaxed awareness that enabled Jordan to be so attuned to his teammates and opponents in the heat of the game.

This quality of Michael Jordan's is distinctly similar to the qualities described in our opening story about the Dalai Lama. Columbia University professor Robert Thurman and his wife, who are close supporters of the Dalai Lama, noticed this profound ability of his to pay absolute attention to everyone and anyone he talked to, completely tuning in to them, while remaining relaxed and open, even after the stresses of a long day in a loud and distracting setting.

What makes people like Michael Jordan and the Dalai Lama such outliers in their unparalleled abilities of relaxed awareness? There are likely many factors involved, such as natural talent, upbringing, and life experiences. But deliberate training and practice of relaxed awareness can also play an important role in developing this quality. One aspect of Tibetan Buddhist practice, of which the Dalai Lama is the lead practitioner, is the development of a state of mind akin to relaxed awareness. The Dalai Lama has spent, and continues to spend, an untold number of hours in meditation practice, including a certain type of meditation described by the Sanskrit word *Shamatha*, which literally means "tranquility," "serenity," or "calm presence." In a practical sense, Shamatha means a "flow of attention which is stable and clear," maintaining a state of mind that is neither agitated, on the one hand, nor dull and sleepy on the other hand, but is balanced in a state of what we would call relaxed awareness.[8] This state of mind enables the Dalai Lama to be more open and ready to engage with whatever happens in the outside world, or in his own inner world of thoughts and emotions.

As the head coach of the Chicago Bulls basketball team from 1989 to 1998, Phil Jackson used meditation practices within his training program. Some players didn't take to it, and some had an interest, but Michael Jordan had a natural aptitude for it, according to Jackson, who himself is a dedicated meditator.[9] So, while it's safe to say that the Dalai Lama is more skilled at meditation, and Jordan is more skilled at basketball, they do have something extraordinary in common—they are both outliers in the ability to access states of relaxed awareness.

How do they do it? How do they acquire this ability and put it into practice? Is acquiring this skill remotely possible for the rest of us "regular people" who are living fast-paced, high-stress lives and don't have access to the specialized training and resources of a hall of famer or a world-famous religious leader?

THE QUIET ALERT STATE

It turns out that you don't have to be Michael Jordan, Michael Phelps, Katie Ledecky, or the Dalai Lama to develop some of this skill. (*Phew.*) In fact, the potential to be in a state of relaxed awareness is quite natural and innate for each of us. Even as infants in the first weeks of our lives, we were already capable of a very basic form of relaxed awareness, which has been called the quiet alert state. Understanding this particular phenomenon can teach us a lot about ourselves, about attunement, and even about how those star athletes achieved seemingly miraculous feats.

The quiet alert state in infants was first described by researchers working in the 1950s, '60s, and '70s: Dr. Peter Wolff and Dr.

Heinz Prechtl.[10] Wolff and Prechtl pioneered the approach of sys-
tematically observing and cataloguing infant behaviors in great detail, in much the same way that biologists made field observations
of animals in their natural environments.[11] In doing so, they noticed that infants tend to cycle through several distinct "behavioral
states." Some of the states occurred when they were sleeping (i.e.,
not aware) or fussy (i.e., not relaxed), both of which don't involve
much interaction with others. In what they called the quiet alert
state—a primal state of relaxed awareness—however, infants experienced the optimal state of mind and body to interact with their
environment and the people around them. In this quiet alert state,
babies' eyes are open and appear bright and attentive, their bodies
are relatively still and calm, their breathing pattern is regular, and
they are aware and tuned in to their environment. It's in this state
that babies interact the most with their parents or caregivers, often
gazing attentively into their caregiver's face, listening to them, and
engaging in some simple imitation of facial expression and some
very basic back-and-forth communication.[12]

So, even in the first days of our lives and continuing throughout our lives, a state of relaxed awareness forms the foundation of
attunement.

REGULATION: DEVELOPING AND MAINTAINING
RELAXED AWARENESS DURING INTERACTIONS

In the quiet alert state, an infant's level of arousal (i.e., level of energy and emotion) is in an optimal zone for interaction—not too
low (not drowsy or sleeping) and not too high (not irritable, fuss-
ing, crying due to hunger, wetness, or cold), but in a middle range,
a sweet spot, in which she can be attentive but calm. To get into this
optimal state, the baby's level of arousal needs to be regulated. The
most fundamental type of regulation involves a parent or caretaker
meeting the baby's basic needs for food, warmth, rest, and contact

comfort (being held). Meeting these needs regulates the state of the baby's body, mind, and capacity for attention, which makes it possible for the baby to get into the quiet alert state. And we know, even as adults, that if we're really hungry, exhausted, or very stressed out, then getting into a state of relaxed awareness isn't really possible. For adults, as well, to connect with others we need to be in that sweet spot in which we're alert, but not very stressed, irritable, or distracted. Meeting our bodily needs is regulation at a very basic level.

Beyond just meeting our bodily needs, there are other, more subtle types of regulation that are necessary for us to be able to *remain* relaxed and aware while interacting with someone. For a baby, lack of attention from the parent, or too much excitement, attention, and stimulation can disrupt the quiet alert state. An attentive, tuned-in parent, noticing that the baby is starting to fuss, can make adjustments to the parent's own behavior (for example, making a bit more or less eye contact), which, in turn, helps to regulate the baby's state. The baby herself also has some capacity to regulate her own level of arousal, for example, by trying to engage a distracted parent in interaction by eye contact, smiling, vocalizations, and movement; by calming herself through sucking on her fist or fingers; or by looking away for a few seconds when she needs a break from all the stimulation.[13] If, most of the time, the parent(s) and other caretakers are reliably available to help regulate the baby in skillful ways, and support the baby's efforts at self-regulation, then, as the baby grows, she develops better and better skills at regulating herself. As a result, she can maintain periods of interaction for longer. Infants who grow up in environments of chronic, severe social deprivation, neglect, or abuse, or places without someone to meet their basic needs in a fairly reliable way, to help them to regulate themselves, are a lot less likely to be able to get into a state of relaxed awareness and attunement with others, and they may develop long-lasting difficulties with emotional regulation and relationships as they grow up.[14]

Relaxed awareness and regulation remain a key to our adult relationships as well. From the perspective of adult interactions, emotional regulation involves some ability to monitor our own emotions and the other person's emotions, and to do something to modify the intensity or duration of our emotions and the other person's emotions.[15] Things come up in our interactions all the time that can disrupt our connection with the other person—a conversation topic that makes us very stressed or anxious; too much eye contact that makes us uncomfortable; feelings of boredom that cause us to lose interest in the conversation; and distractions of all kinds. To keep the sense of connection in a conversation, we automatically regulate ourselves and each other at a subtle level, and we do this without even consciously thinking about it much of the time. To calm ourselves down in the midst of a stressful moment we might take a deep breath. Other times, a glance or a smile will reassure one another during an awkward or uncomfortable moment. If the eye contact is too intense, we look away for a split second; if the topic of conversation makes the other person start to look emotional in a way that makes them or us uncomfortable, we deftly steer the conversation in a different direction; if we sense that we're boring the other person, we try to think of a topic that would interest or excite them more; if we get distracted for a moment, we catch ourselves then return our attention to the other person, with the hope that we haven't missed too many important details.

All of these are ways of regulating ourselves, each other, and the interaction so that each of us is able to stay in the zone of relaxed awareness and keep our connection going. Later in Chapter 5, we'll look more at the interactive, give-and-take aspects of this mutual regulation between two people. We'll see how this process almost never goes perfectly, and how there are often even bigger breaks in the connection, when one or both partners become distracted, dysregulated (i.e., having poorly modulated emotional responses or behaviors), or out of tune with each other. We'll also look at how the two people can learn to repair these ruptures in the connection,

and start again. For now, focusing specifically on relaxed awareness is a good way to understand how each person is able to self-
regulate and maintain a state of relaxed awareness, even as they
experience feelings and emotions. This will set us up to understand
more clearly how regulation works in two-person interactions, as
we get to in Chapter 5.

"HOW DO YOU EXPECT ME TO REGULATE WHEN I'M STRESSED?!"

Let's go back to infancy for a moment. Our relaxed awareness and
regulation abilities first begin developing in the earliest days of our
lives. They grow and evolve in our relationships with our parents,
family members, or caretakers, and then continue to evolve over
the course of our lives. As we grow beyond infancy, our parents
or caretakers typically become progressively less available to regulate our every need. But, if we have the good fortune to have
parents or caretakers who are able to attend to us fairly reliably,
we develop progressively more sophisticated skills for regulating
ourselves.[16] Ordinary, mild stresses don't derail the growth of our
self-regulation abilities or our capacity for relaxed awareness. In
fact, when we deal with the relatively small, tolerable, and inevitable stresses of imperfectly responsive parents, or the various ways
in which external events or internal needs disrupt our pleasant
states, we gain more and more practice in self-regulation. With
these skills in hand—as we become children, adolescents, and
then adults—we have the potential for more sustained forms of
relaxed awareness that can serve as the basis of more mature,
intricate, and skillful interactions with others. As we grow up,
the parts of our brain that help us to regulate our own emotions
and sustain attention—such as our prefrontal cortex at the very
front of our brain—develop a great deal.[17] And this brain growth

and development helps us to develop more sustained and stable relaxed awareness.

Although our self-regulation and relaxed awareness can grow under good circumstances, things don't always go so well. In addition to the ordinary, inevitable stresses of daily life, many of us go through multiple major stresses and traumas that can overwhelm our capacity for self-regulation. Over time, such severe and recurring stress can impede the growth of our capacity for relaxed awareness. Although we usually recover from the immediate effects of stressful situations, severe stresses and traumas like sustained abuse, neglect, systemic racism, loss of parents early in our lives, and the like tend to leave their mark. They accumulate in their effects on us, potentially impacting our ability to regulate and maintain states of relaxed awareness during our interactions with people.

In fact, there is a kind of feedback loop between stress and social disconnection, with each reinforcing the other. Severe stress can sometimes make us withdraw from others, or make us feel less connected to them. In reaction to the stress, we withdraw in order to protect ourselves from perceived threats. Social isolation can then further compound the stress. As we noted in Chapter 1, there is a growing problem with loneliness, social disconnection, and stress in twenty-first-century Western societies.

Stress, and our habitual reactions to stress—ingrained in us over many years—are often major disruptors of relaxed awareness and attunement. The impact of stressors is revealed in our mental state, mood, and responses; but it also leaves a mark physically and biologically, consequently affecting our capacity for relaxed awareness and attunement. Developing an understanding of how stress influences our emotions and behaviors is the first step in training ourselves to respond differently when under pressure. When we improve our ability to self-regulate while under stress, we improve our capacity for sustained relaxed awareness and attunement.

OUR PHYSICAL RESPONSES TO STRESS MATTER

The way we respond to stress has a lot to do with how a part of our nervous system called the autonomic nervous system (ANS) functions. The ANS monitors and regulates the functioning of many of our internal organs, such as the heart, blood vessels, lungs, digestive system, sweat glands, pupils of our eyes, and more. The ANS also regulates body functions that we recognize as being part of our physical stress versus relaxation responses, such as our heart rate, blood pressure, breathing rate, and sweat production. These tend to increase with stress and decrease with relaxation. As the word "autonomic" suggests, the ANS works autonomously, that is, automatically; it is not under our conscious control. When we're confronted with something very stressful in our environment and get a sudden, automatic "adrenaline rush," with a racing heart, sweating, and nausea, that set of physical responses is coordinated by our ANS. The ANS responds automatically not only to the external environment but also to our own internal needs and the functioning of our organs.[18] In terms of its anatomy, the nerves of the ANS are *not* located in the higher brain centers that mediate our thoughts, like the surface layers of the brain (cerebral cortex); instead, the nerves of the ANS are located at the very base of the brain (brain stem) and the spinal cord, and then extend down to our other organs.

The ANS includes two systems—the parasympathetic and sympathetic systems—which function in opposing ways, as kind of counterbalancing yin and yang. Our parasympathetic nervous system (PNS) coordinates a state of relaxation, conserving and restoring our energy and bodies. It slows down our heart rate and reduces our blood pressure. The PNS contributes to the relaxation element of relaxed awareness, and, as we'll explain more in a moment, is important for our openness to social engagement. In contrast, the sympathetic nervous system (SNS) coordinates the "fight or flight" response to emergencies and sudden stressors in the environment. In response to stress, the SNS activates the inner part of the adrenal glands that then releases adrenaline and noradrenaline into our bloodstream, which raises our heart rate and blood pressure and prepares us to respond to the emergency.[19]

The ANS also interacts with another major stress response system in our body, the hypothalamic-pituitary-adrenal (HPA) system. This system includes the hypothalamus and pituitary gland, located at the base of our brain, as well as our two adrenal glands, which sit on top of each of our kidneys. Along with the SNS, the HPA system becomes activated in response to stress, and it releases a cascade of hormones involved in the body's stress response, including cortisol (often considered the body's main stress hormone). On the other hand, the activity of the PNS can reduce the activity of the HPA system.[20]

Relaxed awareness thrives on a balance between the activity of the PNS and SNS, between calmness and alertness: just enough attentiveness and alertness that the SNS is somewhat engaged, but also enough PNS activity that we can be relaxed and open to what is happening in us and around us. In our high-stress society, it seems that most of us have an imbalance such that we are tilted toward excessive stress (SNS activity and HPA system activity) much of the time, and we are tilted away from relaxation (PNS activity). We need a way to rebalance.[21] In order to connect with each other, the relaxation side of relaxed awareness and the activity of the PNS is essential.

The role of the PNS in relaxed awareness and social connection has been a major focus of research for Dr. Stephen W. Porges, currently a professor of psychiatry at the University of North Carolina Chapel Hill and Distinguished University Scientist at Indiana University. Dr. Porges's "polyvagal theory" focuses on the role of the vagus nerve (a major nerve in the PNS) in our ability to engage socially with one another. The vagus nerve runs all the way from our brain stem, at the base of the brain, down through the neck, into the chest, and down into the abdomen. Along the way it sends smaller branches to many of our organs. It enables a two-way exchange of information between our brains and our other organs, coordinates a relaxation response in our bodies, and tends to reduce the "fight or flight" stress responses that naturally occur in more emergent situations. According to Dr. Porges's theory, a particular part of the vagus nerve plays an important role in our ability to communicate effectively with each other. It is involved in the way we use facial expressions and tone of voice, the way we express and recognize emotions, and our ability to listen attentively and respond to each other. This part of the vagus nerve also sends signals to the heart to slow heart rate, tends to reduce the release of cortisol, and is important for a sense of calmness. So the entire system is set up in such a way that there is a positive feedback loop between relaxation and increased vagal tone, on the one hand, and social engagement, on the other hand, with each increasing each other. When we feel safe and relaxed, we can be more socially aware; conversely, social awareness and interaction with someone who is calm and friendly can help to calm us down.[22]

This positive feedback loop between relaxation and social interaction may also involve actions of oxytocin, a hormone in our bodies that plays an important role in our natural physiology of social engagement and bonding. Oxytocin—a neuropeptide produced by specific cells in the hypothalamus at the base of the brain—is sometimes referred to as the love hormone, because it's released during intimate interactions like cuddling, breastfeeding, and sex. Oxytocin is also involved in other aspects of social bonding, such as feelings of trust, generosity, empathy, and understanding.[23] Oxytocin seems to promote a relaxed state, which contributes to social bonding. Oxytocin also balances the activity of the ANS away from stress reactivity (away from SNS activity) and toward relaxation (toward PNS activity).[24] Beyond its role in social bonding and relaxation, oxytocin seems to have a broader role in helping us to be aware of all kinds of cues from other people, and in enabling us to see those cues as interesting, important, and salient.[25]

The opposite feedback loop, in which stress and social disconnection reinforce each other, appears to involve cortisol. For example, experiments conducted at McGill University have shown that a stress response involving cortisol release can block a person's emotional empathy for another person. And conversely, preventing the body's production of cortisol, or blocking the actions of cortisol, can increase empathy.[26] Stanford University neuroscientist Robert Sapolsky pointed out in his book *Why Zebras Don't Get Ulcers* that the body's stress response systems, such as the HPA system, are most useful in responding to sudden stresses, which start quickly and end soon after—such as the way a zebra responds to a lion by quickly running away. When the zebra has made it safely away from the lion, the activity of the zebra's HPA system can ramp down. However, modern human culture has brought us a variety of long-term worries and stresses, and the chronic activation of our bodies' stress systems can have negative effects on our physical health, as Sapolsky points out, and can also have negative effects on our ability to tune in and connect to each other.[27] This continual activation of the stress systems can promote a vicious cycle as stress increases a sense of disconnection; and being isolated and disconnected, in turn, increases stress.

Pressures and stressful events in our daily lives are unavoidable, but the way we respond to stress does not have to be set in stone. Stress doesn't have to inevitably disrupt our connections with others. In order to change how stress affects our way of relating to others, we need a way of retraining our habitual responses. The greats—Michael Jordan, Michael Phelps, and Katie Ledecky—through a combination of talent and training, developed astounding capacities for self-regulation that enabled them to maintain a state of deep relaxation together with sharp awareness, at least while they were engaged in their sports.[28] The rest of us are just as capable of developing more of this ability in our day-to-day interactions.

CULTIVATING RELAXED AWARENESS

Here, we offer you a set of exercises that can help you to develop your own relaxed awareness, buffer stress, and form the basis for greater attunement, even in the midst of the busyness, pressure, and distractions of daily life. When practiced regularly, these exercises can form a new set of physical and mental habits that can help you across a variety of situations. If you are about to go into an important meeting that you're nervous about, about to have a difficult conversation, or about to make a high-stakes presentation, having these habits firmly in place will help you calm yourself down, and help you access that state of relaxed awareness that top athletes can attain before and during high pressure competitions. Also, when you're in the midst of the meeting, conversation, or presentation, you can use these habits to regulate yourself and to remain alert, engaged, and calm. In later chapters, we will show you how to build upon these first exercises, and how relaxed awareness can form the foundation of all the other components of attunement.

Many of the exercises that we present can be considered, from a modern perspective, as forms of mindfulness meditation (i.e., practices that involve paying attention, on purpose, to one's experience in the present moment, with an attitude of nonjudgmental openness).[29] The standing meditation exercise and the silk reeling exercise that we describe are derived from Tai Chi, and they are particular types of mindfulness practices. In general, mindfulness practices have been shown to have a number of benefits in buffering stress, including increases in PNS activity and decreases in SNS activity.[30] Mindfulness practices improve the stability of attention, self-awareness, and the ability to regulate one's own emotions.[31] Mindfulness also causes measurable changes in the structure, connectivity, and function of brain circuits involved in attention, self-awareness, and emotion regulation, including areas of the frontal lobes.[32]

Overall, mindfulness meditation practices have been broadly divided into two main categories: those with focused attention (usually focused internally on the breath or body) and those with open awareness.[33] Tai Chi meditation is distinctive in combining these two approaches: balancing a focused attention on one's body and breath, on the one hand, with a simultaneous open monitoring of one's thoughts, feelings, and surrounding environment, including other people, on the other hand.[34] Tai Chi, other movement practices, and mindfulness meditation can increase awareness of oneself and others;[35] reduce cortisol levels;[36] and boost PNS activity,[37] all of which support the development of relaxed awareness.

With these exercises, the goal is to train both the physical and mental sides of relaxed awareness. At first, they may seem challenging—you might even say there is nothing relaxing about them. Being closely aware of certain aspects of your body structure and posture, and holding your body in a certain way, may feel unnatural at first and can create fatigue, discomfort, and even muscle soreness, all of which will probably feel the opposite of relaxing. But with practice, your legs will become stronger and the exercises will seem easier. We start by developing and practicing an awareness and attention to body structure, and then, while maintaining that awareness—even the awareness of some physical or mental discomfort—we try to relax. The capacity to stay with awareness, even awareness of discomfort, and relax is paradoxical, but it is also an incredibly useful skill that comes gradually with practice. If you're able to find calm during times of discomfort, then you've truly demonstrated the ability to achieve a state of relaxed awareness.

In a state of relaxed awareness, you experience all of your emotions and feelings—you're aware of them, without suppressing them, distracting yourself from them, or overexaggerating them—but you are able to regulate your emotions enough so that they don't overwhelm you and distract you from what's really happening between you and another person. By allowing your emotions and feelings to be there without becoming completely overwhelmed by them, you can direct your energy and emotion into effective action.

We know that this idea of staying in a stressful reality *and* relaxing may feel counterintuitive. How can we relax when we are aware of the very things that are making us tense? The art of teaching, training for, and developing this skill is to adjust the level of difficulty so that it is challenging but not too uncomfortable to continue practicing. As you train progressively, you can gradually handle more of a challenge.

EXERCISES TO DEVELOP RELAXED AWARENESS

The goal of these exercises is to achieve body self-awareness (a balance among body alignment, muscle relaxation, and awareness of breath) and a calm awareness of your surroundings. Being aware of your body, and developing a posture that is upright, aligned, and grounded but also relaxed, is surprisingly helpful in developing attunement. An important part of attunement is physical, whether we're conscious of it or not. Even if we have no physical contact with another person, attunement involves the use of body language, facial expression, and the coordination of our own movements with the other person's.

Please see the Note from the Authors at the beginning of the book regarding undertaking an exercise program.

STRETCHING: RELEASING TENSION, GETTING RELAXED

Virtually all of us carry around layers of tension in our bodies, often without even knowing it. This tension leads to misalignment that can interfere with our ability to tune in to ourselves or to others. The tension can stem from too much time sitting at the computer or using our smartphones, or it can develop from years of chronic stress and trauma that infiltrate our lives to varying degrees. To develop your physical skills of alignment and relaxation, we begin with a series of *stretching exercises* to loosen and release the physical tension from all parts of the body. In order to get the most out of any of the meditation exercises (sitting, standing, or walking), it helps to first warm up your muscles, release tension, and physically relax. If you already have a stretching and warm-up routine that you use for other exercises, go ahead and use those. The suggested stretching and loosening exercises found here are often used in Tai Chi. They emphasize loosening up areas of the body that tend to get tense in our daily lives, especially the neck, shoulders, back, and hamstrings. We describe them briefly here, but you can also find more details and video demonstrations at MissingEachOther.com.

Begin by lightly stretching the following body parts. Try to stretch muscles at about 70 percent of their stretching capacity, rather than pushing yourself to 100 or 110 percent. That's a recipe for getting injured.

Steps

- Neck: Standing with your feet shoulder width apart, knees and hips slightly bent, and with your hands on your hips, gently and slowly rotate your head. Circle your head five times in each direction. Don't let your head fall back too far. Be gentle with yourself.
- Shoulders: Do gentle, circular shoulder shrugs five times in each direction (from back to front and from front to back). Next, starting with your arms reaching down and your fingers extended, circle your arms in front of you, up by your head, and then behind you and back down again. Do five rotations in each direction.
- Waist: Stand with your feet slightly wider than shoulder width apart *and knees and hips bent.* Gently twist your waist from side to side ten to twenty times. Your hips and lower body should remain fixed and stable so that the gentle side-to-side turn comes from the waist. Let your arms naturally move from side to side along with your body.

- **Hips:** With your feet slightly wider than shoulder width apart, your knees slightly bent, and your hands on your hips, gently move your hips in a circle in each direction five times.
- **Back and hamstrings:** Stand up straight with your feet shoulder width apart (or closer if you can keep your balance), then gently bend forward from your waist, keeping your knees straight, and reach with your hands down toward your toes. Let your weight fall toward your shoulders and head, while keeping your balance. Feel the stretch in your lower back and hamstrings and try to maintain this stretch for a count of ten to thirty seconds. Then, slowly and gently, rise back up to the standing position.

SITTING MEDITATION

For this exercise, start by keeping your eyes open and soft (not staring at anything), calmly aware of your environment. Your goal is to balance vivid alertness and awareness of your surroundings, on the one hand, with calmness and ease, on the other hand. In addition, don't use this exercise to shut away thoughts and "clear your mind," but rather use it as an opportunity to notice your thoughts and feelings as they arise. Then, let them pass by. If a thought or feeling is distracting or painful, rather than getting caught up in it, temporarily return your focus back to your posture, breath, and muscle relaxation. Then return your attention back to an open awareness of your surroundings.

Steps

1. To begin, sit on a comfortable surface. It's ideal to use a chair that is standard height and has a firm bottom (i.e., not a squishy couch). Sit a bit forward on the chair seat so that you are not resting your back on the back of the chair. You should be maintaining your own posture.
2. Keep your legs apart at about shoulder width, your knees at about a 90-degree angle, and your feet flat on the floor in front of you.

3. Keep your back and neck straight but not tense, not leaning in any direction, as if your head were suspended from above. Do not arch your lower back.

4. Gently tuck your chin inward, with the very top of your head lifting slightly backward and upward, as if it were suspended from above.

5. Let your shoulders and arms drop and relax, and relax your neck muscles. Relax your face muscles. We usually carry a lot of tension in our face, so this is a good one to focus on for a few seconds.

6. Keep your eyes open, but with a soft, unfocused gaze. Calmly, become aware of your environment, and listen to the raw sounds around you.

7. Breathe in and out through your nose. Make your breath long, slow, thin, and even.

8. Place a hand on your stomach and become aware of the feeling of your belly expanding gently with your inbreath, and relaxing with your outbreath. Take your time and relax during the outbreath.

9. If your attention wanders to other thoughts, that is okay—it happens to virtually everyone. Let the thoughts come and go, and then try to bring your attention back to your breath and the movement of your belly with each breath.

10. Try to count your breaths. Start at one and count to ten, then start again from one. If you catch yourself at a number higher than ten, be kind to yourself and start again.

Advice for Practicing

It may help to **visualize** a point at the center of your body. This point is located in your lower belly, about an inch or two below your navel, and halfway between the front and back of your body. It's a point around which your belly expands on an inhalation and relaxes on an exhalation. You can visualize all the activity in your body and your environment as going on around this point.

As you practice this regularly, you'll get more accustomed to the physical parts of sitting meditation, and you'll quickly be able to get into a meditative state. As sitting meditation comes more easily to you from a physical standpoint, try to develop a feeling of openness and awareness during meditation. Develop a calm awareness of what you are feeling and what is around you.

STANDING MEDITATION

Standing meditation is especially helpful for developing body alignment and strength and for developing the feeling of your body's center. You want your lower body to feel grounded and rooted, while your upper body feels light and relaxed. As you practice this standing exercise over time, you will gradually get a feeling of openness during the session—your body will feel relaxed, grounded, and open; you will feel mentally ready for whatever thoughts or feelings that might arise; and you will feel confident that you can let it come, be with it, and let it pass through you and go. When you develop the ability to access this state of mind, you will be open and tuned in to others without being overwhelmed by what you encounter. Standing meditation (sometimes called standing stake or standing pole) is a core practice of Tai Chi Chuan and various other martial arts; it develops the posture, strength, relaxation, and awareness necessary for skillful interactions with others in a martial arts context.

While standing is a key practice for developing relaxed awareness, standing meditation practice can feel anything but relaxing at first. Finding and holding the correct body alignment can feel difficult and unnatural. Some feelings of muscle fatigue and burning sensations in the leg muscles are normal and generally not a cause for worry. However, the feeling of sharp pain in the knee joint itself is not normal, and it may be due to incorrect posture in the standing position, such as the knees being farther forward than the toes. This should be corrected quickly so as to avoid strain on the knee joint. Those with balance issues may find this exercise difficult, and they should practice it with great care to avoid falling. If your balance issues are prominent, you may be best off skipping this exercise. We recommend starting with a standing position that is not overly low (only bend the hips and knees slightly, not too much). Gradually titrate up—that is, spend more time in the practice and take slightly deeper stances—as you become used to it.

Steps

1. Stand with feet shoulder width apart, feet pointing straight ahead. Balance your weight evenly between both legs.
2. Sink your hips and bend your knees slightly. Make sure that the knees do not extend beyond the toes.
3. As you sink your hips, slowly raise your arms and hold them as if you are lightly hugging a large beach ball in front of you, with the fingers of your two hands pointing toward each other. Keep your shoulders dropped and relaxed. Relax your wrists and hands. Your elbows should be lower than your wrists. Relax your shoulders while your arms are forming the circle in front of your body.
4. Relax your lower back, letting your tailbone tuck in gently, as if you were sitting on the edge of a tall barstool. You will feel your weight mostly in your heels at first, but with practice, you will start to feel it evenly distributed across your feet.
5. Gently tuck your chin inward, with the very top of your head lifting slightly backward and upward, as if it were suspended from above. Let your shoulders drop and relax. With the top of your head lifting gently upward and your shoulders relaxing downward, you should feel a gentle lengthening of your neck.
6. Relax your face muscles. Breathe in and out through your nose, while keeping your lips gently closed.
7. Become aware of the feeling of your belly expanding gently with your inbreath, and then relaxing with your

outbreath. If your attention wanders, that is okay, but then try to bring your attention back to your breath and the movement of your belly with each breath, or try to count your breaths.

8. Keep your eyes open, but with a soft, unfocused gaze. Calmly become aware of your environment, and listen to the raw sounds around you.

9. Imagine your arms are like those on a puppet or marionette doll that are held up by strings attached to your wrists. Your arms are limp and relaxed, and imagine that they are barely held up by the strings attached to your wrists. Relax your back, which is slightly rounded, and relax the chest (do not jut out your chest in front of you).

10. Hold the position for one to two minutes at first. You can gradually build up more time (e.g., five minutes or more) as you practice. At the end of the standing exercise, slowly rise to a standing position.

Advice for Practicing

Allow your thoughts to settle down and become quiet. When you experience other thoughts, you can notice them and let them go. Return your attention back to the gentle expansion and contraction of your lower abdomen and lower back with your inbreath and outbreath. Slowly scan your body in your mind, from your head to your feet. Try to notice any areas of tension, allowing the tension to dissolve and release.

As you practice the standing meditation regularly, you'll get more accustomed to the physical parts of it, and you'll be able to get into the position quicker. As this comes more easily to you from a physical standpoint, try to develop a feeling of openness and awareness during standing meditation. Develop a calm awareness of what you are feeling and what is around you.

WALKING MEDITATION

The purpose of this meditation is to learn to move with relaxed awareness of both your own body and your environment while in motion. In order to bring relaxed awareness into social interactions—which are dynamic, constantly changing situations—we need to learn to maintain relaxed awareness while we are moving, and while things are changing and moving around us. This practice helps us feel the still point in our center while we are moving.

It's especially important while practicing the walking exercise to remain aware of one's surroundings so as to avoid tripping, bumping into things or people, and the like. When first learning this exercise, walk very slowly in a private place. Take a step forward with one foot, pausing while the back foot has its toes on the floor and the heel lifted. Then take another step, pausing while the back foot has its toes on the floor and the heel lifted. This very slow walking is a good way to learn it at first. Later, practice by walking out in public at a more typical pace. While walking, keep these relaxed awareness principles in mind.

Steps

1. Begin to walk.
2. Keep your back and neck straight but relaxed, not leaning in any direction.
3. Gently tuck your chin inward, the crown of the head lifting slightly backward and upward, as if it were suspended from above.
4. Let your shoulders drop and relax.
5. Relax your neck muscles, and feel free to move your head or neck as needed in order to see where you are stepping.
6. Relax your face muscles.
7. Breathe in and out through your nose.
8. Feel the breath go into your belly.

9. Keep your eyes open, listen, and remain calmly aware of what is around you as you walk, including sights, sounds, and where you are stepping.

10. As you walk and remain aware of your surroundings, try to notice any areas of tension in your face or body (e.g., neck, shoulders, or back). Allow the tension in any of these areas to dissolve and release.

SILK REELING

In Tai Chi Chuan, one purpose of silk reeling is to maintain relaxed awareness while being physically challenged (like in the standing exercise) *and* while in motion. Silk reeling exercises enhance our ability to maintain relaxed awareness in all kinds of situations. Along with standing meditation, silk reeling is a basic, foundational exercise in Tai Chi Chuan. Standing meditation trains the basic elements of posture and body alignment and relaxed awareness in stillness. Silk reeling trains the fundamental movement principles of Tai Chi, while maintaining awareness and the body alignment principles established in the standing practice. Like the walking practice, silk reeling helps to develop awareness of oneself and one's surroundings during movement. However, silk reeling uses a more complex and less familiar movement pattern, and in this way it increases the challenge of maintaining your concentration and awareness.

Silk reeling involves standing with your feet a bit wider than shoulder width apart, with hips and knees bent, and carrying out a specific sequence of weight shifts and turns of the waist. One hand remains on your hip, while the other hand and arm move in a spiraling pattern along with the weight shifts and waist turns. For detailed steps and videos on how to practice silk reeling, as well as videos and tips on troubleshooting all the exercises described in this chapter, please go to MissingEachOther.com.

CHAPTER THREE

LISTENING

From a Dan Rather (DR) interview of Mother
Teresa (MT):

DR: "When you pray, what do you say to God?"

MT: "I don't say anything. I listen."

DR: "Well okay . . . when God speaks to you,
then, what does He say?"

MT: "He doesn't say anything. He listens . . . and
if you don't understand that, I can't explain it
to you."[1]

BEING A GOOD LISTENER IS
HARDER THAN YOU THINK

The ability to listen may seem mundane and easy to do—like a ge-
neric skill to which we barely give a second thought. But is genuine
listening really that simple? To *hear* something is simple and automatic: it's a biological function in which your ears, and the basic
functions of your brain, process sound. To truly *listen* is a more
complex, challenging, and frankly undervalued ability. Most of our

everyday routines include moments of partial listening. Maybe we reply to a text while half listening to our friend recount a story, or maybe we start thinking about adding something to the grocery list as we hear about our partner's day. While we may glean enough of the main points to piece together a response, we are so rushed, distracted, and preoccupied that it's difficult to focus on the whole message someone else is communicating—words, emotions, and all.

The moments in which we feel heard are memorable. It's not often we experience someone *attentively* listening to us for more than a few seconds, or maybe a minute. They may partially understand what you are trying to say before interrupting you, or before they get distracted by someone else or by their phone. It can seem like a miracle to enjoy someone's attention for five minutes or more, when they let you do most of the talking, as they listen in an open, nonjudgmental, receptive way, and while they genuinely try to understand your experience and your point of view. Listening, at an elevated level, is rare and precious. As Ernest Hemingway once wrote, "Most people never listen."[2] More often than not, we don't listen because we get lost in our own thoughts, get distracted by the noise around us, or haven't had the opportunity to practice foundational components of deep listening.

In this chapter, we describe three important elements of listening. We break it down in order to help you build up your own listening skills. The first element of listening involves focusing your attention on the other person. We use the word "listening" to mean not just using your ears to hear the sound of someone's voice, but, much more broadly, we mean using your attention and concentration to absorb all aspects of what the other person is communicating. Listening means paying attention to the words that the other person is saying, while also noticing the nuances in their tone of voice and the pacing and pauses in their speech. It means looking at them and noticing their facial expression, the direction of their gaze, how their body is held, how they move, and the distance between you and them. Each of those subtle elements gives the listener information about the speaker's mood, emotion, and intent. Deep listening involves being open enough to let another person affect you, and being willing to get on their wavelength. Listening in this way requires you to be less preoccupied with the many distractions that vie for your attention so that you can direct more energy to understanding someone. When you focus your attention on what someone else is communicating over a sustained period of time, you create a space that's welcoming for the other person to share and be heard—you are offering a gift that we all hope to receive.

The second important element of listening is "synchrony," which means that, as we listen to someone closely, our facial expression, body language, and tone of voice start to mirror the other person's to some extent. This mirroring happens automatically in many of us as we listen—we may not even be aware of it—but it is also a skill that can be developed with practice. Synchrony is an important part of listening because it shows the person we're listening to that we are affected by them, that we're not merely observing them at an emotional distance. As we listen to someone well, we resonate with them—even the rhythm of our own brain's electrical activity becomes similar to the other person's.[3]

The third element of listening is emotional empathy, which is the ability to resonate emotionally with another person. Having emotional empathy means that you feel emotions similar to the other person's, and you realize that these emotions came from the other person. While listening and emotional empathy involve close attention to another person, they don't mean completely losing yourself in the other person's experience. As a good listener, you still need to maintain a sense of yourself *while* attending to the other person. In fact, full use of your capacity to listen involves being aware of the effects that the other person is having on you, something to which we don't always pay conscious attention. This doesn't mean getting distracted by your own random thoughts, or by what you want to say to the other person—instead, it means "listening" to your own thoughts and feelings *that are evoked in you* by the other person, even as you are primarily paying attention to the other person.[4] What you yourself are thinking and feeling in response to what you're hearing can be a kind of emotional mirroring of the other person—even if we sometimes don't realize it's happening.

> **Edward ("Ted") once had a vivid experience of emotional mirroring when catching up with a close friend:**
>
> *It started off like all the other lunch conversations I've had with Brian in the past, sitting down to check in on our lives. This conversation, though, was memorable in the way it left an impression on me. Within a few minutes of Brian telling me about his week, I began to notice myself feeling a bit sad and nervous. I was left confused, since our conversation had only touched on mundane topics, nothing remotely emotional. I was perplexed by where that feeling was coming from, especially since I had been in a pretty good mood earlier that day. But then, moments later, Brian started to shift uncomfortably as he described to me the sad news that he and his wife were separating. In retrospect, I had picked up on some subtle body language or facial expressions of his, and resonated with his sadness, even before we started talking about the separation.*

A note of caution here: while it's good to notice what you're feeling, it's hazardous to *assume* that what you're feeling must be exactly what the other person is feeling. Your own feelings may give you a hint of something going on with the other person, or between the two of you, but it's important to stay open to what you are seeing and hearing from them. So "listening," in the broad sense in which we're defining it, includes two highly intertwined aspects of an interaction—listening to the other person *and* to yourself.

Both are necessary for garnering the deepest view of what is happening between you and the other person.

You might be thinking that this idea of inner and outer listening seems difficult or even unrealistic. How can you listen to yourself *and* listen to the other person at the same time? It's challenging, and it doesn't come easily to many people. A lot of what we think and feel is not easily accessible to consciousness or is hard to put into words. If you're not sure what you're feeling as you listen to someone, it can be a useful start just to notice the sensations in your body. For example, you can notice how fast your heart is beating, or if there is any tightness in your shoulders. Noticing what is happening with you physically is a first step toward formulating what you might be feeling. In order to notice all this, you can use many of your powers of perception to sense what is happening both internally and externally.

Listening is built on a foundation of relaxed awareness. As you begin to develop relaxed awareness, your listening abilities will start to improve naturally. The relaxed awareness exercises develop the skill of "listening" to ourselves by getting us to deliberately release tension in our bodies, focus on our posture, pay attention to our breath, and become aware of our thoughts and emotions that come and go. The relaxed awareness exercises also prepare us to listen well to others. By releasing some of the tension in our bodies and developing an upright but relaxed posture, we're better able to use our body orientation and body language to express our attentiveness and openness to what the other person is saying. By practicing relaxed awareness of our own thoughts and feelings without pursuing them or holding on to them, our mind is clearer and at ease, less distracted and preoccupied. You're now better able to listen to the other person without getting stuck on what they just said, and you're more likely to remain open to hearing what they are saying now and whatever they might say next. This clarity enables you to listen more attentively to what the other person is *really* saying, and it helps you to be less distracted by what you *want* or *don't want* them to say. This clarity enables you to listen with the intent to understand the other person, rather than the intent to reply.[5] You're also better able to check in with yourself while listening to them. If something they say is really upsetting, you can self-regulate by returning your attention to your body and breath for a few moments to calm yourself so that you are not overwhelmed when you return your attention to them. The Buddhist teacher Ajahn Brahm once wrote that "total listening," or what we would call relaxed awareness while listening, "means putting aside all of the history, all the past and all the future, not having an internal commentary, not trying to second guess what [he or] she's saying, but having such stillness and such openness, that all the lines of communication are open."[6] It's a tall order, but it's possible with practice.

LISTENING—A WAY OF FOCUSING YOUR ATTENTION

There is virtually an infinite amount of stimuli that we *could* pay attention to in any situation. The world around us presents us with a constantly changing kaleidoscope of sensory stimuli. As such, we have to figure out efficient ways to selectively attend to the most important information in the particular interaction we're in. For a typical conversation between adults, the most important information may be what they are saying and seem to be implying, the expression on their faces, their tone of voice, and the many aspects of their body language. If the objective is to understand what your teammate is doing on the basketball court, then body language is paramount. If you're playing music with someone, then the subtleties of sounds become the priority, with some emphasis on body language too.

We gain critical information when we look at someone's face in a live interaction. Seeing someone's lips move helps us decode their speech. Likewise, we pick up all sorts of cues from their face—their emotional expression, the direction of their gaze, the level of flushing in their skin—that influence how we interpret someone else's experience. Other people's eyes often provide one of the richest sources of social information, and they are a key to understanding others. Looking at someone's face also signals to the speaker that we're paying attention, that we're listening to what they are saying. Making some eye contact and expressing genuine interest during even the most casual conversation invites the other person to feel free to express themselves fully. Of course, there is a balance to be struck—ideally, we make enough eye contact to pick up on cues and express interest, but not so much continuous eye contact that we are staring in a way that makes the other person uneasy. Unfortunately, it has become uncomfortably "normal" for us not to make much eye contact at all—to glance away from a conversation at our cell phone, to check a message, or to keep our eyes on the television when our partner or kids tell us a story from their day. The less we invest in being in the same place with someone and directing our full attention toward them during an interaction, the less practice we have with this type of exchange. As a result, we become less familiar and potentially a little uncomfortable with the practice of sustained attention. You can imagine this is amplified for newer generations who have had access to smart devices and touch screens since birth. They may not have as many opportunities as previous generations have had to practice the sustained attention that's so important for meaningful, live interactions.

Genuine, focused attention on another person can be tricky to sustain even in the most ideal conditions. But it's trickier still when we add negative emotions into the mix, either your own or those of the other person. Stress, distractions, and insecurities can sometimes go unidentified and can consequently hinder your ability to understand each other. If I'm caught up in my own stress or disappointment about something, then I'm less likely to have the mental space to try to listen to you. Or when someone feels hurt, low, or is grieving, it can feel uncomfortable to look directly at them. It's not uncommon for folks to shrink away from a person who becomes teary and emotional in front of them. Maybe we think they'll feel embarrassed if we draw attention to their distress. Or maybe we have trouble managing our own reaction to their pain and, in turn, look down or away to avoid that awkward feeling. Consistent practice of relaxed awareness, genuine attention, and strong eye contact in positive or neutral moments will allow you to strengthen your emotional muscles and increase attunement, making it easier for you to remain attuned in both positive *and* emotionally challenging moments.

Glancing at your phone or replying to one more email while talking to someone may feel inconsequential at the time, but those small moments add up and can have a detrimental impact on a relationship as a whole. Diminished eye contact and attention to someone's face over time sends the message that giving someone your attention is not important to you, which ultimately can make someone feel like they are not a priority to you—even if that wasn't your intention. You might not be training your focus on them because you're nervous about delaying an email response to your boss or because preparing these lunches *now* is essential to making sure the morning routine is not as chaotic as it was yesterday. Each is a well-intentioned act, but each is also a behavior that will cause you to miss fleeting emotional reactions on your loved one's face or make it difficult to interpret their response to something. All this is not to cause unavoidable guilt for all you multitasking kings and queens—but it is a reminder of the power that these micro moments and small behaviors have on developing and maintaining attunement.

This power of paying attention results in a much deeper connection that elicits a reciprocal pattern of open communication. Few are as good at this as Oprah, an interviewer who is consistently present and avoids distractions that would pull her away from the moment as she's conversing with her interviewee. From her days on *The Oprah Winfrey Show* to her current *SuperSoul Sunday* series, she's conducted countless interviews that illustrate her uncanny ability to make a connection and draw out genuine conversation. An interview setting is more controlled in some ways, as the main purpose is to converse, connect, and elicit information. It potentially lacks the random distractions more common in day-to-day interactions at home or at work. Yet even in an interview setting, variables like limited time, the need to touch on specific questions, tracking camera angles, or unexpected emotional reactions, all could impact Oprah's capacity for sustained attention on her subject. Nevertheless, her priority is to show interviewees that their perspective matters—that she treasures every moment in order to develop their connection. The greatest stories she's ever elicited come from her awareness that every single person shares the desire to be validated, seen, and heard. Understanding that principle and training herself to direct her focus and attention toward them has kept the stories flowing and given her a reputation that comes close to the Dalai Lama's in terms of her ability to be with someone as they speak.

LISTENING BY GETTING IN SYNC

We tend to think of listening as what occurs when one person quietly attends to another person who is speaking. But the most basic type of listening can occur without speech. Sometimes listening can happen between you and another person when neither of you is talking— like when you're walking together, hand in hand, with someone you love; or when you're holding them in your arms and really paying attention to them in an undistracted way. You are both quiet but very attuned to each other, sensing each other, in sync. There is an emotional and even a physical "resonance" between the two of you.

Listening often involves actively synchronizing the movements of your body to the rhythm or activity of another person. You can see this in the way that one dancer follows the movements of another, or the way that one musician plays in rhythm with their bandmates. This temporal coordination of actions during social interactions, called synchrony, has become a growing subject of research by psychologists and neuroscientists, as it has a lot to do with social rapport or attunement in our daily interactions with each other.[7]

You may have noticed that when you're having a conversation with someone who you're getting along well with, you and the other person tend to mirror each other, at least to some extent. Maybe you have the propensity to start using hand gestures similar to whomever you're conversing with. It's not intentional, but happens automatically, outside of your awareness. Another example occurs often when we're talking and walking with someone, and we unconsciously synchronize our footsteps as we move along together. Not only do we tend to imitate each other's movements, but, if we're getting along well, we tend to pick up on each other's use of language, and, over time, we start using words and terms in common. Sometimes this will lead two good friends to develop their own shared language, like an "insider's" way of communicating that only they both understand well.[8]

People tend to feel more positivity, mutuality, and rapport toward someone whose movements synchronize with their own, a phenomenon that's been called embodied rapport.[9] In good conversations, there is some imitation and mirroring that goes on between the two people, but it doesn't feel like one person is completely imitating the other. Synchronization in excess can interfere with rapport. You may recollect some experience you've had of talking with someone who imitates you almost completely. Every time you nod, they nod. Every gesture you make, they make. Their facial expression doesn't seem to come as a natural expression from within themselves but as a mirror of you. That is imitation and mirroring taken to the extreme, and it can leave you feeling disconcerted. But when someone is attuned to you in a more balanced way, the mirroring that they do conveys that they are closely attending to you, but the non-mirroring that they do also indicates that they are a separate individual who is there with you, listening and appreciating what you are saying from their own perspective.[10]

Synchrony has become a hot topic in autism research, because it is so important for social connections. We have been collaborating over several years with an autism research team led by Professor Robert Schultz at the University of Pennsylvania and the Children's Hospital of Philadelphia to study the way pairs of people in conversation tend to synchronize their postures and movements with each other automatically. To measure motor synchrony, Dr. Schultz's team developed a system of sophisticated cameras and computer software that can analyze very precisely the subtle movements of facial expression and body language of two people in conversation. The team is beginning to map the ways that motor synchrony and embodied rapport differ across people, including people on the autism spectrum and others.[11]

Musicians or dancers also give us insight into the psychology and neuroscience of synchrony and embodied rapport.[12] Years ago, there was a story about a conductor of the Juilliard Pre-College Orchestra who got frustrated because the orchestra wasn't playing in sync during a rehearsal. The orchestra members weren't really listening to each other in the way that the conductor wanted. To demonstrate what he meant by true "listening" and true ensemble playing, he asked one of the violinists to stand up and walk with him as the rest of the orchestra watched. At first the conductor demonstrated what he *didn't* want: as the violinist walked, the conductor walked along with him, but always just slightly behind him, so that it was obvious to the observers who was leading (the violinist) and who was following (the conductor). Then he demonstrated what he wanted: the violinist started walking and the conductor stayed exactly in sync with the violinist so that it was impossible to tell who was leading and who was following—they moved as a unit. It was clear, even then, that that the conductor's ability to synchronize took a high level of awareness of himself and the other person, as well as sustained "listening" to follow in real time.

By listening and watching each other, musicians coordinate the rhythm of the music, as well as the emotion they're expressing through the music.[13] One researcher has found that musicians who play together in groups need to develop three core skills to achieve synchrony: (1) anticipate what each other will do, (2) divide attention between their own actions and sounds and those of their group mates, and (3) be flexible enough to respond in real time to unexpected variations in the way their group mates play.[14] So musicians who want to be in sync can't just set a beat at the beginning of the music and then forget about each other. They have to continually stay in touch with each other and be ready to adjust in response to one another at any time.

Attempting to listen closely while dividing your attention between your own actions and other people's actions can seem awkward and difficult, especially at first. But with practice, your abilities can grow. We'll offer you some simple exercises for developing this ability at the end of the chapter, ones that anyone can do and that don't require you to be a trained musician. Step by step, the process comes more naturally until it is no longer frustrating, and certainly not dry and tedious. Just the opposite—achieving this deep level of listening—whether in music groups, in dance, or even just in a conversation—can be a very emotional, transcendent, even ecstatic experience. Contemporary sitar virtuoso Anoushka Shankar once described how, onstage with her group, mutual listening and synchronization makes her feel "alive, distilled, poured into the very essence of myself. Drunk on chemistry, heightened by sound vibrations, empowered by connection with my core and that same core in others."[15]

When this kind of listening finally "clicks," the process of coordinating your actions with the other person doesn't feel constricting, or like you are simply following the other person's rhythm. Instead, it feels co-creative, like the two of you (or you together with the group) are creating a coordinated action in real time, and where you have the freedom to move together flexibly as a group. For example, the Berlin Philharmonic orchestra's synchronous performance was once described as extraordinary, not just due to their "clarity of sound, nor their crisp articulation, but the level of freedom with which the players move as one, each tracking the other like swallows in flight."[16] The connection was so palpable that the audience could easily sense it.

THE FOUNDATION OF SYNCHRONY

Just as relaxed awareness has its roots in the very beginnings of our lives, so does listening. We seem to be hardwired for these elements of attunement from the time of our earliest days, suggesting they are critical to good social connection. Babies, for example, begin to imitate other people's mouth and face movements in the first weeks of their lives, most often when they are in the quiet alert state.[17] Then, an exciting moment comes around two months of age when most babies start to smile back in response to their caregiver's smile. Parents and caregivers are usually thrilled by that first smile back at them. After many sleepless nights with a new baby, a blur of feeding, rocking, and exhaustion, suddenly, unmistakably, your baby smiles at you. You can't believe it. Did that really just happen? You suddenly forget all the weariness and stress, and you feel the joy of that breakthrough and a new level of connection. That small act has a powerful impact on the mutuality of your connection.

By about two to four months of age, infants start developing more complex, socially engaging behaviors, like mutual gazing with their caretakers, vocalizing together, and matching a greater variety of emotional facial expressions with their caretakers (sometimes called affect synchrony).[18] This imitation, called perception-action coupling, may help the infant to begin to understand other people's actions and intentions and to share emotions with them, forming the earliest roots of empathy.[19]

Not only does the infant mirror her parents, but an attentive parent or caretaker also reflects back to the infant what they see in the infant, leading to a kind of mutual, reciprocal, back-and-forth imitation. In the 1960s, English pediatrician and psychoanalyst Donald W. Winnicott viewed this parental mirroring of the infant as crucial for the infant's psychological development. Parental mirroring signaled to their baby that they were seen, listened to, understood, responded to, and cared for.[20] More recent research shows that synchrony between parents and babies can be seen at the level of body rhythms. For example, when a baby and parent synchronize their movements, emotional expressions, and vocalizations, their heart rhythms, which are affected by the autonomic nervous system, also coordinate with each other.[21]

Caregivers and babies can also get in sync by following each other's gaze, and by sharing the same focus of visual attention (i.e., looking at the same thing). This capacity, called joint attention, begins to develop in babies typically around five to nine months of age. If the parent looks at some other object, like a toy, the baby will follow the parent's direction of gaze and also look at that toy.[22] Experts in child development argue that joint attention is the early foundation of learning to take another person's perspective.[23] In general, synchronization of gaze between adult and infant—whether by looking directly at each other or by sharing a focus of visual attention—seems to foster a feeling of social connectedness between them. These types of synchrony are important in the way that adults attune to each other too.

ON THE SAME WAVELENGTH

When we listen closely to another person, we synchronize the rhythmic, electrical activity of our brains with the rhythm of their speech. One of the ways that scientists have documented this is using a technique called electroencephalography (EEG), in which electrodes on the surface of the scalp measure the rhythmic electrical waves (i.e., oscillations) generated by groups of brain cells as they "fire," or become electrically activated. When we're sitting in silence, not listening to anyone, our brain is still electrically active. It has its own natural rhythm of electrical waves. But when we start listening to someone talking, our brain entrains its electrical rhythms to the rhythms of the other person's speech. Our brain is actively anticipating the next words it will hear.[24] A similar process occurs when we listen to music—our brain entrains its rhythmic electrical activity with the rhythm and beat of the music, a phenomenon called neural resonance. Our brain waves fire *in expectation* of the pattern of the beat, rather than simply responding passively to the sound.[25] This resonance has been documented not just in one person's brain in response to another person's speech but also between two people's brains when they are listening and synchronizing to each other. When we unconsciously synchronize or mirror our body posture, movements, or facial expressions when talking with each other, the electrical activity of our brains becomes more synchronized.[26]

The brain is also naturally prone to sync with another brain such that, even if we're physically still and not actively imitating another person while watching them, our brains seem to "simulate" the other person's actions. During the late 1990s, a group of Italian scientists at the University of Parma, including Vittorio Gallese and Giacomo Rizzolatti, discovered a specific set of brain cells (i.e., neurons), called the mirror neuron system (MNS), that become activated *both* when we carry out a certain action *and* when we're still but observing another person carrying out the same action.[27] So these cells would fire when we do something, like picking up a book, and they would also activate when we sit still and watch someone else pick up a book. In the latter example, our MNS gives us a "first person" understanding of, or empathy for, the actions and goals of the person we're watching. It's kind of like understanding the other person from the inside. As we sit still watching, our MNS helps us to know what it would be like to pick up a book without actually doing it ourselves.[28]

The evidence from all these studies on brain synchronization demonstrates the depth to which two people can connect when they use broad, deep listening skills. When you're relaxed and able to direct genuine attention and interest toward another person, the interaction becomes mutual, even if you're doing more listening than speaking. Our brains have a natural way of invisibly connecting, linking up, and even "speaking" to one another during social interactions.

I FEEL YOU MAN: EMOTIONAL EMPATHY

As we listen deeply, not only do our bodies synchronize, but our emotions "resonate" with the other person's emotions. It's a process called emotional empathy. If you listen to someone who feels hurt, you often start to feel their pain and feel a bit saddened yourself. Emotional empathy can be thought of as a kind of emotional mirroring, in which you feel emotions similar to the other person's expressed emotions, accompanied by the recognition that the other person is the source of your emotional state.[29]

Emotional contagion isn't limited to sad or painful emotions. You've probably had the experience of hearing people laughing, and then starting to laugh yourself, even though you didn't know what got everyone laughing in the first place. We've worked together for years, and we can remember many times when one of us started laughing about something and we couldn't stop, even though we were in a situation where laughter would be inappropriate, like a class or a serious meeting. We could usually hold in the laughter to not make a scene . . . but if we made the mistake of looking over, seeing the other person trying to hold in their laughter would cause our own laughter to bubble up again. Similarly, when meeting someone for the first time, discovering that you find the same things funny can help to break the ice and make you feel a bit more relaxed, making it easier for you to develop rapport. It's no coincidence that we're drawn to friends or romantic partners because they can make us laugh. Emotional resonance can occur among people in larger groups who don't even know each other. This occurs through a shared interest or experience, like rooting for the same team, seeing an emotional movie scene together with the rest of the audience in a theater, or living through some kind of emotionally intense experience together.

Emotional empathy involves the activity of a set of interconnected brain regions within the limbic system, which is heavily involved in emotions and memory.[30] Neurons in these regions extend to the other brain regions and send signals to each other through chemicals called neurotransmitters and neuropeptides. Several of these natural brain chemicals have a role in emotional empathy, including endocannabinoids, serotonin, and oxytocin.[31] The "love hormone," oxytocin, does more than just make you feel relaxed. It boosts several aspects of "listening," including emotional empathy, behavioral synchrony, and synchronized brain activity in people who coordinate their activity.[32] The MNS also seems to be involved in emotional empathy. As we watch another person who is making emotional facial expressions, the MNS in our brains automatically simulates the activity of the observed person's brain, even if our face doesn't outwardly mirror the other person's facial expressions.[33] It's like our brain is smiling or frowning, even if our face isn't.

Emotional empathy is a powerful force that contributes to compassion and ethical behavior, a sense of consideration and respect for the feelings of others, and a disinclination to harm others. If you can feel what another person is feeling, you tend to avoid causing them pain and distress, in part because their pain would elicit pain in you as well. Virtually all of us have lapses of emotional empathy, moments of insensitivity or callousness toward others, especially when we're so stressed, distracted, or caught up in something else that we don't internalize the other person's feelings. But the idea of seriously harming someone who has never harmed you, and is not threatening imminent harm, is something most of us would not consider doing. The same can't be said for those with psychopathic traits, individuals with a major defect in emotional empathy. Without that empathetic inclination, they tend to disregard or violate the rights of others—exploiting, manipulating, dominating, or harming them—without remorse, and show a callous-unemotional response toward other people's feelings. Psychopathic individuals may intellectually understand that another person is feeling distressed, but they generally don't share the other person's emotion or feel it in their gut. Typical people would feel distressed and show a spike in activity of the amygdala (a brain region involved in emotion) while witnessing someone else's distress— they feel *with* that other person. But a psychopathic observer would feel little to no distress, and show much less amygdala activation.[34] Highly psychopathic individuals lack the ability to have truly mutual, intimate relationships—to really get emotionally close to another person, to be genuinely attuned to them. Without emotional empathy, attunement isn't possible.

LISTEN TO YOURSELF

Through careful attention, synchrony, and emotional empathy, we're able to register what another person is feeling and communicating on a deep level. But, while tapping into other people's feelings in these ways is essential for skillful listening, this *doesn't* mean we should get completely swept away by other people's emotions or totally lose touch with our own thoughts and feelings. Research has shown that maintaining a sense of yourself, and being able to distinguish your own feelings from the other person's feelings, are *also* crucial for good listening and empathy. In fact, if you lose sight of yourself completely and become consumed by the other person's feelings, you actually reduce your ability to empathize, which may seem paradoxical.[35] Think of it this way—there needs to be a *you* there, as an individual, in order for you to empathize. If you get completely consumed and swept away by the other person's feelings, there is less of you available to be helpful to that other person. So, as you listen attentively to the other person, it's important that you mentally check in with yourself to gain some awareness of your own reactions to that person. Also assess your own feelings, which may be somewhat different from the other person's feelings. Again, the key to attunement is balance—we need to try to balance awareness of others with awareness of ourselves.

You might think that awareness of yourself would be the easy part, but it can be surprisingly challenging. Sometimes you may have trouble knowing what you're feeling, and there may be times when you want to avoid certain feelings. For example, perhaps you have been under stress and in a sour mood, but you didn't even realize it until someone else pointed it out to you. This has definitely happened to us. We have had times during a meeting about our research study when one of us noted that the other seemed "off" or stressed. "Really? No, no I'm fine," the other would reply. It was only later that evening, with some quiet time to sit, relax, and let go of the tension of the day, that the so-called "fine" person would become more aware that something had been wearing on them emotionally. Even if you're reasonably aware of your own emotional state much of the time, it's natural to suppress or deflect difficult or overwhelming emotions in one way or another. It may be adaptive and useful in certain circumstances to hold your own emotions at bay so that you can function and not feel overwhelmed. If you're in the midst of an emergency—say your house is on fire and you need to get yourself and your family out of there—your fight or flight reaction allows you to go into action mode and not be overwhelmed with panic or other emotions. But chronic unawareness of your own emotions, especially during nonemergency moments, can negatively affect your ability to attune to yourself and others.

People vary in their awareness of their own emotional states, and their ability to describe them, even when they are in a non-stressed state. On one end of the spectrum, some people are very self-aware emotionally almost all of the time. On the other end of the spectrum are those with a condition called alexithymia, meaning that they have great difficulty being aware of their own emotions or describing them. Many of us fall somewhere in between, with some moments of emotional self-awareness and other moments of unawareness. What's even more interesting is that difficulty in recognizing our *own* emotions seems to be associated with difficulty in recognizing *other* people's emotions.[36] This suggests that the capacity to listen to ourselves is necessary to be able to optimally listen to others. "The way out is in," Zen teacher Thich Nhat Hanh once said.[37] If we want to be in touch with others, we first have to learn how to be in touch with ourselves. For example, if we're irritable but aren't aware of it, we're probably not going to be very aware of what's going on with other people around us at that moment either.

One of our patients, Bill, had difficulty in picking up on his wife's emotions. It later became clear that Bill also had a lot of trouble knowing what he was feeling himself. Bill and Kate were having some difficulties in their marriage. From Kate's point of view, Bill was often preoccupied with his work or hobbies, and he didn't listen or pay attention when something was starting to upset her. The more he didn't seem to notice, the more upset she got. It was only when she got really upset and angry at him that he noticed, and even then his response was muted and not what she would have hoped for. From Bill's point of view, everything was going along fine, and then all of a sudden Kate was yelling at him, seemingly out the blue. He really cared about Kate and their relationship, and he felt bad that she was mad at him, but he didn't really know why she would suddenly get so mad. He also didn't know how to respond, and so he would freeze up and not say much while she vented her anger. In our conversation, Bill acknowledged that it was hard for him to pick up on Kate's feelings short of a full-blown argument, and that during the argument it was hard for Bill to be emotionally expressive, because he wasn't really sure what he was feeling himself. Bill's difficulties in sensing his own emotions and in sensing Kate's emotions seemed to go hand in hand.

Some researchers have argued that those with alexithymia, like Bill, have difficulty with "interoception," which is a difficulty sensing or "listening to" our own physical feelings or bodily state.[38] Interoceptive awareness means the extent to which our sensations and feelings (for example, the feeling of our own heartbeat) reach our awareness.[39] Many of the same regions of the brain's limbic system involved in interoception overlap with those involved in emotional empathy. This suggests that there is a close relationship between the way that our brain senses our own emotions and the way it senses the emotions of others.[40]

If you have difficulty being aware of your own emotions, start by trying to pay attention to your physical feelings that are a part of the experience of emotion. These physical expressions include rapid heartbeat, quickened breath, feeling cold or hot, perspiration, or tearing eyes. Consistent efforts and practices to develop mindfulness of your own bodily sensations can improve the accuracy of your internal perceptions and can improve your awareness of your own emotions.[41] Author Yuval Noah Harari, a devoted practitioner of mindfulness, has commented that one of the things that makes us feel alienated from each other is that we have difficulty with perceiving our own internal feelings. He notes that the alienation many people feel may not just be from social dynamics. It may also be related to how disconnected we feel from the sensations in our own bodies.[42]

Interoceptive awareness can also improve with consistent training in a movement practice, such as dance, Tai Chi, or yoga.[43] As you become more aware of your own physical feelings and emotions, you can start to notice your own reactions more when you interact with others. Learning to "listen" more accurately to ourselves, through interoception and awareness of our own emotions, may actually help us have more emotional empathy toward others.[44] So listening to the other person versus yourself does not have to be a zero-sum game; instead, with practice in balancing the two, they can reinforce each other. While some people have difficulties with interoception and emotional self-awareness, others experience the opposite extreme. These people are hyperaware of small body sensations, and they struggle with anxious self-preoccupation and worries. What we are aiming for is a happy medium—a balance between awareness of yourself and the other person, all built on a foundation of relaxed awareness. By discovering where you tend to have difficulties, you can work on restoring your own balance.

TRUE LISTENING: NOT FOR THE FAINT OF HEART

Sometimes, listening well can be its own reward. It can be wonderful, even ecstatic: like two musicians or dancers moving in sync, like a parent and baby sharing smiles, like lovers whose hearts beat faster when they look at each other and feel their silent connection. But listening isn't always easy or pleasant. Even with someone you love, it can be hard to listen to them during tense moments—when you're fighting about bills, when someone is angry at you or criticizing you, or when someone is telling you about an upsetting or scary event they went through. We've both experienced times when people close to us told us things that were so difficult to hear that we nearly shut down and became numb so as to protect ourselves from the consequences of what they were saying. Even simply sharing other people's experiences or points of view can be anxiety-provoking, offensive, or just hard to handle at times. That's one of the reasons that listening needs to be built on a strong foundation of relaxed awareness. Champion swimmer Katie Ledecky is one inspiring example of someone who knows the importance of staying relaxed, especially when experiencing the physical pain that accompanies the final stretch of a 200m freestyle sprint. Getting anxious, nervous, or stressed would only take away energy she needs for a photo finish win. In a similar way, we non-Olympians can strengthen our capacity to stay relaxed and open even when what we're hearing, or resonating with, is unpleasant. The ability to continue to wholly listen, even while "taking heat," is exceptionally useful for achieving more effective communication. If we're arguing with someone, relaxed listening skills, rather than heated, uncontrollable emotion, opens the door for us to advocate fruitfully for what we want, because we will have a clearer understanding of what that other person is trying to communicate. It's not uncommon to get so lost in your fury or frustration or disbelief at what someone is saying that it derails the possibility of negotiation or compromise.

As a female, a person of color, or a member of any other vulnerable minority group, relaxed awareness while listening can be lifesaving. If you're in a situation while talking with someone and things start to feel "off" or worrisome, oftentimes the first response is to brush it off or dismiss it and doubt your intuition. Women and racial/

ethnic minorities, in particular, often try to avoid coming across as overly sensitive to potential unease caused by unwanted sexual attention or racial microaggressions. There's a societal pressure not to "cause a scene" or be "dramatic." Some of the most contentious #MeToo movement stories are filled with debate, because listeners can't imagine why the person in question "didn't just remove themself" from the situation. The less explicit experiences we hear about from public celebrity encounters or anonymous survivors on Twitter contain shades of subtlety that clearly illustrate how culturally curated anxiety, insecurity, or shame can overtake a marginalized individual's clarity and power in that moment. For racial/ethnic minorities, chronic experiences with implicit bias and discrimination are often exacerbated by the risks that accompany speaking up, which include verbal reprimand at best, or physical assault, even death, at worst. Practicing relaxed awareness while listening gives you the power to feel a little bit more in touch with your unease, release the anxiety that accompanies wanting to maintain societal decorum, and trust your gut. Doing so, consequently, gives you the presence of mind that it's time to go. And when the situation allows, it gives you the strength to excuse yourself, advocate for yourself, or look for assistance.

That's not to say the offenders don't hold the responsibility for long-term change. If sexual offenders or those exercising both implicit and explicit bias were to develop more capacity for attunement themselves, then they could have greater awareness of their own behavior and its impact on others. For the naive perpetrators, specifically the ones who claim to have had no conscious ill-intention yet seem to "misread" the situation, relaxed awareness and listening to the other person's verbal and nonverbal messages could enable them to see, with empathy and without ego, what is truly in front of them, rather than what they may want to see.

While we've spent the chapter emphasizing the importance of using good listening, we don't mean to suggest that we should be attuned to others all the time. Quite the contrary. Attuned listening includes being aware of your own needs just as much as the needs of those around you. This awareness means knowing when things feel uncomfortable or disturbing while you're talking with someone else, when "enough is enough," and when it's time to walk away to catch your breath, reregulate, and figure out your next step. We're human, which means there will always be moments in which emotions consume us and impact our ability to listen to those around us. Listening is a surprisingly active process and not just a passive reaction; it is a skill that can be developed and strengthened through practice. As our ability to listen carefully to ourselves improves, we may decide that certain people are so intrusive, troublesome, manipulative, or toxic that we don't want to continue listening to them, at least for the time being. Having enough relaxed awareness to listen to them, for at least a little while, enables us to get the information we need about the person and the relationship to make an informed decision about our next steps.

EXERCISES FOR CULTIVATING YOUR ABILITY TO LISTEN

RELAXED AWARENESS WHILE LISTENING*

Practice relaxed awareness while listening to someone speak to you. Many people will feel more comfortable sitting while listening to someone, but you could also do this while the two of you are standing. The goal of this exercise is to build directly on the still relaxed awareness exercises (sitting and standing meditation) and add a listening component. In the earlier sitting and standing meditation exercises, you went from an initial focus on your body alignment,

---

*Indicates that this is a partner exercise. Choose a partner to practice with. This partner could be a friend, spouse, significant other, family member, neighbor, etc. This partner should be someone you trust and feel comfortable explaining the exercise and practicing with in a nonjudgmental manner. Please see the Note from the Authors at the beginning of the book.

breath awareness, and muscle relaxation to adding on an "open awareness" of your own thoughts and feelings and the surrounding environment. Now, as an additional step, you'll broaden that awareness to conversation. A one-way conversation (you listening to the other person) can give you the space you need to practice each component of relaxed awareness and listening without feeling the strain of having to respond to what the other person is saying. This practice should act as a foundation to help you utilize these steps when you're engaged in an active, two-way conversation.

Steps

1. Refer to the Sitting Meditation exercise in Chapter 2 to review the body posture and breathing techniques that should be used during this exercise.

2. Ask your partner to talk to you for roughly two to five minutes about anything on their mind or about something that recently happened to them. While listening, use the same principles of posture and relaxed awareness that prior exercises have developed. You don't need to verbally respond back to them as they speak.

3. As you listen, try to put aside distractions; maintain your focus and concentration on what they are saying, with care, but not with intensity or strain. Notice not only the words they are saying but also their emotional expressiveness— their pace of speech, the tone of voice, their facial expression, and their body language.

4. Try to consider what they are saying and expressing to be the most important thing to you at this moment.

5. From time to time, try to "listen" or pay attention to yourself by checking in on your own posture and breath, and by noticing the sensations in your body, your thoughts, and your emotions, much as you do in the sitting meditation. If it helps, set a timer for thirty seconds. When the timer goes off, check in on your posture, breath, and relaxation for a few seconds.

6. You may not agree with some things that the other person says, or you may even find them upsetting, but try not to get stuck on that or hold on to any of it. Instead, "stay with" the other person while they talk. If necessary, check in on your posture, breath, and relaxation for a few seconds to help deal with any difficult emotions, and then try to return your attention to the other person. This process of momentarily returning to relaxed awareness is a kind of self-regulation routine that will help you to not feel so overwhelmed that you have to disengage completely from the exercise.

7. At the end of listening, if they are interested, allow your partner to practice listening as you speak to them.

SYNCHRONIZED WALKING*

The goal of this exercise is to maintain relaxed awareness and "listen" to the other person while in motion with them. In Chapter 2, we learned a solo walking meditation exercise. In this next level of the walking exercise, in addition to awareness of our own body and the general environment, we extend our awareness to a partner who is also in motion, while maintaining physical coordination with that partner. This is an exercise to help you stay aware of the other person and yourself in a moving, changing situation. Initially, practice this with a trusted partner who understands that you are doing an exercise with them. Over time, you can try to discreetly use this exercise when walking with colleagues in the office or with friends on the way to get coffee or a meal together. Notice the way in which actively syncing with their pace impacts your communication and overall attunement with them.

Steps

1. First, both you and your partner should review the basic principles of the walking practice and relaxed awareness described in Chapter 2.

2. You and your partner should stand with about one to two arms lengths between you, with both of you facing in the same direction.

3. For each walk, one person will be the leader and the other will be the follower.

4. The job of the follower is to pay careful attention to the leader, and to try to walk in sync with the leader (same foot moving in the same way at the same time)—not lagging behind, and not anticipating (i.e., not being ahead of) the leader.

5. The leader should also maintain awareness of the follower so that there is a mutual awareness.

6. Initially, the leader should walk at a moderate, steady pace. It also helps to start with a "one, two, three, go" and know that both people will begin by stepping out with, say, the left foot first.

7. Once both parties are comfortable in walking at a steady pace, the leader can unpredictably change the walking pace. The job of the follower is to change pace along with the leader, while staying in sync in terms of which foot is moving.

8. As the follower tries to stay in sync with the leader, the follower may start to tense up because of the effort to pay attention. Instead, the follower should work on trying to remain relaxed and aware while trying to stay in sync.

9. If you get out of sync and have trouble getting back in, it's no problem. You can stop and begin again together.

10. Partners should change roles, with the leader becoming the follower. Try to practice this with several different partners, the more the better. Getting in sync will probably feel a little different with different people, and it may be easier or more challenging with different partners.

SYNCHRONIZED SILK REELING*

The goal of this exercise is to extend your awareness of your own body in motion and the general environment to your partner, who is also in motion, and to try to move in time and in sync with that partner. This is accomplished through silk reeling together. Tai Chi is often practiced in a group in which members coordinate their movements in time with each other. Participating in this flowing movement as part of a group can develop a feeling of relaxation, as well as a close awareness of one's own body position in space, one's own body movements, and how one's body is moving together in time with others. Silk reeling is, of course, less natural than walking, and performing it requires an additional level of self-awareness and attunement to others. This additional challenge is useful because the interactions and situations that we find ourselves in during our daily life can be challenging, unpredictable, and stressful at times.

See the exercise section of Chapter 2 for a brief description of silk reeling. For detailed steps and videos on how to practice synchronized silk reeling, as well as videos and tips on troubleshooting all exercises described in this chapter, go to MissingEachOther.com.

CHAPTER FOUR

UNDERSTANDING

"A hundred cares, a tithe of troubles and is there one who understands me?"

—JAMES JOYCE, *Finnegans Wake*[1]

TO FEEL UNDERSTOOD IS TRULY A GIFT. When someone genuinely listens to you and understands what you're saying, you feel heard, seen, and frankly, loved. Often that type of listening within relationships ebbs and flows, and it isn't consistent. In the low moments, we can sometimes be surrounded by people but feel alone, disconnected, or unseen. But then come the good moments, when someone breaks through the usual barriers to reach us. They've used enough relaxed awareness and listening skills in order to really see something about us and to let us in. And for them to truly *understand* us, they probably had to have some understanding of themselves, as well. Let's break it down.

Most of us want to feel understood, at least by those who we care about, and we feel much closer to them when they really seem to "get us." Take the universal experience of being an adolescent or teen. During this phase in development, we long to be recognized and understood for who we really are—by our parents or caregivers, siblings, friends, and teachers. Being recognized in that way can give us a greater sense of ourselves as we build our identity. Most teenage angst is born from a feeling of being disconnected and misunderstood, which is amplified by the shame of feeling like we're the only ones who long to be seen. It's unfortunate how long it takes us to realize that we are all in the same boat, yet somehow we think there's no one else riding along with us. Sometimes, it's long into adulthood before we finally get how much we have in common with others. It goes to show what a powerful impact feeling understood has on our own sense of self and our ability to confidently navigate life. Sometimes a member of another species can help us to find that feeling too. The American writer Gertrude Stein once said, "I am I because my little dog knows me," suggesting that being accurately known and understood—even by her little dog—enabled her to be her authentic self. A furry friend is a good start, but even a small increase in mutual understanding in our human relationships can make our connections far deeper and stronger than we might have imagined.

The phrases "they get me" or "I totally get where she's coming from" can seem like abstract concepts. What does it mean to "get" someone or for someone to "get" me? Most of us have experienced moments in which we really *connect* or understand someone. This can occur with making new acquaintances, when you might feel an instant connection or "friend-love" at first sight that makes you excited about the possibility of this new relationship. You might have a conversation with them in which you feel like you've known them for longer than you actually have. Other times, you may have a good, deep chat with an old friend and come away with an appreciation for how much you understand and support one another.

When we take a microscope to these moments of mutual understanding, the elements that make up this dynamic process consist of both quick, unconscious processing of the information that we take in, and more deliberate thinking and responding to each other. In every millisecond of an interaction, our senses and brains are processing the social information gathered and exchanged, both verbal and nonverbal, in order to convey your perspective and understand the perspective of another person. What's more, how you each give and receive this information in a live interaction is enhanced or clouded by our moods, biases, and prior experiences.

THE SOCIAL BRAIN

The amount of information that we're seeing and hearing during a social interaction is endless . . . as is the number of ways in which that information can be interpreted and responded to. It's safe to say that most people have, at some point or another, fallen prey to the classic example of crossed signals. A patient of ours, Sienna, once recounted a story about this. She had been casually chatting with her close friend Aaliya at work one day, talking about how their respective weekends went. Sienna had taken a trip to New York for a family celebration. A couple of weeks earlier, she had invited Aaliya to go on that trip to New York with her. Things got busy and they never confirmed the plans, so Aaliya didn't join. After they finished chatting about their weekend and parted ways, later that night Aaliya sent Sienna a message apologizing because she thought Sienna was upset at her for not coming to New York. Sienna was stunned. She tried to replay their conversation from that day in her mind to find any cues she had missed or any responses she had made that may have given Aaliya that impression. In reality, Sienna was not upset in the least, because she knew Aaliya decided not to join for myriad valid reasons. In that example, it's difficult to say exactly where things went sideways that led to the two women not understanding one another, but it's safe to say it was a combination of a breakdown in relaxed awareness, attentive listening, and true understanding. Have you ever been there? Have you ever encountered a moment when you couldn't understand how your signals crossed and you sailed right past each other?

Social-emotional understanding, or the way we interpret and respond to another person's social cues, can seem like a poetic, indescribable phenomenon at times; it's something we feel or experience yet can't explain. Many people describe themselves as being very good at "reading" people. Whether they are accurate or not, that fairly vague characterization refers to a skill that has been broken down through psychological science and is called social cognition. It's how we think and process information in social situations. Social cognition has been an area of very active research in recent decades—including some of our own research—both in typical child and adult development, as well as in individuals on the autism spectrum.[2] The more that social cognition has been studied, the more researchers have realized how intricate and multifaceted it is.[3] Our brains carry out a wide range of cognitive processes during interactions with other people. Social cognition is essentially a set of tools that we use to help make sense of our interactions.[4] In our framework for attunement, social cognition is the process of listening (perceiving lots of different kinds of stimuli from the other person and yourself), trying to understand, and then responding.

Take the example of casually meeting a new person at a party. During the interaction, you naturally utilize every sensation you have. Your eyes *see* their outfit (blue jeans and a striped, blue button up) and hair (combed back lightly with a dollop of hair gel). You *hear* the sound of their voice as they introduce themselves, you *smell* their body spray, and you *touch* the texture of their skin as you both lean in to shake hands. As light waves, sound waves, olfactory signals, and touch from the other person reach your senses, your brain processes them as perceptions (e.g., color, pitch, smell, sensation) that you put into the context of your prior experiences of sensations.[5] Ultimately, you organize and use all these small sensations and perceptions to make decisions about how you should best respond. When the partygoer puts their hand out, you see it, and you identify it as a welcoming gesture you've seen in the past that is typically used to introduce yourself and become familiar with a new person. Your brain moves at lightning speed, processing that information and interpreting it to be a safe gesture that demands a response, directing you to return the favor and put your hand out to shake theirs. You then process, store, and represent in memory this experience to use in the future when interacting with the world. It seems technical, but even for something as mundane as a handshake, we're processing every little detail, encoding it, interpreting it, and identifying an appropriate response.

Our social cognitive abilities include processes that focus on things like identifying emotions expressed on people's faces, reading body language, making social decisions (is this person a friend or a stranger?), and choosing social responses (should I smile or should I get out of here now?).[6] At times, we are aware of these cognitions, but more often than not they are unconscious processes that our brain carries out automatically. In Chapter 2, we mentioned how we automatically regulate ourselves, even on the most subtle, unconscious level imaginable. One of the examples involved redirecting the conversation away from a topic that seems to be boring the listener. This redirection happens quickly, without us even thinking about it. But it's a response that we, as speakers in a conversation, have acquired over time by recognizing the social cues indicating that the other person is bored (for example, when they yawn, show less eye contact, start looking around at other things, or check their phone). Recognition of these cues, in and of itself, is a powerful ability that we have as social creatures. While it may feel easy to identify someone's boredom, there are a multitude of small steps that brought your brain to that realization.

RECOGNIZING EMOTIONS WITHIN OTHERS *AND* WITHIN YOURSELF

In the previous chapter, we talked about "listening" to emotions through emotional empathy for others and through listening to yourself. As a reminder, "listening" means being aware of emotions at the level of feelings and physical sensations. In this chapter we want to tackle the next step, which is *understanding* those feelings. The first step toward understanding is to recognize each individual emotion. This kind of emotional intelligence may seem basic, so much so that you don't need to give it a second thought. But recognizing emotions in other people and in yourself can be a surprisingly complex and challenging task.[7]

People express emotions mostly through nonverbal communication, less so with words. These nonverbal communications include facial expressions, body language, and tone of voice. Neuroscience research has shown that specific parts of our brain, such as the amygdala, process and integrate information from multiple senses—like what we see in the other person's facial expression, and what we hear in their tone of voice—and this integrated information helps us to recognize emotions.[8] Activation of the vagus nerve of the parasympathetic nervous system (PNS), which increases relaxed awareness, appears to facilitate both recognition of other people's emotions and the ability to distinguish among different emotional expressions.[9]

So a key to recognizing emotions is trying to stay relaxed and aware, and paying attention to what you're taking in through your senses. If you're not looking at someone, then you can't catch their quick glance at the clock that indicates their boredom. If you see their slight eye roll but don't notice the tone of their voice, it may be hard to know whether they're laughing with you or at you. By paying attention and integrating these visual and auditory "streams" of information, we can get a sense of the other person's emotional state. Understanding emotions from facial cues enables us to navigate dynamic, varied social interactions quickly and skillfully.[10] Being able to interpret the other person's boredom from their expression allows you to make an instant judgement and either quickly become more interesting or change the topic altogether!

Recognizing other people's emotions, as well as your own, is also the first step to being able to regulate and cope with emotions better. It takes certain skills to be able to identify your own many emotions when you're upset, stressed, overwhelmed, nervous, and so forth, and then to know how to regulate those emotions and come back to baseline. One of the challenges in disentangling our own emotional state, or that of others, is that sometimes people feel a complex mixture of emotions.

Humans begin to develop the basic skill of recognizing emotions and discriminating among different facial expressions of emotion starting early in infancy. In fact, by four months of age, many infants can discriminate angry from happy faces,[11] and show a preference for looking at positive versus negative emotions on faces.[12] Babies will tend to scream or cry at a scary face, suggesting their ability to discern emotions. Within the first year of life, infants can also adjust their social behavior to the emotional message inferred from other people's facial expressions.[13] Often, parents who are feeling sad or hurt are surprised when their small toddler picks up on their feelings and comes over to sit with them or offer a hug. Children and adolescents who are better at interpreting emotional cues tend to have more positive coping skills, interpersonal relationships, and overall well-being.[14] On the flip side, lower levels of emotion recognition have been linked to poorer psychosocial adjustment in adolescence.[15]

Reading facial expressions to determine emotions can be a challenge at times, even for adults. Consider examples in your own life: maybe there was a time when you were unsure if someone liked the idea you pitched at work. Was that stern look on their face a reaction to your idea or were they just thinking about something else? Boredom is another emotion that can be tricky to discern. To recognize expressions of boredom in another person, we look for myriad cues, such as wandering eyes, pursed lips, deep sighs, shifting legs, crossed arms, fidgeting bodies, heavier sighs, attempts to interject or change the subject, and so forth. It's a miracle that our brain can process each individual piece of information and holistically comprehend the combination to mean, "*Red alert*: this person may be bored. Change your behavior before you lose them!" With enough experience, most of us seem to acquire the ability to integrate all this sensory information quickly and effortlessly to recognize boredom.

But the skill of recognizing other people's emotions may not work well when you are distracted by your thoughts, or when your conversation partner is trying to conceal their emotions and feign others. Microexpressions occur so fast that past researchers had to film people in conversation and then slow down the replay in order to observe the almost imperceptible changes in expression. This is an area that facial expression researcher Paul Ekman has pioneered—identifying the microexpressions that reveal true emotions, even when people are trying to conceal their emotions. How many times have you felt bored and immediately tried to cover it up by shifting position or doing your best not to let the other person see you check your watch? Sometimes you'll get away with it, and sometimes you won't get so lucky. On the other hand, if the other person is covering up their true feelings or not being forthcoming, how are you supposed to understand them? There's no easy answer, of course. But if you notice that something in the pattern of their cues doesn't seem to fit, or if they are saying one thing but giving off different nonverbal cues—like saying "that's interesting" but seeming to look away more—then that may be a hint toward understanding their true emotions. So if you develop your relaxed awareness and listening skills, you'll be in a better position to start to perceive these hints. The skill of understanding involves paying attention to these hints and cues, and noticing the patterns. Of course, the fallout from the COVID-19 pandemic has made this all the more challenging, since a lot of our interactions with colleagues, friends, and family, in recent months, have been mediated through face masks or via online video conferences that obscure the subtle, instantaneous nonverbal cues that communicate so much. All we can do is to adapt the best we can, trying to be as attentive as possible to the cues we can glean, while appreciating how valuable in-person interaction really is.

We all have moments in which we fumble, lose our attention, and don't pick up on the clues someone is dropping for us. We can all use strategies to attune better to each other. We can accomplish this if we focus our attention in a more mindful way and enhance our ability to understand one another and "pick up what they're putting down." The key is paying attention and getting in the habit of noticing, moment-by-moment, the patterns of the other person's facial expressions, body language, and tone of voice, as well as paying attention to feelings in ourselves. At the end of this chapter we lay out some step-by-step exercises that you can try in order to develop these habits.

COGNITIVE EMPATHY VERSUS EMOTIONAL EMPATHY

Your social brain utilizes a series of complex processes to analyze and interpret social information about yourself and about other people.[16] Once we look at someone, our brains process social cues and emotional expressions from the other person at lightning speed. These processes help us to understand and connect with other people, and a key part of doing that involves having empathy for others. In Chapter 3, we talked about *emotional* empathy, which is sometimes called emotional contagion or emotional resonance—the capacity to *feel* what another person is feeling at a gut level, to resonate with them emotionally. Emotional resonance is activated

quickly and automatically, as soon as you get the sense that someone is feeling a certain way.

Here, though, we emphasize another side of empathy called
cognitive empathy—the capacity to know and *understand* intellectually someone else's point of view, what they are thinking and
feeling.[17] It can be useful to think of emotional empathy as "hot"
and cognitive empathy as "cool." Cognitive empathy includes the
ability to understand and predict people's behavior by inhabit-
ing their perspective.[18] This involves something that can be really
challenging—consciously switching back and forth between reflect-
ing on your experience, that of someone else, and back again to
yours, to understand in what way your perspectives may be similar
and in what way they're different. Cognitive empathy works best
when you have a curiosity about how the other person views the
world and what motivates them, an openness to considering what
it's like to be in their shoes, and a tolerance of the idea that their
perspective might be very different from yours. When you think
of it for a moment, being able to step out of your own perspective
and see things from another person's point of view are really high
achievements of social cognition.

Both emotional and cognitive empathy are important in understanding and connecting with others, especially if they are having a
hard time. It would be hard to cultivate a meaningful relationship
without both understanding how the other person is thinking and
feeling as well as having compassion for them and the motivation
to want to help them. When emotional and cognitive empathy are
working together, you're able to step beyond your own subjective
experience and go into a shared subjective experience between you
and the other person. When that happens, you experience a mutual recognition of each other's perspectives, a phenomenon that
psychologists call intersubjectivity.[19] Research shows that the most
responsive caregivers are those who are high in both emotional and
cognitive empathy.[20] Although they ideally would work together,
the emotional and cognitive sides of empathy aren't one and the

same. Some people are strong in one type of empathy but not in the other. Similarly, evidence suggests there are independent developmental paths for emotional versus cognitive empathy, meaning these abilities develop, change, and decline in different ways as people age, which would indicate they are separate capacities.[21] And there's strong evidence that the two types of empathy involve the activity of different sets of interconnected brain regions.[22]

In Chapter 3, we mentioned that emotional empathy involves the activation of a set of brain regions in the limbic system, some of which are deep in the brain, and which are involved in emotional feelings and memories. Cognitive empathy involves activation of its own network of interconnected brain regions, mostly regions on the surface of the brain, the cerebral cortex, which is involved in thought and reasoning.[23] However, one area of overlap in the emotional and cognitive empathy brain circuits may be in the mirror neuron system. The "embodied simulation" carried out by the mirror neuron system when observing another person's actions may also be important for understanding the intentions of their actions.[24]

To understand cognitive empathy better, let's take a look at something psychologists have called theory of mind, or the ability to take someone else's perspective and understand their thoughts, beliefs, intentions, and nonverbal social cues.[25] Essentially it's the brain's way of realizing that another person's perspective may be different from our own, and helps us to metaphorically step into the other person's shoes. We act based on how we think and how we think other people think; and again, it's something that we develop at a very early age.[26] Typically, children around the age of four or five start to understand that different people think and want different things; and around that age, kids will start to act in ways to get what they want based on this understanding.[27]

The Sally-Anne story is the classic assessment of theory of mind in children. Describing to you the Sally-Anne story can give you a better sense of what we mean by perspective-taking, and why it's important for attunement throughout our lives. In this assessment, a child is introduced to two cartoon characters, Sally and Anne. In the cartoon, they see Sally take a marble and hide it in her basket. Then Sally leaves the room and Anne takes the marble out of Sally's basket and puts it in her own box. Sally comes back to the room and the child is asked, "Where will Sally look for her marble?" Those children who answer "in Sally's box" are thought to have a strong handle on understanding someone else's perspective. Children who've developed theory of mind realize that Anne put the marble in Anne's box, but that Sally was out of the room when that happened and so Sally wouldn't know that—Sally has a different perspective.[28] This assessment illustrates the key idea that different people have different views of the world, depending on their own experiences and backgrounds. Although this idea may seem obvious, recognizing it is necessary for us to be able to connect with others, and ultimately for us to form and maintain relationships. It's very difficult to be attuned to others if we're only able to see the world from our own perspective and assume that everyone else must agree with us. Although children begin to develop theory of mind around age four or five, it can remain an ongoing challenge throughout our lives to remember to take other people's perspectives into account, especially as we get into the intricacies and messiness of adult interactions. Over the course of a lifetime, our views of the world can become colored by attitudes and opinions derived from our own unique life experiences, thereby making our views more rigid and inflexible. To foster attunement, it's helpful to try to remain open and curious about other people's perspectives, without necessarily giving up our own.

When we take someone else's perspective, we're trying to infer their thoughts, beliefs, desires, or intentions. Then we use this information to interpret their speech and actions—asking ourselves what they are trying to communicate—as we try to anticipate their next move. This includes situations like reading and responding to someone's intentions, reading someone's level of interest as we communicate, detecting someone's intended meaning (are they sincere or sarcastic?), and imagining how they might be perceiving us. A lot of our research has focused on investigating how perspective-taking is impacted in autism, because individuals on the spectrum often struggle with reading emotion in others or anticipating what others might think of their actions. However, perspective-taking skills can be difficult for some neurotypical people as well. Fortunately, those skills are malleable and they can be improved through mindful awareness and practice.

We can do our best to interpret someone's intended meaning, but our efforts, while sincere, don't always hit the right mark. That's because our own biases, emotional states, or the context through which we view a situation impact the quick assumptions or calculations we make based on the limited information we have about another person. More often than not, we use quick strategies that help provide an explanation for the motive or cause of other people's behavior or our own. Psychologists file this quick approach under something called attribution theory. These, usually unconscious, strategies are used to "attribute" meaning to why someone is acting the way they do. It's a comforting technique that makes the world a more predictable place. There's nothing worse than not understanding why someone has acted the way they did, especially when that action seems negative. There are two options you can choose from: an internal or dispositional attribution, which means a person's behavior is due to some aspect of the person's character or personality; or an external attribution, which indicates that behavior is explained by some aspect of the environment. Let's say our coworker Elina didn't get the promotion she's been working toward. An internal attribution about her would be: "Elina doesn't work as hard as George; she really doesn't deserve to be promoted right now." An external attribution would be: "Maybe with so much male leadership in this office, Elina's qualifications were underestimated due to gender-based bias." One perspective blames Elina for her lack of progress, and the other takes into consideration external, sometimes hard-to-see factors within the system.

Attributions can help or hinder our ability to understand each other. These attributions can become distorted and unhelpful when people experience stress, anxiety, depression, or other forms of psychopathology that may lead them to focus more heavily on the negative. If you're in a cycle of depression accompanied by pessimistic, negative attributions, your negative attributions could, in turn, be maintaining your low mood state. For example, you could be feeling depressed, leading to an attribution like, "That's how it goes in the world. Nothing ever works in the long run," which in turn could contribute to feelings of depression. Misattunement can be reinforced by a feedback loop between stress and social disconnection, and negative attributions can be part of that mix. Similarly, tendencies to make negative internal attributions can also leave you feeling less connected to someone, as well as making that person more likely to withdraw from you. For example, any of us could experience a bias toward over-attributing someone's behavior to internal factors rather than to external or environmental variables. It's called the fundamental attribution error. Let's return to the example of Elina and the promotion she was denied. It's much quicker and frankly easier to assume that she didn't get the promotion because she wasn't qualified than to actively think about all the potential systemic issues that could have impeded her progress within that particular corporate environment.

Consider another example of two former college classmates, Naomi and Oliver, who recently reconnected and decided to meet for coffee to catch up. Oliver suggested they meet at 2:00 p.m., and Naomi arrived a few minutes early and found a nice spot by the window to wait. Oliver ended up arriving fifteen minutes late. Naomi, understandably, was rather shocked, since Oliver was the one who suggested their meeting time, but she ultimately shrugged it off and moved on. Interestingly, Oliver didn't mention anything about being late when he greeted Naomi, and instead breezed right into the typical niceties and asked if she had ordered already. As Naomi tried to hide her disbelief while they finally sat down with coffee in hand, Oliver quickly stopped to say hello to his coworker who was seated at the table next to them. A little while later, as the two classmates were catching up, Naomi asked how Oliver's job hunt was going since he had mentioned that he was looking for a new job when they originally ran into each other. Oliver started to look a little uncomfortable and quickly brushed it off with a general reply, and then pivoted to describe the new home he and his fiancé had just purchased last month. Despite Naomi's best attempt to give him the benefit of the doubt, it quickly felt like Oliver was showboating a bit.

In that quick vignette, how many opportunities did you notice that Naomi had to make either internal or external attributions about Oliver? When he was late, she could have given him the benefit of the doubt and maybe thought traffic was to blame . . . or she could have automatically thought of him as a "late-person" who isn't considerate of other people's time. In reality, maybe Oliver misremembered their meeting time and thought he and Naomi had agreed to meet at 2:15 p.m., meaning it was all a simple mistake. The breeze-by of the job hunt topic? Naomi's internal attribution could be that Oliver is closed off, hiding something, and/or possibly didn't trust her as a close-enough friend with whom he could share personal details of his life. Naomi's external attribution could be to acknowledge the presence of Oliver's current coworker at the table next to them, realizing that he may feel uncomfortable disclosing that he is looking for a job while still at his current position and while in earshot of his coworker. Attributions can also be clouded by our own emotions, consequently causing us to make pessimistic assumptions about others. Remember when Naomi thought Oliver was bragging about his new home? Checking in with your own emotions is important so you can consider whether they may be clouding or influencing your interpretation of someone else's behavior. Had Naomi checked in with herself, she could have wondered whether maybe she was a little sensitive to this topic, because she was self-conscious about still being a renter and not being as close as her peer to owning a home. Acknowledging those remnants of disappointment and/or shame are necessary to avoid the trap of becoming prone to negative, internal attributions of others. Your own emotions are always valid, but not being aware of them in the moment, or leaving them unchecked, will undoubtedly decrease your ability to attune to the joy and excitement of others.

Our processing patterns happen fast in order to accommodate all the rapid-fire social information we're taking in. This makes us susceptible to choosing what could be the most obvious cause for something. It takes time, energy, and cognitive processing effort to slow down and identify potential external variables that are playing into a situation. Internal attributions are usually automatic forms of cognitive processing—we do it quickly and not always accurately. Our accuracy plummets even further when the internal attribution is distorted by bias. External attributions that could be impacting the situation require more controlled processing that takes longer and necessitates more thought in order to file through potential reasons and weigh all the information about the context of the situation. It would take your brain a few more seconds to consider traffic or miscommunication than if you just assume someone was late because they are inconsiderate of your time. Sometimes we can't process it all perfectly in the midst of the interaction, and we need to rethink things over a bit later. Or maybe we make one assumption in one moment, but just a few moments later realize that we may have misunderstood the situation. Developing mindful awareness of these automatic thoughts that we all have is a necessary step toward being able to reflect on them and to modify their impact on how we relate to people.

As you start to identify the role of attributions in your social interactions, consider how your leniency changes as the level of intimacy differs across relationships. In the previous vignette, those were Naomi's responses toward an old classmate, someone who she was not extremely close to and in whom she may not endow the same level of trust as a partner, family member, or best friend.

With less intimate relationships comes a greater level of formality that makes you more careful with your language or more likely to consider external attributions. We're more personally involved and more sensitive to how we are perceived by people who we are closer to. As a result, it might be easier for you to lose your temper with them or to use internal attributions more often, because you have higher expectations of those you love and of their love for you. It's easier to expect our partner to "just get it," and we often lose patience more quickly when explaining something to them than we would with a friend. If someone you're intimate with doesn't seem to be paying attention to what you have to say or isn't understanding you, then you may be quick to label them as being self-absorbed or less empathetic, when instead you could pause to consider if they were distracted or whether you could have rephrased something in a clearer way. Try to observe how you attribute motivations to behaviors of your casual friends versus your intimate relationships. The exercises at the end of this chapter will be helpful in practicing that awareness. Deep understanding skills are built upon balancing mindful attention of yourself and others, and upon an ability to reflect on ourselves and the experiences of another person. This balance and reflection enables us to interpret what happens between people more effectively, to better understand someone's intentions, and to generate a more proactive, useful response to one another.

BREAKING THE CHAINS THAT BIND US

Humans are reactive—it's deeply ingrained in our nature. We process and communicate quickly, and we often use heuristics or shortcuts that help with how we process, interpret, and respond to people. But when we are too quick to react, especially in negative ways, this reactivity can become an impediment to understanding rather than an advantage. When we experience stress or heightened emotions, or when we are distracted, it's much easier for us to respond automatically. Maybe you snapped at someone for something they said, because you weren't able to consider their perspective before responding. Such a reaction could result in you making more internal, negative attributions about someone, which could then lead to a less attentive and/or compassionate response, taking you both down a road to a place where neither person feels seen, heard, or understood. To understand deeply, try to consistently practice being more reflective and utilizing more controlled responses when engaging in conversations and interpreting someone's responses. We can improve our ability to understand each other through reducing the reactivity we experience within a dynamic interaction.

Humans have been trying to grapple with our own reactivity, and the impact that has on our interactions and relationships, for literally thousands of years. About 2,500 years ago, the Buddha taught that human suffering comes from misunderstanding ourselves and the world—from not recognizing our relational nature, how highly interconnected we are with other people and living things, and from wishing and expecting life to be how *we* think it *should* be, rather than the way it is. We want life to be and go a certain way; we don't want things that we value to change; and we want people to be and act a certain way—and since life almost never goes as perfectly as planned, it frequently fails to live up to our expectations and desires. Suffering is born from the way we constantly and automatically react to life as it unfolds, sometimes fighting against what is. Something happens, we react, and then that reaction becomes the stimulus to our next reaction. It's like a chain of events with no clear ending.

Conversations are like a microcosm of life. Because two or more people are involved, we only have so much control over how conversations go. When they don't go the way we want, we tend to react emotionally, rather than with intention. This reactivity can become a vicious cycle that impedes our ability to stay relaxed and aware, which can consequently have cascading effects on our capacity to listen and understand. It's remarkably difficult to do the opposite of what comes naturally—to try your best to give up your attachment to the outcome of a situation, especially when you fear that things won't go your way, and instead, learn to respond patiently. This is what Dogen, the thirteenth-century Japanese Zen master, described as making "effort without desire."[29] Our amygdala and the other parts of our brain's emotional response systems are programmed to react quickly when we feel threatened by fear, guilt, outrage, disappointment, or shame. This quick reaction causes us to fight or flee. It's difficult to acknowledge or identify this response pattern in the moment, especially when emotions flare or when stress gets the better of you.

Sometimes partners in a relationship, close friends, or family members jump to conclusions in a conversation or argument because of so many repeated patterns from past interactions. We develop expectations of what we think someone is trying to say or what they mean based on other encounters we've had with them. While those expectations may be accurate at times, they could also sometimes make us jump to the wrong conclusions. Other times, quick reactions can be born from irritable moods or from a desire to take out our frustration from another situation. Maybe in a different moment, a particular conversation wouldn't have annoyed you, but being in a bad mood can really tip you over the edge. Emotional reactivity can even stem from underlying cumulative resentment or guilt over a totally different situation that is being projected onto the current one. Consider this example: imagine your housemate was upset that you left the lights on when you went to work that day. Come evening, the housemate walked into the house, saw the lights on, and blew up in frustration. Then you came home, and you got an earful. In reality, one instance of carelessness should not have provoked such an extreme reaction, but it did. Upon reflection, the answer is revealed: the housemate's reactivity grew from a brewing resentment about you not having helped clean up around the house in general for the last few months.

It's usually easier to identify a cycle of reactivity when it's not happening to you. A patient once described a particularly vivid example of this. Marcus was visiting his parents one weekend. He was puttering around in the kitchen with his mom when his dad walked in after running some errands. His parents initially began talking about something fairly banal. But then the conversation slowly began to brew into a simmering argument between his parents. Time started to slow down for Marcus. At this point in his retelling, Marcus mentions, for context, that his parents have been married for almost thirty-five years and have what he considers to be an exceptional example of a strong, communicative, loving partnership. But no one's perfect, he conceded. On this occasion, as they argued over something that has since probably become a forgettable blip on their timeline as a couple, Marcus could easily see the chain of events unfolding, as each stimulus bred a reaction that then became the stimulus for the next person's response. His father was annoyed at his mother for doing or not doing something and proceeded to gripe about the issue. Stimulus. His mother quickly responded with the reasoning for her choice, in a defensive tone of voice, which became the next stimulus for his father to react to. As the bickering continued, Marcus could see them both becoming less relaxed and more agitated. The annoyance and irritation rose in his father's eyes like a dark fog that started to cloud the edges of his vision and develop a filter over his senses. As each of them became enveloped in tunnel vision, their awareness of their own emotions decreased, which consequently reduced their capacity for controlled processing. He was filtering her responses through a cloud of negative emotion that biased his interpretation of what she meant. Her annoyance increased with her confusion about his responses that didn't make sense to her. Their attention became biased toward each negative aspect of the other's argument and their internal attributions about each other's actions quickly grew. It was like watching a cartoon strip of a character rolling a small snowball down the hill, and the snowball gaining traction until its size and speed were uncontrollable. The chain of reactivity kept going until they decided to just walk away from the conversation in order to take a breath and cool down.

It was easy for Marcus, as an outsider, to see the chain reaction unfolding. But it's not so easy when you're the star of the show. How many times have you found yourself in the snowball, convinced there was no other path other than to keep rolling down the hill? The magic of mindful attention is that it allows you to identify the chain as the links grow, and to use that moment to pause. The emotional discomfort that comes from any heated conversation, like the one between Marcus's parents, is so great that our minds are susceptible to just reacting to the pain, whether it be by snapping back, saying something we regret, or making an impulsive decision. Buddhist teacher, lay minister, and podcast host Noah Rasheta uses the phrase "mind the gap" when thinking about how to break the chain reaction of stimulus and response.[30] The phrase "mind the gap" was popularized from the warning announced in the London Underground subway system when the doors of the train cars open. The phrase is a reminder to focus your attention as you step from the platform to the car or vice versa. Rasheta noted that "mind the gap" can be a helpful saying to remind you to pay attention to the gap in between a stimulus and reaction, the gap in which you can pause, process, and deliver a more controlled response. It may not happen within the first few chains in the link of reactivity, but the important part is that it happens at some point. In the case of Marcus's parents, one example of minding the gap could have been that one of them took a breath, paused, and noticed their emotions were boiling up, and that the back-and-forth was going nowhere. The pause alone is powerful because it gives you more options for how to proceed, instead of rolling down the hill.

We would argue that building relaxed awareness and deeper listening skills set the stage for your capacity to "mind the gap."

This is especially important because negative reactivity happens fast, and, depending on the person, it can be a challenge to start to notice the chain building and find enough awareness to pause. This is not to say that you shouldn't have a negative reaction. If your colleague challenges you by pointing out a biased or implicitly racist comment you made in a team meeting, it's completely understandable to feel upset, disheartened, worried, guilty, and so on. Meditative practices, like the ones we describe in Chapter 2, are meant to bring awareness to all emotions; they are not meant to stifle them and force you to feel peace, joy, and happiness 24/7. Instead, practicing relaxed awareness and listening to yourself should allow you to notice yourself becoming activated when receiving critical feedback. A moment of self-awareness can help you to prevent your emotions from consuming you and restricting you from hearing what your team member is saying. For example, reactivity might lead you to become defensive of what you said such that you start immediately disagreeing with the colleague before you have a chance to even hear and understand the impact your words may have had. At some point in the conversation, finding a moment to check in with yourself and notice how you're reacting to the feedback provides you with a chance to "mind the gap" and regulate yourself before the chain of unchecked negative reactions grows longer and inhibits your ability to listen, understand, and communicate effectively with this team member. That's the level of strength necessary to confront challenging emotions and to tackle difficult conversations.

Mindfulness of breathing is essential for developing mindfulness of emotions. Our brains aren't evolved in a way that makes it easy for us to consciously manage our emotions and identify them in ourselves and others. The emotional part of the brain is not easily interfered with or controlled by the conscious, rational part of our mind. That's why it takes consistent effort and practice to learn and develop ways of recognizing emotions and emotion-driven impulses.[31] Breathing is an automatic process, just like emotional reactions. We aren't required to focus on our breath—the body does it by itself. So when you first learn to practice mindful breathing, it can be extremely difficult to focus for even thirty seconds without your mind wandering to other thoughts. The practice of mindful breathing allows you to build and strengthen neural pathways that generate the capacity to be attentive to other automatic processes, like emotional impulses. The practices aim to heighten your awareness of physical changes that occur within your body when you are becoming emotional (e.g., tension, creased forehead). Relaxed awareness and listening may also help you identify and respond to the facial expressions or nonverbal cues of those around you. Relaxed awareness and listening truly are superpowers, but are ones that don't just develop overnight. You need consistent practice, like doing the exercises we present in this book, to develop these new habits and skills. The changes in your patterns may seem glacial, but when you start to recognize and reap the rewards in your everyday interactions, the experience is truly magical.

BALANCE BETWEEN OURSELVES AND OTHERS

In addition to trying to understand others, coming to understand yourself can also really improve the quality of your connections. Taking the time to reflect on yourself, your life experiences, and your past relationships can help you to better understand your own strengths and vulnerabilities and your own style of relating to other people. Do you tend to be an introvert, an extrovert, or some combination? What kinds of interactions come more easily for you, and what kinds are more difficult? Have your relationships, romantic or otherwise, tended to fall into certain patterns? Do they tend to begin, progress, or end in a certain way? Do you tend to blame things on others a lot, or do you take all the blame and responsibility on yourself? What situations tend to trigger an emotional reaction in you and set you off? By coming to understand yourself, and what you "bring to the table"—by looking at these aspects of yourself with some kindness and tolerance, as you would view a dear friend—you can gain a greater understanding of what happens between you and others, and work toward improving the quality of your connections. Gaining perspective on yourself can be very challenging though. It's hard to see yourself with clarity. And sometimes there are things that we feel ashamed of, that we'd rather not see in ourselves. Sometimes, feedback from people you really trust, like friends or other loved ones, can help. And psychotherapy with a skillful therapist can be a great way to come to a greater understanding of yourself.

Attunement involves not just cognitive empathy for the other person, but also keeping in mind *both* the other person's *and* your own feelings and perspective too, even if there is disagreement.[32] Part of "understanding" involves processing both the information you glean from listening to the other person and the information you get from listening to yourself; trying to disentangle which thoughts and feelings come primarily from you, from the other person, and from you "resonating" with the other person as you listen to them. Understanding means you recognize that your two perspectives are interdependent—as you elicit thoughts and feelings from each other in your interaction—and yet you recognize they are distinct. Attunement does not mean trying to reconcile the two different perspectives of you and the other person in order to make one, merged "right" perspective, nor does it mean losing yourself in the other person's perspective. Sometimes understanding one another requires stepping back and gaining a "30,000 foot" perspective. Ideally, we want to use cognitive empathy to imagine someone else's perspective without losing sight of and respect for our own thoughts, feelings, and values. While empathy is really important, it's problematic when it goes too far such that you completely lose sight of yourself. The ideal balance for understanding is similar to the type of balance we promote in Chapter 3, where your goal is to listen attentively to another person while still being aware of yourself and your own thoughts and feelings.

There's a lot of variation across cultures in how people prioritize themselves versus others. As we mentioned earlier, people in Western cultures, like the United States, tend to be more individualistic, and they value the freedom, needs, and priorities of the individual over relationships or the collective culture. However, when this individualism is taken to the extreme, it can lead to self-centeredness, as well as a sense of loneliness and disconnection. Indeed, these conditions seem to be growing in the West. On the other hand, people from some Eastern cultures, such as South Korea, have traditionally placed more emphasis on the collective rather than on the individual. From an early age, Korean youth are taught the art of *nunchi*, which includes the skills of being especially attentive to other people's thoughts and feelings and responding accordingly. In Korean culture, there's an emphasis on being able to "read the room" and quickly attend to those around them. Those with nunchi tend to stay present with others and demonstrate their deep understanding of them by attending to their ever-changing words, gestures, or facial expressions. As the social information they receive changes, they recalibrate their understanding of the other person's emotional state and perspective in order to readjust their own behavior to be in line with the social code.[33]

In its essence, nunchi is a philosophy that promotes conscientiousness and respect, and it places emphasis on how others are feeling. Korea's collectivist culture values interdependence, and thus part of a Korean individual's sense of identity may develop *through* their relationships or social connections. Disruption of group harmony, or failing to act with nunchi, is not only frowned upon, but could potentially lead to being ostracized from your family unit, friend group, or work team. While in some ways nunchi promotes social connection, some native Koreans have described how, in excess, it can lead you to lose sight of yourself. While children are encouraged to "act with nunchi," those who act without it or make what could appear as inconsiderate choices, are frowned upon as not being aware of their impact on others or offending others. A Korean friend of ours taught us another expression, *nunchi bo-in-da*, which is used in conjunction with nunchi and translates literally to "I see/sense nunchi." This phrase is used by those who feel self-conscious about what others would think of their actions or about acting in ways that don't follow societal norms. For instance, it is still somewhat socially frowned upon for women to smoke in Korea. Women who smoke on their lunch break may say, "I sense nunchi"; meaning, "I feel anxious about what my boss would think of me if they found out that I was a smoker and they held the societal belief that women shouldn't smoke." Taken to an extreme, the tendency to prioritize or pay more attention to the comfort of others over one's own individual needs or desires may play a role in strong interpersonal connections but it may also take a toll on an individual's own emotions.[34] In the current generation, many Korean families acknowledge the importance of balancing the needs of the self with those of others in order to foster greater confidence, assertiveness, and calm.

These progressive families are also coincidentally promoting a key component of deep understanding and, in turn, high quality attunement. When a Korean child is consumed by acting with nunchi and directs all his energy toward identifying other people's emotions and figuring out how he can respond in a way that is pleasing to others, the child can lose touch with himself. He doesn't notice the increase in physical tension or anxiety brewing during social encounters, and he is less likely to respond in ways that will protect his own needs and vocalize his own opinions. Finding the balance between yourself and another builds the connection and strengthens the relationship.

The ability to balance awareness of the other person's perspective and your own is highlighted in the work of Dr. John Gottman.

He is known for his research on couples, and for identifying contempt within couples as a predictor of divorce. He also studies parenting. He conducted thousands of hours of interviews with over one hundred married couples with four- to five-year-old children and identified how specific ways of listening and understanding affect attachment between a parent and child. Through observation, questionnaires, interviews, and biological samples (heart rate monitoring, respiration, blood flow, sweating, urine samples, and the like) that were collected multiple times as the child grew older, he analyzed a mountain of data that eventually painted a picture of how parenting related to child development and outcomes later in life. Gottman created four profiles of the types of parents he saw, three of which weren't the most successful. Those three types were dismissing parents (who disregard, ignore, or trivialize negative emotions), disapproving parents (who are critical of negative feelings and punish kids for emotional expression), and laissez-faire parents (who accept and empathize with their child's emotions but don't provide guidance on how to respond/behave). The children of these three profile types didn't do as well over time—they demonstrated more behavioral and social problems and lower self-esteem. The common thread among these profiles is the inconsistent ability of the parent to listen, acknowledge, and validate their child's emotions while also modeling appropriate behavioral responses for them.[35]

The most successful parents, which Dr. Gottman dubbed the Ultra-Parents, used emotional coaching strategies that accepted a child's feelings and helped them figure out the best way to respond. They unknowingly embodied the core of attunement; they were aware of their own emotions as well as their child's. Dealing with a child who is emotional or has reacted emotionally can be an overwhelming experience for any parent, and the child's strong emotions can make it difficult for parents to see clearly and respond with compassion. The ability of a parent or caregiver to be aware of their own perspective and feelings, those of their child, and also the relationship between the two—an ability that psychologists Peter Fonagy and Arietta Slade have called mentalizing or reflective functioning—has been found to be associated with secure attachments in infants.[36] Infants benefit from parents who are better at accurately identifying an infant's internal state (like stating the infant likes the blocks if she smiles when he sees them) and who make minimal nonattuned inferences of (invalid assumptions about) their child's perspective.[37] The same can be said for adult relationships. Bonds develop more easily when someone is attuned to your emotional state (like noticing that a dip in your energy levels may be related to feeling down) and avoids making ill-informed assumptions due to a lack of paying attention.

Mutual understanding between caretaker and child gets even harder when the infant grows up to become a sullen teenager. Decoding their emotions may seem impossible for anyone except a top-level NSA agent. Adolescence is full of moments ripe for misinterpretation and remains a prime example of a time in development in which reading emotions, and understanding how someone feels, is critical to a deeper connection. A parent's behavior or a child's behavior may have a certain intention, but they may convey a very different meaning to the receiver. The late Nobel Prize–winning writer Toni Morrison once talked about the example of mothers who look their children up and down when they come downstairs, dressed and ready for the day. In a mother's mind, she is looking at her child with care, concern, and love, searching for any shirts untucked, zippers unzipped, or hair out of place so that the child can present their best version to the world. What a child sees is their mother's scrunched nose, wrinkled forehead, and seeming disapproval, ready to criticize. This profound example of how our interpretation of a situation can be significantly off from one another, despite our best intentions, proves yet again the value of focusing our attention on our nonverbals and syncing our intention with our method of communication. Morrison said, "Let your face speak what's in your heart." It's a reminder to adjust your expressed emotions to more accurately represent your intended message. In adulthood, mentalizing—that ability to hold in mind your own perspective as well as the other person's—gets easier in some ways, as we develop more experience and skills. But it also gets harder, as we gather experiences and history that shape our personalities and may make us more set in our patterns of behavior. To really understand ourselves and others, it's important to have some awareness of our own patterns of relating to people, and to come to understand other people's patterns as well.

UNDERSTANDING YOUR UNIQUE LENS

Through our own temperaments, and our experiences from early childhood and on through our lives, we develop expectations about how close relationships will go, something that psychologists have called our own, personal working models of attachment. It's our own pattern of the way we tend to view close or caregiving relationships in terms of how available, stable, or dependable we expect them to be. Our working model of attachment influences how we perceive, feel, and behave in close relationships, and it affects our ability to understand what someone else is thinking and feeling. For example, experimental research has shown that when someone tends to have insecure attachments in which they are often afraid of being vulnerable or of being abandoned, this significantly impacts how that person perceives social support from their romantic partner.[38] If the person feels insecure in their relationship, they would interpret messages of support from their partners as unsupportive, no matter how objectively supportive their partner actually is.

This type of filtered reactivity stems from long-term emotional needs, wounds, and patterns that we've developed over the course of our lives. It doesn't mean they are immutable, only that they seep into our relational dynamics, and it's important to recognize them if we want to change our patterns of behavior. Our own temperament, prior relationships, and things we've lived through have shaped us a certain way that predisposes us to react in our own, habitual ways. These ingrained reactions are powerful in that they can get in the way of understanding, disrupt attunement, and take a toll on romantic relationships and friendships. Sometimes these kinds of wounds and attachment patterns impact people's relationships to the extent that they seek out psychotherapy, which, with a well-qualified doctor or therapist, can truly help an individual become aware of their own patterns and work toward new ways of coping and relating to others.

We've observed the story of Eric and Greg, and it may resonate with experiences from your own life. These two young men worked together at a startup tech company for a few years after college. Since joining the company, Eric had really wanted to break into Greg's circle of friends. In Eric's eyes, Greg oozed a smooth confidence that made Eric feel cool by proxy. As they became better friends, they hung out a lot and had each other's backs during the many ups and downs their company experienced as it started to really take off. After a few years of grinding away at this job, other opportunities drew each of them away from the company. They went their separate ways, eventually moving to different parts of the country. This made it impossible for them to talk as much as they once did when their desks were just feet away. Eric, who, by nature, wanted to stay in close, frequent communication with his friends, was disappointed when Greg became less responsive to his texts and calls over time. Greg, by nature, was the type of person who needed more space and time to himself. You can imagine what happened. Greg's latency to reply resulted in Eric expressing growing frustration and annoyance, which led to Greg's increasing distance and unresponsiveness. Eric's personality craved attention and bonding with friends, leaving him feeling rejected when he didn't receive the kind of responsiveness he desired. Greg, on the other hand, found expressed neediness hard to handle, causing him to shut down and avoid Eric altogether. Similar to the research on insecure partners, each friend interpreted the other's behavior through his personal lens, which caused him to lose sight of the bigger picture. Sometimes attunement means sensing and understanding that the other person needs some space or understanding that the other person needs a quick check-in. We all have our own personal lens through which we view other people and relationships, a lens that is usually invisible to ourselves. This lens affects our perceptions of others and the way we react to certain situations in relationships. Becoming more aware of your own reactivity opens the door to being able to identify how it's triggered. Over time you may even feel comfortable and trusting enough to communicate what your triggers are to others so that they can respond with more insight and understanding.

The deeper level of understanding we've been describing is derived from a multitude of skills that include social cognition, and the cognitive and emotional forms of empathy. Many of these elements are largely unconscious, automatic, and deeply ingrained—like our own working model of attachment—but we can still become more aware of these processes in order to grow and develop. Understanding ourselves and others comes more easily to some people than others, and there are certain moments or contexts in which we're better at it or worse at it. But because many aspects of understanding are more thoughtful, conscious forms of processing, understanding is an element of attunement that can certainly be developed and grown with attention and practice.

Some of this thoughtful reflection happens before or after the interaction, when there is more time to think. During an interaction, things often are moving so quickly that there's less time to reflect. It's challenging to develop understanding in real time during a rapidly unfolding interaction. Think again of the examples of a fast break on the basketball court, jazz musicians improvising together, or even normal conversation between friends. Pairs of basketball teammates, jazz musicians, or close friends ideally know each other so well that their understanding is often immediate and not always conducted at the level of conscious verbal thought. To get to that level of virtually instantaneous understanding, they almost certainly have had to spend lots of time together to get to know each other, to reflect on their way of relating to each other, and to work out many misunderstandings. But with this hard-earned practice and familiarity, their mutual understanding has become increasingly unspoken, subliminal, and embodied, which enables them to make use of this understanding quickly and effortlessly during the interaction. When you know someone really well, you often can read their cues and subtle signs quickly and easily.

LEVELS OF UNDERSTANDING

Understanding is not just important for close relationships; it's also important for dealing with people we don't know well. Our capacity for understanding helps us to interpret the intentions and communications of the other person and to determine the extent to which they seem trustworthy. At times, this kind of understanding can be a crucial survival tool. Our understanding informs us how to skillfully navigate our interactions with them, and to decide whether or not we might want to get to know them better.

So there are different levels of understanding another person. You can have a quick, superficial understanding or "reading" of another person who you don't really know or care very much about, which can be useful in navigating through life. There are also much deeper levels of understanding of another person who you've come to know very well. These deeper levels are a kind of love, or at least they require loving that person. And that is quite a positive force! Most of us wish for some people in our lives who really "get" us. They've known us long enough, and have gotten to know us well enough, that they mostly understand our ways of thinking and feeling. They know our strengths but also our flaws and foibles, and they accept us and love us for who we really are. This is a deep and precious understanding. It's this kind of understanding that can really help to dissipate the loneliness that we talked about in Chapter 1.

But even if we feel that we have a deep understanding of someone, it's important to stay humble and open-minded. Deeply understanding someone is always a work in progress, never a finished task, if for no other reason than the fact that we're all continually changing, growing, and evolving. It's hard enough for us to try to understand our own thoughts, feelings, and impulses as they arise, moment to moment. But it seems even more difficult to ever fully understand another person whose complexities and nuances, whose shifting thoughts and feelings, are much less accessible to us. So it is realistic to view the process of understanding ourselves or another person as a dynamic process that needs to continue over time. Inevitably, there will be some misunderstandings, and we may need clarification or more information. It's best to approach the challenge of understanding with a mindset that is interested, open-minded, nonjudgmental, curious, not set in stone, and always willing to update or reconsider our understanding based on new information.

Despite the difficulty of understanding others, and the need for appropriate humility, in good relationships that grow over substantial periods of time, a deep level of understanding of the other person, and yourself, can develop. Sometimes another person can see potential and possibility for growth in us that we at first can't see ourselves. For example, we may see some good quality in a caring parent, teacher, mentor, or friend that we can't imagine in ourselves. But they are able to recognize that quality in us, or another potentiality, and their recognition of that quality in us helps us to develop it and start to see it in ourselves. That kind of understanding and recognition, at a deep level, could be considered a kind of love.

EXERCISES TO DEVELOP UNDERSTANDING

UNDERSTANDING IN CONVERSATION*

The goal of this exercise is to build on the listening exercises from Chapter 3, and to incorporate the component of understanding. While aspects of this exercise can be done when in conversation with anyone, at any time, try to practice with someone who knows you're working on these skills. This will allow you to pause and reflect on your skills during the conversation without it being awkward. As you practice the listening exercise from Chapter 3, pay more attention to your partner's nonverbal communication—their facial expressions, tone and pace of voice, and body language, and the variations in those.

Steps

1. Refer to the Sitting Meditation exercise in Chapter 2 to review the body posture and breathing techniques that should be used during this exercise.

2. Ask your partner to talk to you for roughly two to five minutes about anything on their mind or about something that happened to them recently or in the past. While listening, use the same principles of posture and relaxed awareness that prior exercises have developed. You don't need to verbally respond back to them as they speak.

3. Keep about 80 percent of your attention on listening to the other person and keep about 20 percent of your attention on your posture and the feeling of your breath expanding and relaxing your belly.

4. If something that the other person says makes you feel nervous or upset, return your attention for a moment back to

---

*Indicates that this is a partner exercise.

your head—which should feel like it is gently suspended from above—drop and relax your shoulders, and let the gentle expansion and contraction of your belly move with your inbreath and outbreath. When you begin to feel calmer, return your attention to the other person.

5. Check with the other person on what you heard them say. You may think that they said one thing, but it's possible that you misunderstood, or that they were not aware of how you were understanding them. So it is helpful for the two of you to check in. If there was a misunderstanding, then they can clarify what they were trying to communicate.

6. At the end of this exercise, if they are interested, allow your partner to practice listening and understanding you as you speak.

Advice for Practicing

Consider one or two of the following prompts when practicing this exercise:

- Contemplate how the other person may be feeling as they are speaking to you. What might be motivating them? How might they see you?
- What emotions do you sense from them?
- What emotions do you sense in yourself? How are your emotions different from theirs? How much might the two of you be eliciting these feelings in each other?
- Do these emotions seem typical for you, or unusual?
  - If the emotions are typical for you, do they seem to fit the situation, and do they seem to fit what is going on between the two of you? Or could the feelings be part of your own long-standing patterns of relating to others, rather than the feelings that really fit the situation?
  - If the emotions are not typical for you, could there be something about the other person, and what they are

doing or saying, that are eliciting these unusual feelings or reactions in you?

At least momentarily, as you listen, try to imagine what it's like to be the other person, and try to imagine their perspective. Then return your awareness to your own feelings and perspective. How much of your feelings might be due to each of your personality styles, or what has happened in your lives over time, or what's happened to you recently? Try to let go of a rigid view of them or of yourself, and remain open to updating your understanding of them and of yourself as you listen. With your partner, take turns in who speaks and who listens and tries to understand. After the listening period, the listener can check in with the speaker to see if their understanding is accurate.

Evidence suggests that the learning process involved in exercises like this can change the structure and function of our brain circuits that are responsible for understanding ourselves and others.[39] Strengthening this social understanding "muscle" will make it quicker and easier for you to access and use it in more emotional situations in which the stakes are higher.

PUSH HANDS*

One goal of push hands, an exercise derived from Tai Chi, is to develop a physical sense of relaxed awareness, listening, and understanding during interaction with a partner. Sometimes called sensing hands, this exercise involves coordinated, cyclical movements with one or both arms in contact with the arms of a partner. The practice of push hands can be a complex practice for seasoned Tai Chi practitioners, but we will focus on one foundational push hands exercise that should help you develop your ability to tune in to yourself and others. The exercise develops relaxed awareness of your own and the other person's body. It also develops careful "listening" to (i.e., acute sensing of) the movement and force of the other person, which varies in pace, force, and direction. Finally, it strengthens your capacity for "listening" to sensations in your own body, which in turn helps you to develop an increasing understanding of what your partner is trying to do and how to manage your own response.[40] Ultimately, this type of partnered movement, similar to dance or other martial arts training, increases our understanding of other people's body and emotional states, as well as our own.[41]

Steps

It's challenging to describe push hands without seeing it. Before reading on, check out some video examples and detailed explanations at MissingEachOther.com.

1. Arrange your body position in relation to your partner's body position, as shown in the videos.
2. As your partner pushes toward you, use a turning of your waist to redirect the force a bit to the side and then back toward the partner, and vice versa, in a continuous cycle. The challenge here is to do this without developing much tension in your shoulder or arm. The more you develop your relaxed awareness, listening, and understanding, the less tension you will have in moving with your partner.
3. To an observer, this exercise looks less like two people trying to push each other and more like two partners moving together in a fluid, cyclical, almost dance-like way. Within each cyclical movement of push hands, there is a turn-taking of who is leading by pushing, and who is following and redirecting.
4. Regardless of whether you are leading or following in any particular moment, you continue to "listen" to each other's movements and maintain physical contact with each other at your arms.

Advice for Practicing

In the solo exercises, like sitting and standing, you worked on developing a feeling of a still point in your center. When you practice push hands, try to maintain the feeling of this still point while simultaneously trying to develop awareness of a second point, the point of connection between you and the other person where your arms touch. Your goal is to try to develop an awareness of your own center as well as to maintain a continual awareness of the point of connection with the other person. Things will change— your position, the other person's position, the particular situation— but in the midst of this change, you try to maintain awareness of both of these points, your own center, and the point of connection. With practice, the skills used in push hands will become more natural and should generalize to your ability to remain in control in a peaceful and relaxed manner even while you're in more difficult, seemingly uncontrollable social situations.

You can think of push hands as a bit like dancing—something we can all do, at least to some extent! But when you practice dance, or push hands, you learn to develop and maintain a connection and understanding of each other. In the tango for example, dancers are taught to remain rooted in their individual axis while also maintaining connection to their partner. The combination creates a dialect that seems magical. When someone leads in dance, it doesn't mean they just do whatever they want in a way that is disconnected from the partner, and it's the partner's responsibility to follow. Instead, the leader has to pay close attention to the partner and sense the connection between them from the beginning (before even starting to lead), and then continue to pay attention to the partner throughout the process of leading. So within the process of leading, there is also a bit of following. And the person who is following has to show the other person that they're following, which involves a bit of leading.

When first practicing push hands, most people have a tendency to be tight and tense, focusing intensely on getting the movement right. As you practice and the movements start to come more easily, the next step is to try to do the movements while remaining physically relaxed, without much tension in your arm and shoulder. Staying relaxed is challenging and counterintuitive—when someone pushes at you, your instinct will be to tense up, resist, and push back. But you start to learn that tensing up makes it harder to listen and respond, and that tension messes up the connection between you and the other person. On the other hand, if you can remain relaxed and listening, you can maintain the connection such that you're ready to respond to anything that your partner might do. The goal of push hands, much like most of life's experiences, is to listen, understand, and respond and act without creating additional resistance. When you experience a difficult interaction, whether it be a slight disagreement or colossal meltdown of communication at work, remaining grounded and responding with controlled calm allows for the situation to be neutralized rather than ignited. Push hands, much like life, succeeds when the two partners are in sync and are able to stay connected.

CHAPTER FIVE

MUTUAL RESPONSIVENESS

"The true self arises in our meeting, in our connection."

—NORMAN FISCHER[1]

MUTUAL RESPONSIVENESS: REACHING THE HEIGHTS OF ATTUNEMENT

When you witness highly attuned people in action—dancers gracefully flowing in sync across a ballroom floor, volleyball players fluidly passing and setting up for the spike, or close friends engrossed in deep conversation—what is most apparent is their almost instantaneous communication and responsiveness to each other, their moments of synchrony, and the ease of their back-and-forth exchange. They are connected, but they maintain their individuality within that connection—if anything, they seem even *more* themselves in the context of that connection. Mutual responsiveness is the culmination of attunement, and when people move and connect in such elegant and intricate interaction, it's magic.

Part of the secret behind this magic comes from what you already know about attunement—the development of relaxed awareness, listening, and understanding. Relaxed awareness is the foundation of attunement, the key state of mind. Listening lets the information and the feelings in. Understanding gives us insight into our own perspective versus the other person's frame of mind. But mutual responsiveness is what we actually *do* in the interaction to keep the seemingly effortless connection going. Mutual responsiveness is how we act in relation to the other person and ourselves, and the magic happens when our responsiveness is guided by relaxed awareness, listening, and understanding. With that guidance, our actions land on target, and our responses are more effective and impactful in enhancing communication. "Responsiveness," as we're defining it here, does *not* mean having a passive, automatic, reflexive response to the other person. Rather, it means taking initiative, and that is done when we direct our actions in a more conscious way.

MEET ME WHERE I AM

Mutual responsiveness is initiated when at least one person "meets the other person where they are," or ideally when two people meet each other halfway. Unless you're dancing the tango or practicing Tai Chi, this doesn't mean to literally physically meet them, but rather to meet them mentally and emotionally. You pay careful attention to the other person—using your skills of relaxed awareness, listening, and understanding—in order to actively gauge where their mind is at the moment, and what they're interested in. Then you try to engage with them on that topic. Instead of being preoccupied with what you want to communicate, with your own agenda, or with what you want the other person to do, you see what's on their mind, what's important to them, and meet them there. The idea is to *meet* them, without asking much else from them, at least at first. This willingness to meet them is a way to begin engagement that will open up communication, which increases the likelihood that they will reciprocate in the same way.

In the 1993 movie *Falling Down*, a Los Angeles police officer, Sergeant Martin Prendergast, on his last day of work before retirement, and his partner, detective Sandra Torres, are searching for an active shooter on the loose. By quickly stitching together bits of evidence, they deduce that the shooter is William Foster, a middle-aged white man who "lost it" after recently getting divorced and laid off from his job. The pressure is high to track him down, as the rampage accelerates. They go to Foster's mother's house, and when she opens her front door, the less-experienced detective, Torres, starts insisting that they need to ask her some questions. In response, Mrs. Foster becomes defensive, uncooperative, and asks them to leave. Sergeant Prendergast takes a different approach. He pauses a moment to notice the large and lovingly tended collection of glass sculptures that Mrs. Foster has displayed. He asks her about it, admiringly, looking at each piece closely. Given the desperate situation and the clock ticking down, Prendergast seems to be wasting precious time asking her about something so irrelevant. But as the scene unfolds, the wisdom of Prendergast's strategy is revealed. Rather than being swept up by his intense need for immediate information, and demanding information from her, Prendergast "meets" her at something that is clearly very important to her—her treasured collection. The simple act allows him to establish some connection and rapport with her. This paves the road for Mrs. Foster to open up and eventually share enough information to help the police stop the string of violence.

Sergeant Prendergast's tactics were not only a great example of meeting the other person where they are, but also were potentially ahead of his time. By his use of this fundamental principle of attunement, Prendergast de-escalated the situation and made force unnecessary in this encounter. This approach is just the type of re-form called for in real life in the wake of protests against police brutality following the May 2020 killing of George Floyd, when a police officer knelt on Floyd's neck for eight minutes and forty-six seconds during an arrest due to his alleged use of a counterfeit bill. Activists across all fifty states marched for weeks, demanding that police departments ban excessively forceful tactics, and prioritize de-escalation training, which, research demonstrates, keeps both police officers and community members *safer*.[2]

With the right intentions, meeting someone where they are can lay the foundation for trust, vulnerability, and open-heartedness. In our American culture that often values assertiveness and "leader-ship," the idea of meeting the other person where they are may seem meek or passive. But true assertiveness is not about overpowering someone to acquire what you want. Real assertiveness balances the rights, desires, and needs of yourself with those of the other person. This approach is surprisingly effective at both the macro and micro level. Hamdi Ulukaya, founder and CEO of the yogurt brand Cho-bani, demonstrates this approach: he has eschewed prevailing busi-ness values that promote profits for shareholders above cultivating a dialogue among leadership, employees, and consumers. Instead, Ulukaya replaced what he calls a fundamentally flawed business model with the "anti-CEO" approach that leads with humility and gratitude, that asks permission to enter communities, and that lis-tens to the needs of the community and of employees. As a result, the company maintains a dynamic approach to listening. Ulukaya meets community members and employees where they are, which is a communication style that requires leaders to place their egos to the side. With this strategy, Ulukaya led Chobani in igniting the Greek yogurt craze, which went from 1 percent of the total yogurt market in 2005, when Ulukaya founded Chobani, to 50 percent of the yogurt market in 2017.[3]

At a more intimate level, Phil Jackson maintained a similar per-spective when he coached the Chicago Bulls. He recognized the importance of setting aside his tendency to try to dominate or control his players, and instead he developed a coaching style of meeting his players where they were—what he called "listening without judgment"—to get a feel for the players' concerns and develop a rapport with them. Although this was a counterintuitive coaching approach to use when under the pressure of a high-stakes industry, the payoff was clear. "Meeting someone where they are" was stunningly effective, as evidenced by Jackson's six NBA championship wins with the Bulls.[4]

Placing your ego to the side can sometimes be the most difficult part of meeting someone where they are, but it is also your most powerful communication tool. Even if you're engaged in an argument or conflict and need to assert yourself verbally, violating someone's rights by diminishing their voice ensures you will be met by defensiveness like that of Mrs. Foster in the movie Falling Down. If you barge in and bully someone with your words, they will likely push back, not listen to you, or shut down. You haven't convinced them or "won" the argument. Maybe you've overwhelmed them temporarily, seemingly "winning" the immediate battle, but you've lost the war. As Phil Jackson put it, "If you push too hard to control what happens, resistance builds and reality spits in your face."[5]

This is exactly what we've seen across countless episodes of police brutality, which exemplify the way in which attunement breaks down and unjust violence ensues. In the case of Sandra Bland, a twenty-eight-year-old African American woman who was pulled over for failure to signal a lane change, video and audio footage of her arrest allows for a frame-by-frame analysis of the degradation of attunement. In his book Talking to Strangers, Malcolm Gladwell carefully assesses the back-and-forth exchange between Bland and the arresting state trooper, precisely highlighting how each verbal response and nonverbal cue from both individuals might have triggered the other's consequent reaction. Of note, the exchange is ripe with moments in which the officer attempted to assert himself by talking past Bland, without taking a moment to register her current experience, which quickly incited miscommunication and ignited emotional reactions rather than thoughtful responses. In the heat of the moment, it can be extremely difficult to find the humility necessary to meet someone where they are—something that becomes exponentially more messy and complicated when the interaction is colored by structural inequalities and systemic bias.[6] But the regular practice of relaxed awareness can foster greater mindfulness of your own biases and negative attributions in those moments. There is power in realizing that extending the olive branch in order to de-escalate a confrontation can actually be in your best interest in most circumstances. By meeting someone where they are, talking with compassion and with the intention of helping them understand your point of view, you increase the likelihood of effective communication.

Even if you know a lot more than someone else, and are trying to teach them something, things work better if you meet them where they are. One of the greatest living Tai Chi masters, Chen Xiaowang, knows the value of this when beginning to work with a new student. He doesn't begin by trying to impose his knowledge, experience, and agenda on the student. Such an approach wouldn't be engaging to them, and the novice student wouldn't easily understand what he was talking about. Instead, rather than flaunting his knowledge, Chen starts by asking the student what got them interested in Tai Chi, what they want to learn. He begins formulating his teaching strategy with that information. If they want to learn how to manage stress through meditation, he starts with that. If they want to learn how to throw a better punch, he starts with that. Meeting them where they are, at what interests *them*, is a good entry point to teaching the fundamental principles of Tai Chi. As Chen starts to teach a punching technique, and the student gets a sense of the power of Tai Chi's movement principles, it increases their interest and desire to learn more of the art. As Chen describes it, "First I follow the student. Later the student understands, and the student follows me."[7]

Understanding each other's motives, what drives each other's interests and state of mind, is a powerful tool for building attunement. Teachers and clinicians build rapport with their students and patients by exploring what motivates each of them as individuals. Most people feel some degree of warmth when another person is interested in the driving force within them. Starting from a young age, we crave the attention and interest that's on our level. Consider an adult trying to communicate with a young child. Rather than the adult standing up and talking at the child or down to them, adults can build a small connection with a child by getting down to the child's level and trying to initiate or join in some play that interests the child. And this makes the child much more likely to return the favor by talking with the adult and listening to them. From this micro-moment of give-and-take, a mutually enjoyable interaction evolves. Parents have the common experience of coming home at the end of the day and asking their children how their day at school was, just to hear them say…"good." And if they dare to ask their children what happened during the day, they get informative echoes of "nothing" or "not much." But things can be wildly different on the days that parents join their kids in doing something together that the kids find interesting, like coloring, playing a game, or baking. Within a few minutes, the kids may spontaneously recount important things that happened that day, or things that have been on their minds for a while but that they haven't felt comfortable to share before. Parents who expect that kids immediately respond in the way they want them to, on demand, are often disappointed. But meeting their kids where they are, and joining them in doing something that's fun and interesting for them, gives parents a much better shot.

You may have noted that this isn't just true for interactions of parents with their kids. At any age, conversation is most easily elicited when you feel someone engaging with relaxed awareness, listening, and understanding in a way that signals to you, "I want to find out where you are, and meet you there." In the Buddhist

tradition, the Sanskrit term for this strategy of engaging others—
upaya—translates to "skillful means" or "artfulness." Finding a
way to engage and connect with others is an art form. It's the art
of tailoring your approach to the particular interests, motivations,
and personality of the other person. It's the art of engaging and
meeting the other person at a level and to a degree that is comfortable for both people, which fertilizes the soil, so to speak, for a
deeper connection to blossom.

Some of you might be more reluctant to engage or you might
have a tendency to be less verbose, even with those closest to you.
You could just be having an off day—at which point you hope
someone meets you where you are, either by drawing you out in a
way that feels helpful to you or by giving you the space you need.
But maybe it's more than that. Maybe you're consistently the less
effusive and expressive one in the relationship. Maybe you have a
partner or family member who's always on your case about not
engaging enough or often pleads with you to share more with them.

When practicing the exercises described in this book, take a moment to consider whether there might be something holding you
back from being more expressive. Some people just tend to be more
introverted in temperament. Others have had repeated life experiences that leave them feeling less comfortable being open, and
they may need more time than others to process things for themselves. Diversity of personality styles is something to be valued.
There's no need for us all to be extroverts. But some of those who
fall along the lower end of the open and expressive spectrum may
be holding tight to protective emotional "armor" that served them
well in earlier life situations. These individuals could be working
overtime to protect themselves, and their defenses may actually be
impeding their ability to connect, even when it's safe for them to
try. Vulnerability can be fertile soil for connection, but the seeds
can only be planted when the soil is tilled and ready. The relaxed
awareness exercises from Chapter 2, when consistently practiced,
may gradually help you feel more centered, grounded, and calm so

that you are more ready to open up with others in your life who have proven to be most trustworthy. But beyond these exercises, if you think that your emotional armor may be standing in your way in some relationships, you may find it helpful to discuss the life experiences that have left you feeling less safe with a well-qualified therapist.

Part of the artfulness of meeting someone where they are is knowing when not to push too hard, and realizing when it's *not* time to try to meet them. Sometimes people don't want to engage with you about some issue, or they need some space for themselves. Teenagers often don't want their parents or teachers deeply involved in certain aspects of their lives. They have more need for privacy, independence, and space—a need to differentiate themselves as individuals and to invest more in peer relationships. At that stage of their lives, their parents often seem to be about as uncool as a human being can possibly get. And having a parent butt in can seem to be the last thing they would want. Even younger children, who more generally seek out their parents' attention, often want some play time to themselves. So, as a parent, if you use your attunement skills, you're more likely to get a sense of when to push and when to draw back. If you try to meet your children and you get rebuffed, you may take the hint to give them the space that they want, especially if there's no safety issue. If they know you're interested and available, but not intrusive, chances are that they may want to talk with you about it later. And there are probably other topics on which you can connect in the meantime.

How to handle being rebuffed is an art form as well. Trying to connect with someone and receiving either coldness or anger that is clearly meant to reject your advances is *rough*, and the sting is immediate. The more intimate the relationship—with your child, your partner, or a close friend—the more sensitively you may perceive rejection. It takes vulnerability to try to connect with someone. Mutual responsivity may mean that you use your relaxed awareness skills to hear their emotion and give them space, without letting their reaction get under your skin. If your teen is irritable or your partner is cold, it's natural to feel rejected. As a response to that rejection, our self-protective nature often goes into defensive, reactive overdrive, causing us to fire back the same bitter pill we just received. Instead of snapping at them or turning your back on them, find focus on your breath, notice the tension that's rising in your body, and pause for enough of a moment to separate their emotions from yourself. It doesn't necessarily mean you did something wrong, and their anger might not even be directed at you. The hardest pill to swallow is the realization that sometimes it's not always about you. Breaking that chain of reactivity creates space for you to find compassion and understanding, and to accept that this person needs space. By doing something as simple as not reacting, you give yourself more energy and resources to connect (at some point). It's not easy. It never is. This is why practicing each attunement skill individually, and then with partners, helps you to gradually assimilate these skills and makes them more easily accessible to you when you're in the heat of the moment.

You might be wondering why you should always make the effort to meet *them* where *they* are. Maybe this doesn't seem fair. Why don't they meet *me* where *I* am once in a while? "Why do *I* always have to be the one to extend myself?" you may ask. We agree, it would be nice if the other person were always willing and able to meet you where you are. Probably, the ideal situation is if both people meet each other halfway. Sometimes those moments happen, and when they do, you will feel it and appreciate it. But being able to meet another person in this way takes a particular frame of mind and skill, and many people can't or won't be capable of it much of the time. Which leaves you to meet them. So if you want to be effective in communicating with others, you may need to take the initiative and develop this skill in yourself, and then be willing to make the first move yourself. One way to look at it is this: if they meet you where you are, great; if they meet you halfway, fine; but if they don't, then you can try to meet them where they are. In any case, the only place you can meet them is where they are at that moment.

Of course, there are appropriate limits to how generous you may be in your willingness to meet people. Realistically, you won't do this for all people at all times—we only have so much time, energy, and interest. And if someone never seems to reciprocate over extended periods of time, then your willingness to meet them may, understandably, diminish. In situations in which you feel that someone is trying to draw you into some kind of dysfunctional and hurtful interaction—getting overly personal with you before you know them well, "gaslighting" you, exploiting you, or manipulating you in some other way—then you may wisely choose to step back and leave the situation.

CONTINGENT RESPONSIVITY

Once you've developed the ability to meet someone where they are, the next key step in mutual responsiveness is what psychologists call contingent responsivity. This means that one person says or does something *in response to* the other person's speech and action, and vice versa, in a turn-taking exchange between the partners: *I* do this, in response to which *you* do that, in response to which *I* do something else, and so on, in a continuous, reciprocal, but somewhat unpredictable loop. Imagine two people playing tennis. Each player responds to the other player's shot, and both of them have to be connected to the nature of each shot—its location and speed—or they'll miss the ball. Importantly, contingent responsivity is different from the mirror-like synchronizing we do with another person's speech or activity when listening, which we discussed in Chapter 3. Contingent, mutual responsiveness has more of a back-and-forth, turn-taking quality in which the actions of the two people don't happen simultaneously and are not necessarily identical. In contingent responding, one person's speech or action is clearly *related* to, or *builds* on, the other person's speech or action. In a conversation, when you say something, and then the other person responds by saying something that builds on what you just said, then it signals to you that they really paid attention and heard you. They are responding to you, rather than going off on their own tangent, unrelated to what you just said, or just simply reflexively mirroring you.

Tina Fey and Rachel Dratch, both outstanding actors individually, exemplify contingent responsivity as an elevated art form in their work as a pair. When training together at The Second City theater troupe in Chicago, Tina Fey noted how improvisational comedy worked best when her mindset was to serve her partner, as opposed to showing off herself. Improv comedy actors accept or embrace the offers made by the other performers in order to advance or move the scene forward. You don't respond to what you hoped your partner would say or what was in your head—you respond to what they actually did or said, the offer they made. Successful comedy partners, like Fey and Dratch, emphasize the importance of trust, because improv succeeds when the performers are attuned to their partner's rhythm and patterns of thinking. Fey says she discovered a certain joy and freedom that comes with letting herself free-fall into the uncertainty of which direction the interaction will go. With practice, you can reach a seamless back-and-forth exchange in the moment, no matter what the "sketch" calls for.

Though the concept of contingent responsivity is fairly simple, it's tricky to get right. Fey and Dratch's comedic magic looked effortless, but it only appeared that way because of the energetic and active awareness they had of each other in each moment while on stage. Many of us, on the other hand, often function as if we're on autopilot, or are so stuck in our own heads that we don't really listen to or understand the other person. Maybe we interrupt and talk over them. In these cases, our responses feel like they come out of the blue to the other person, because they seem to be unconnected to what the other person is talking about. Contingent responses show that we are in tune with the other person, and that our responsiveness is *to* them and *for* them. Someone who responds to us by "accepting" or internalizing what we've said with the intention of advancing the conversation forward can make us feel heard and recognized. Although mirroring a person is an important component of listening, research indicates that it's the *contingency* of the actions between two people, rather than mirroring, that is more powerful in creating feelings of connection and closeness between them.[8] When someone mirrors us, it indicates that they must be listening and paying attention, at least to some extent. But when someone responds to us in a way that thoughtfully builds upon what we just said, we know that they are not just on autopilot— they are really there, really engaged, and they've understood us and are putting something of themselves into the interaction. It's one of the best feelings.

Think back to a recent conversation in which you felt a real sense of rapport with the other person. We bet you'll find that it had this quality of contingent responsivity, this turn-taking in which each response built on the previous one. When you replied to the other person, you may have automatically used some of the same words that they just used and incorporated them into what you said—which is another way of showing that you're responding specifically to what they said and building a common ground between the two of you, thereby creating a shared understanding of the meaning of what you were discussing. This convergence of language between the two conversation partners is called interactive alignment.[9] With your close friends or family members, you may have developed a lot of this alignment over the years so that you have your own shared, idiosyncratic way of speaking to each other. You may even have your own "code words" that reference shared experiences or funny stories from your past. While there might be some shared language between people, contingent responsivity doesn't mean that there is pressure to agree with each other in conversation or to follow a rigid script. If the conversation is going really well, we feel ready to deal with whatever comes up, flexibly, spontaneously, and genuinely.

Neuroscientists have begun to map out the brain circuits that are involved in contingent responsivity. They have studied the brain function of pairs of people while they are engaged in a live, fairly natural interaction. The regions that are active during contingent responsivity include some of the same regions that are involved in aspects of listening (emotional empathy), understanding (cognitive empathy), and feelings of pleasure.[10]

Contingent responses often involve taking some new initiative in the interaction, expressing yourself, asserting yourself, or even arguing and convincing the other person of something—but doing these things in a way that connects with the other person, and connects with what the two of you have just been talking about. Contingent responses can steer the flow of the conversation in a new direction, but they usually aren't very abrupt or way out of proportion to what the other person just said or did. Although responses are most effective when they're connected to the other person, part of the art of this is gauging the optimal level of directness and intensity—strong enough that your message will be heard and effective, but not so strong or abrupt that the other person can't handle or receive it. You can gauge your responses using the guidance of your own attentive listening and understanding of the other person. If you sense, during your conversation, that the other person can't handle or receive what you are saying—that you've hit an emotional sore spot for them—you may choose to back off a bit in your intensity and directness, and perhaps even gracefully move the conversation to a different subject and try to bring it up again in a different way later.

When we worked together at the University of Pennsylvania, we trusted each other for feedback on how things went in presentations and meetings. After one particularly tense meeting, we asked each other for critical feedback about how we each handled some tough personalities. Although we did have some honest feedback for each other, we were able to calibrate the intensity of what we said so that each of us could receive the other's message clearly and without taking it personally. There were no harsh insults or "are you kidding me with that!" jabs. Any good manager knows harsh tactics are the quickest way to making a person feel defensive, hurt, and closed off.

Certainly, there are situations where very blunt, tough love is absolutely necessary, such as in emergencies, life-or-death situations, instances of major injustice or abuse, or situations in which someone needs to be quickly brought to their senses. In those extreme scenarios, toughness and bluntness are called for and *are* proportionate to the situation. But if you went around in a full-on, blaring, tough-love mode all the time in your personal life, you are not likely to effectively communicate with most people. Not many people could tolerate it. They might start to tune you out or avoid you, and as a result you wouldn't have the impact that you were hoping for. That's why, most of the time, contingent responses that are roughly proportionate to what's come before in your interactions are most effective at both getting your message across and keeping your connections intact.

The art of proportional, contingent responsivity follows us everywhere. It's with us in the workplace, outside of work, and in our most intimate relationships. In the world of dating, contingent responsivity is the glue that keeps conversations and dates alive, enough for the next one to occur. There's usually a moment, after you've been casually dating someone, when you start to wonder if the feelings you have for them are mutual and to the same degree. There's often a kind of flirtation or "dance" in which you say or do something as a "trial balloon" to see how they might react, to see if they will reciprocate in some way or if they might even take things a bit further. Maybe it is something small—just a look or a playful comment—or maybe you take a bigger risk and ask them something more serious, like to go to a wedding together or to meet their family. Their response will tell you something about their feelings.

Those small acts are usually proportionate to the speed at which the relationship had been advancing, and probably don't involve suddenly blurting out, "I *love you*!" after the second date. You may have felt it or had the impulse to say it, but your motivation to avoid overstepping or driving them away kept you on an even path. That subtle back-and-forth of contingent responses brings much steadier waters, making it easier for you to see where things might head. To engage in contingent responsivity, you have to continue to listen (in the broad sense) to the other person and to yourself, to gauge your reactions during the back-and-forth exchange, and to make adjustments as needed.

KEEPING PACE AND STAYING IN THE FLOW

People often say, "Go with the flow" as a means of promoting harmony within relationships. "Just relax, chill out," they say. We'd argue that going with the flow can sometimes lead people astray, because it encourages them to be passively carried along by events.

Instead, attunement is strengthened more by what we call "staying in the flow," or keeping up awareness and engagement with what is actually happening in the interaction, while still being an active participant in shaping the interaction. In order to do this, you focus on interpreting what someone is communicating while being ready for whatever will come next. That focus shouldn't be intense, rigid, or stressful by any means. With relaxed awareness comes the ability to more calmly perceive the other person's social cues in the current moment, which allows you to automatically anticipate what the person might think, feel, say, or do next. It's much like the way your brain automatically and unconsciously predicts where a ball in flight will go next so that you can be there to catch it. But to stay in the flow, you can't rely too much on the accuracy of your own predictions or be too distracted or too directed by them. You also need to remain aware of what's actually happening and be flexible enough to respond to what the other person really does, not just to what you predict they will do.

Think back to a time when you were nervous to talk to someone about something. You might have imagined what could happen in the conversation, and to reduce your anxiety, you may have actively practiced what you were going to say. You might have even come up with a plan A and plan B, depending on how it goes. But if you stuck too rigidly to your prepared script, and did not respond to the things the other person *actually* ended up saying, then you probably came across as stilted and mechanical and out of tune with the other person. Although a general strategy can be planned ahead of time, conversations usually go best if you can be open to the unpredictable things that might happen. You need to be flexible and responsive enough to make adjustments as things actually occur, ready to say or do what fits the reality of the interaction. This is true for lots of different types of conversations, from job interviews to difficult conversations with a partner, a family member, or a friend.

Megan, a medical student at New York University, rediscovered the importance of this when she was beginning to do patient interviews. In her first career as a professional violist, she had learned to stay in the flow of what was happening between her and the other chamber group members, even when something unexpected happened. This is what Yannick Nézet-Séguin, the music director of the Philadelphia Orchestra and the Metropolitan Opera, has described as being "open to the moment."[11] When Megan transitioned careers to become a medical student, she found that preparing for each medical interview was helpful, but, much like playing a duet, she soon realized that she also needed to stay in the flow of what was happening between her and the patient, and be ready for unpredictable things that patients might ask or say. "As much as I've prepared and I think I know how [the patient] might reply, chamber music teaches that it could be completely different than what you expected. Knowledge and technique help you prepare your inner thoughts, like how musicians need years of practicing etudes and scales, but you can't use that diagnostic knowledge if you aren't truly listening to your partner's thoughts and responding attentively."[12] In the words of the Dalai Lama, "I am open to the guidance of synchronicity, and do not let expectations hinder my path."[13] Easier said than done! But this is where your work in developing relaxed awareness, listening, and understanding pays off. Whether it's a conversation, playing music, or dancing, your work will guide you so that you don't get ahead of your partner or lag behind—you will stay *with* them, even as unpredictable zigzags in direction and changes in pace occur.

The distraction of our own thoughts, worries, and emotions can make it hard for us to stay in the flow of the present. One of our patients, a woman in her early thirties named Melanie, had a lot of difficulty staying in the flow, because she would get extremely distracted by her own thoughts that arose when she was interacting with someone, especially when that someone was a potential romantic partner. This became a real problem when she was having coffee with Angela, someone she was getting to know. As they were talking and Angela would say or do something, Melanie would become preoccupied in wondering what Angela meant by that, why she said that, or if that could mean she was interested in her. While Melanie was wondering about those things, she fell way behind in the conversation to the point where she was only half paying attention to what she and Angela were saying. While this probably happens to a lot of us in these situations, it happened to Melanie to such a great degree that it derailed her in the conversation. Suddenly realizing she had fallen behind in what they were talking about, Melanie would try to jump ahead, not only to what Angela was saying in the moment, but ahead two or three steps in an effort to anticipate and guess what Angela might say. So instead of staying in the flow, Melanie was either lagging behind or jumping ahead. In our therapy sessions, we took a look at this situation together and brainstormed about another way that Melanie could handle these situations. We did a kind of thought experiment together, making use of a soccer analogy, since Melanie loved to play soccer, and thinking about soccer was much more relaxing to Melanie than the actual topic of how Angela might feel about her. In this experiment, Melanie imagined that she was a soccer player on defense, and that an offensive player on the other team was dribbling the ball down the field, heading straight toward Melanie. If we freeze-frame that moment, Melanie might be wondering about the other player's intentions. What was her opponent going to do next? Would she try to break right or left around her? But soccer moves quickly, and if Melanie were to become so preoccupied with that question, so much so that she was no longer in the flow of what was actually happening, then it would be easy for her, in this distracted state, to lose contact with the other player and for that player to speed past Melanie toward the goal. On the other hand, if Melanie noticed the question in her mind but quickly returned her attention to what the player with the ball was actually doing, then Melanie could stay in the flow and be more effective as a defender. The anxious thoughts were sucking up her reserve of energy and attention that she could use to respond to whatever happened next. Melanie was actually good at this when it came to soccer—she could get into a flow state and become relaxed and aware, ready to respond to whatever the opposing player did—so she knew she was capable of having that kind of mindset. But how could she bring this to a situation that she wasn't so comfortable in?

We talked about how it was perfectly natural for Melanie to have those questions about Angela's potential interest or intentions arise in her mind while she was talking with Angela. In fact, having some awareness of her own thoughts and reactions could be really useful and important. But the goal was for Melanie to try to take only a brief notice of her thoughts, and then try to return her attention to what Angela was actually saying or doing so that she could stay in the flow with her. But how could Melanie really do this when she got so nervous? We started by practicing the fundamental skill of relaxed awareness, and we worked on helping her develop this skill and incorporate it into her daily life, in moments with and without Angela. It would be unrealistic to expect Melanie to skillfully manage her anxiety in what she perceived to be a high pressure scenario when it was still difficult for her to regulate her thoughts during more mundane situations. Through a lot of practice in therapy sessions, and by practicing in her daily life, Melanie got better at noticing her anxious thoughts, briefly moving her attention to the feeling of her belly on an inbreath and relaxing her shoulders. This sequence helped her to let go of the worry and to physically relax for a second, which then helped her get better at returning her attention to what was actually happening in the moment. The ability to notice your own thoughts and feelings but to also stay in the flow with the other person, plus the ability to be open and flexible enough to respond to whatever arises in the interaction, is challenging! But acquiring even a little of these abilities can really pay off in many areas of your life. The strategies that Melanie worked on in therapy were ways of regulating herself, of adjusting her level of emotion, so that she could stay in an optimal zone of relaxed awareness, listen, and stay in the flow.

REGULATING EACH OTHER TO STAY IN THE FLOW

In addition to regulating themselves, people who are interacting can also regulate *each other* to try to stay in this optimal zone. This is a process called interpersonal regulation that's often natural and automatic and not necessarily deliberate.[14] Here's a really simple example of this: we (the authors) are on a flight that hits turbulence. We are cool with flying in most circumstances, but as we've gotten older, we've become less cool when the plane suddenly dips or gets tossed around. In recent years, we've both become more consistent about practicing our relaxed awareness exercises, which has done wonders for maintaining our cool on choppy flights. But when turbulence hits a certain level of intensity, both of us agree that, despite our best efforts to self-regulate, tensions rise. Often, around that time, Ted will look to the calm and comforting movements of the flight attendants to find some relief. Just their calm demeanor is soothing to him and helps regulate him. Ashley, on the other hand, tends to keep her eyes down to avoid the possibility of witnessing a passenger or a crew member start to freak out. Seeing people clench their armrests or hearing them let out little frightened squeals can make her tension and anxiety worse. Witnessing the reactions of others doesn't regulate Ashley, but dysregulates her instead.

Regulation and dysregulation occur at a primal level, and they don't require verbal conversation as such. Regulation can happen even between humans and other mammals, like when your dog senses your mood is low and comes over and lays its head on you, or when a horse and rider keep each other calm. Ali Schultz, cofounder of the coaching company Reboot and an avid horseback rider, described how she and her horse could each sense "when the other was tense and what was needed for reassurance to return to calm and connection so we could be with each other and flow together."[15]

Interpersonal regulation goes on during conversations too, of course. For example, if you tell someone about a topic that is anxiety-provoking to you—say some work project that you're really stressed about, or a family matter that's worrying you—and the other person really listens and understands you, and further projects a calm manner in what they say and how they react, then you will probably begin to feel calmer. But if you talk with a person who becomes even more anxious than you are, due to concern for you, then your anxiety may ratchet up even further. What's the difference between the first person who calms you down and the second person who riles you up? Person number one listened to you attentively and resonated with your feelings, with both emotional and cognitive empathy. Despite being empathetic, they didn't simply mirror you by joining you in your anxiety. That probably wouldn't help much—you'd both end up stewing in your anxiety together. Instead, they were able to "hold" your anxiety—to perceive it, be stable and grounded without being overly affected by it, and they remained interested and responsive to you. They were able to stay calm, which then is reassuring and calming to you. This describes one direction of interpersonal regulation, in which the other person regulates you. But ideally this process is mutual, such that you can both regulate each other.

Members of teams can help to regulate each other's emotions—sharing the highs and lows of, say, a long basketball season, a hard endurance bicycle race, or a grueling trek up and down a Himalayan mountain—and ideally supporting each other along the way, motivating each other at challenging moments and calming each other down during moments of high tension and stress. During the multiyear adventure of writing this book, we experienced this interpersonal regulation, even when working from different cities. By sharing the exciting moments, buffering each other's worries, and encouraging each other along the way, we were able to stay in the flow long enough to get the book written.

Yet even if you utilize the strategies outlined here and regulate yourself to perfection (which would be a feat unto itself!), it doesn't necessarily mean every exchange will be agreeable and flow with ease. Sometimes the people you encounter won't be able to connect with you. For example, they may have a personality or be in a mood that doesn't allow them to be positively influenced by your approach. After all, attunement is ideally a two-way street, a mutual dance that requires two (or more) active partners. But, we can promise that if you are able to regulate yourself and exude an energy of interest in connecting, you create the possibility for a ripple effect to occur, influencing yourself and those around you.

With time and consistent practice of the exercises, you can start to take note of the influence you have on others during your interactions. Ashley found herself noticing interpersonal regulation in action at a friend's birthday celebration:

> I joined Luna and her friends, many of whom I did not know, briefly for lunch on a sunny Saturday. We were all gathered around a picnic table and I was frankly a bit nervous, especially when the only person I knew left the table to pick up their food from the counter, leaving me alone with an older couple. I was anxious and unsure if I would have anything interesting to say. Having practiced the exercises presented in this book for a while, at that point, I had gotten much better at accessing the strategies and was able to regulate my breathing and emotions, unclench my shoulders, and relax the rest of my body. Once I got my nerves under control and put my self-consciousness at bay, I had more energy to put toward making eye contact, introducing myself, and exuding genuine, open-hearted interest in making conversation. My initial few conversation bids were met with shy reactions from the couple. Had I not been able to balance my attention between their responses and calming my own nerves, I would have been discouraged by their reticent and awkward reactions and been dissuaded from prodding the conversation forward. But I found it in myself to persist, and I asked a few more questions and made comments to try to engage them about their recent time abroad. Finally, there was a moment when I tangibly noticed the husband physically relax and show a burst of positive energy in his reply. It revealed his genuine interest in the topic and his desire to continue the conversation with me, which kept the reciprocal exchange alive. It

wasn't a life-changing conversation by any means, and we didn't leave the table as friends. I may never see them again. But the connection in that moment around the picnic table felt deep from its warmth and the joy I was left with. I remember walking home feeling rejuvenated, in a way, from experiencing the power of attunement even at this micro level.

LAPSES IN RESPONSIVENESS . . . AND LEARNING TO BEGIN AGAIN

Even with our best efforts to be responsive to each other, perfect and continuous attunement between two people isn't possible over a sustained period of time, no matter how hard we try or how much those people love and care about each other. Everyone needs some time to themselves. And even during the times we want to engage with each other and we try our best to connect, we inevitably miss each other, at least occasionally. We'll be out of tune with each other, misunderstand each other, or do or say something that leads to a lapse in the connection for just a moment, or for longer periods of time. If these things happen, even after working on the exercises in this book, don't be too hard on yourself. It's impossible to avoid completely and forever. So, in addition to developing the skills of mutual responsiveness, it's equally important to learn the skills of reconnecting and beginning again. The situation is similar to the practice of relaxed awareness exercises, in which we ask you to pay attention to your breath. Inevitably, your attention lingers off to some other thought. In those moments you direct compassion to yourself for losing focus, notice the thought, let it go, and start again to pay attention to your breath. Our connections are the same. There will be moments of deep, continuous flow, and there will be moments of disconnection.

The beauty comes from noticing the breaks more and more, so that there are more chances to start again.

In momentary loss of connection, you should relax, listen, and see if you can quickly understand what happened. Did I just space out for a moment? Did one or both of us become distracted or dysregulated? Did I misunderstand them, or did they misunderstand me? Did they hear that differently from the way that I intended it? Whatever the case may be, you can begin again, tune back in, and try to meet the other person where they are now, and try to clear up any misunderstanding. If you did or said something that was inadvertently hurtful to the other person, you may need to address this directly with them in order to clear the air and begin again. You can acknowledge what went wrong, and acknowledge what you did, and be willing and humble enough to take responsibility and apologize so that you can try to repair any damage done. Fully repairing a bigger rift can take time, and the other person may need some space to think it over. But your willingness to take responsibility and your openness to begin again, when they may be ready to do so, can go a long way toward healing the connection. Beginning again requires the willingness of both people, and if you insist on it or push to restart the connection before the other person is ready, that may be counterproductive. You can try to be as attuned as possible to the signs of when the other person might be willing to try to reconnect, and you can give it a try then. Ali Schultz even talks about rifts she had in the attunement with her horses, on days when the connection seemed to be gone, "when both horse and I looked at each other like we were from opposing planets with no direct line between us, nor an interest to find one."[16] In those cases, attempts to force a reconnection seemed futile, even counterproductive. There had to be a mental shift inside one of them, so that they could reach out to the other in a different way—with less anxiety and with more trust—and begin again.

Kendrick was a patient who found himself in a situation in which his good friend at work, Abe, got really mad at him for something that was seemingly benign. The anger caught Kendrick by surprise, because the issue was something that Kendrick never would have guessed would upset Abe. Abe was so mad that he abruptly started avoiding Kendrick. Kendrick's early attempts to reengage Abe went nowhere. So Kendrick gave it time, and over a few weeks the ice gradually started to melt, so to speak. Abe started to seem less uncomfortable around Kendrick, and he began to smile and laugh a bit more with the group at work when Kendrick was in the room. Around that time, Kendrick was able to strike up some bits of conversation with Abe again, brief ones at first, but then the ice continued to melt. Ultimately, they were able to hash out what happened that started the whole thing, and share each of their perspectives, make amends, and move on. They went on to become even better friends than before.

It's hard to predict for sure how situations like this will turn out. Sometimes you can repair things, and the friendship can seem even stronger for it. And sometimes repair seems impossible, and the friendship is never revived. A lot of it depends on the particular personalities and situation involved. But developing the capacity to try to begin again won't be a waste of time—it will end up being needed in any relationship that you hope to sustain over time.

RESPONDING TO YOURSELF

In addition to responding to the other person, respect and responsivity to yourself, to your own thoughts and feelings, should be a priority for you. Frankly, not responding to yourself can often be what blocks your capacity for staying in the flow. If you don't give your own feelings and perspective the respect they deserve, you can ultimately hurt a relationship.

Let's return to the story of Melanie and Angela. Despite the communication challenges at their first date, Melanie and Angela met for a second coffee date. Melanie had, by this time, learned not to get *too* distracted by her own thoughts and feelings during the flow of a conversation—she had learned to take quicker notice of them so she could then refocus on her conversation partner and stay in the flow with her. Melanie did not ignore her thoughts and feelings completely; instead she managed them by catching herself when she got lost in thought and quickly redirected her focus back to Angela. Melanie left the date feeling like she was much more present, which allowed her to really understand Angela better. And Angela seemed more engaged in the conversation, probably because Melanie was more present with her during the flow of their interactions.

Even though taking note of your feelings may need to be quick in order to stay in the flow, like the story of Melanie shows, observations of your own feelings are really important. Listening to your own inner experience and understanding yourself can give you guidance on what's best for you in the interaction and in the relationship as a whole. If you notice that you feel comfortable and safe with someone, that observation may lead you to become a bit more open with them. If that person makes you feel attended to and cared for, you may be more inclined to reciprocate. But if that person makes you feel uncomfortable, and you truly pay attention to your own discomfort, you may choose to be more cautious with them. And if they're being unfair or mistreating you in some way, you can stand up for yourself. So your own gut feelings are extremely valuable, and sometimes they can guide you in how to respond to the other person.

Alice, a patient in her early thirties, had been in a relationship with Jake for quite a while. They seemed to fit together in a number of ways. But over and over, Jake would make subtle but unmistakably critical comments about Alice's appearance and weight. She took his words to heart, and they started to affect her confidence and self-esteem, even though she really wasn't overweight. She didn't tend to feel bad about her appearance in other contexts, but she certainly did in those moments with Jake. After discussing this in therapy and with her friends, Alice began to realize that Jake's obnoxious habit of doing this might not *really* be about her appearance. Instead, it might be about Jake feeling insecure about himself and their relationship, and him trying, in a dysfunctional way, to get Alice to feel like she was lucky to be with him. That insight was helpful, but it was not quite enough for Alice to break out of the usual pattern. When Jake started in once again with the comments, despite her efforts, her embarrassment and low self-esteem took the wheel—her responses, it seemed, were still so instinctive and habitual. At times when Jake was not being insulting, she tried to talk with him about how much his criticisms of her appearance bothered her. But trying to discuss it with him out of context seemed to go nowhere. Then one day, Jake started in with the sarcastic comments again, but this time, in the midst of the interaction, Alice was able to take a mental step back from it to sense in real time what Jake was doing. She sensed in herself that her usual emotional reactions were starting to happen. With that greater perspective, born of a moment of heightened relaxed awareness, listening, and understanding of what this pattern was, Alice didn't feel bad about herself, but instead recognized Jake's intentions and decided to respond to her own feelings and perspective by setting some limits, and not give him the satisfaction of getting her to feel bad about herself. She recalled saying, "Jake, I'm tired of your criticisms of how I look. My body is not yours to control. If you have something to say, say it. Do it directly and with respect. I'm done with your passive-aggressive comments." Jake was stopped in his tracks, and at least for a little while, the patterns in their relationship shifted. Alice, like most people, needed time and practice to make even a seemingly small change. Even small changes may not happen overnight for you, but the consistent practice of being responsive to yourself and your own feelings can help you identify troubling or dysfunctional patterns. Eventually this can help you stick up for yourself and assert yourself in relationships.

Responding to yourself can also mean choosing not to engage in an interaction, or choosing to step away from an interaction. If someone is provoking you, attributing things to you that you feel are false or inappropriate, or otherwise trying to draw you into a struggle, you can "listen" carefully to your own discomfort, understand what the other person is trying to evoke in you, and "respond

to yourself" and your own feelings by setting a limit on it, not engaging in it, or walking away to give yourself a break.

HOW MUTUAL RESPONSIVENESS
BEGAN, EARLY IN OUR LIVES

Like the other components of attunement, mutual responsivity in
relationships starts way back at the beginning of our lives. As infants, our parents or caretakers (hopefully) met us where we were,
and noticed and attended to our needs. As infants, we were too
helpless to be able to meet our parents where they were, so we
needed them to take the initiative. But amazingly, even as infants,
we started to engage in contingent responsivity with our parents or
caretakers, probably within the first few days or even the first hours
of life, with very basic, turn-taking exchanges of actions, facial expressions, and vocalizations. This is how we and our parents first
got to know each other and solidified our bonds with each other.[17]

This contingent responsivity with our parents grew and grew,
and by the time we reached about two to four months of age, we
had created with our parents our own unique way of playfully exchanging smiles, gestures, and vocalizations.[18] Although we didn't
have any "real" words or language yet, the rhythms of the turn-
taking vocalizations between us and our parents were very similar
to the rhythms of conversations between adults. So our capacity to
coordinate the timing of our vocalizations with a partner (in this
case, our parents)—to take turns in vocalizing and be mutually
responsive—is even more primal than language itself.

Some of the classic research on mutual responsiveness and attunement between infants and mothers was done by an American
psychiatrist, Dr. Daniel Stern, in the 1980s. He studied the way that
mothers responded to their babies' vocalizations and actions by
matching them—either by imitating them or matching the emotion
that the baby was expressing. This matching, Stern argued, was a

form of attunement, a way that mothers shared feelings and experiences with their babies. Stern argued that the mutual responsiveness and attunement between mothers and babies in the first year of the babies' lives taught the babies a crucial lesson: "that internal feeling states are forms of human experience that are shareable with other humans. The converse is also true: feeling states that are never attuned to will be experienced only alone, isolated from the interpersonal context of shareable experience. What is at stake here is nothing less than the shape of and extent of the shareable inner universe."[19]

But Stern also observed that there were many instances in which mothers didn't match their babies' behaviors. Some of these instances were deliberate and some were accidental. In some cases, mothers purposely over- or under-matched the infant's intensity of behavior, with the intention of increasing or decreasing the infant's level of activity or emotion. For example, the mother might respond less intensely than her baby, in order to bring down the baby's level of excitement a bit. These instances of deliberate mismatches were a form of interpersonal regulation, which helped to keep their babies' emotions and activities within a certain optimal zone so they could stay in the flow of mutual responsiveness.[20]

In other cases, parents showed mismatches of their babies' behaviors accidentally, because of the parents' occasional, understandable lapses in attention (after all, everyone needs to take a moment for themselves from time to time). They got out of rhythm in the turn-taking responsivity, misread the baby's signals about their emotional state, or were unable to get into a similar feeling state as the baby. Just as with adult interactions, there is no such thing as perfect attunement sustained over time between parents and babies. Temporary lapses in responsiveness are inevitable. One study of three- to nine-month-old infants found that mother and infant were in mismatched states (out of sync, not attuned) 70 percent of the time.[21] An important skill that infants and parents learn together, through these breaks in connection, is how to begin again and reconnect. These mismatches and repairs between babies and parents are important learning experiences, because the inevitable breaks in connection and repairs will be a part of their relationships throughout life.

MANAGING CONFLICT BY BUILDING ATTUNEMENT

The versatility of mutual responsiveness, and attunement as a whole, is truly amazing. Not only is attunement crucial for cultivating close and loving relationships, and for improving the quality of more ordinary interactions, but it's also extremely helpful in managing conflict. It seems counterintuitive to want to be attuned to someone who you're in conflict with and/or dislike intensely. Paradoxically, an ability to attune to your opponent, to connect with them, will put you in a much stronger position in managing a conflict with them. This is a basic principle of the martial art of Tai Chi Chuan.

Anger and conflict are often fueled by misperceptions and mis-understandings of each other, and are often driven by fear. Let's say someone at your workplace gets mad at you due to their own misimpression of you, and they accuse you of doing something that you didn't do. Naturally, you'd then get mad at them for falsely ac-cusing you, and you might also fear that others at your workplace could believe their false accusation. Instinctively, you might react by lashing out verbally at the person who accused you. They might lash out right back at you, and the whole thing escalates.

But let's say that, instead of shooting from the hip, you're able to keep your wits about you, staying centered and grounded in a zone of relaxed awareness, even when you're accused. Not easy to do, but let's imagine it was possible. In a state of relaxed awareness, you feel more solid and secure. You feel less need to lash out at them, or to pull back and run away from them. You can stand your ground. Your ability to be more centered and grounded can help to calm down the situation. With a clearer head, you're in a better position to listen and under-stand your accuser, and to see more clearly where their perceptions of you and the situation went wrong. Once you can see and understand the misperceptions, you're in a much better position to correct them, to clear them up, to address the root of what started this conflict in the first place. Using the components of attunement, you can de-escalate the conflict and defend yourself more effectively at the same time. The skill to defuse conflict is the skill of a martial artist, even when only words are used. The Chinese character that means "martial" actually means literally "to stop the spear" or "to stop the fight." The goal of true martial arts is to skillfully manage and minimize conflict and aggression, to minimize harm to self and others.

Let's imagine that the situation is even worse. Let's say the co-worker is not accusing you due to any honest mistake or misperception. Instead, they know that you didn't do anything wrong, but they're purposely, manipulatively accusing you of something for malicious reasons just to "throw you under the bus" at work, to harm you, to get you in trouble, or even to get you fired. In this case, there's no honest misperception to clear up. If you lose your cool and lash out at them suddenly, then they've likely gotten exactly what they wanted by provoking you and making you lose your bearings and your better judgement. They might even capitalize on the opportunity to gaslight you, which can cause you to cast doubt on your perception of events. In most cases, as difficult as it is, you'll be better off staying in a zone of relaxed awareness so that you can listen, see, and understand clearly, and know the most effective way to respond. (Sometimes that response might necessitate making your voice heard by seeking support from a trusted supervisor, human resources, or maybe placing a more prominent spotlight on the coworker's behavior.) Attuning to the person you're in conflict with doesn't mean liking them (necessarily) or becoming close with them. It just means giving yourself the best chance you can to manage the conflict skillfully. By connecting with them and using the principles of mutual responsiveness, you can keep your balance, focus your energy to keep your actions on target, and direct your countervailing response. Again, this is a basic principle of Tai Chi and some other martial arts. If—through your relaxed awareness, listening, and understanding—you clearly perceive someone to be truly threatening in some way, you may however decide wisely to avoid them completely and end the interaction.

What's astounding is that the principles of attunement are useful even for outright combat. We're not suggesting that you get into fistfights, but it's interesting to take a look at this in order to appreciate the full versatility of attunement, and the role it can play in managing all kinds of conflict. Take the example of boxing or some other fighting art. Your ability to meet the person where they are (rather than at a misperception of where they are), to respond proportionately and with the right timing, and to stay in the flow of the interaction, enables you to manage the fight more skillfully. When you need to be forceful, it's better that the force be directed by an accurate perception of the other person. Maintaining a connection by listening to and understanding that person in the course of the conflict helps you to do that. The martial artist Kanishka Sharma said that, "Anyone can learn to kick and punch. The true artist reads the rhythm of his opponent. He is a master of distance and timing." So the *art* of martial arts is really in reading the rhythm of one's opponent—the art is in attuning to them. One of the things that surprises beginners of Tai Chi or some other martial arts is how much they emphasize relaxed awareness. A novice student may think, "Wait . . . I wanted to learn how to fight. What's all of this relaxation and meditation stuff, and what could it possibly have to do with fighting?" But it's a relaxed body and mind that is much more capable of reading the opponent, and of generating a response (e.g., a punch) that's not blocked and impeded by your own stiffness. A state of panic will not help you in a fight. As you will remember, relaxed awareness is the foundation of attunement. The contemporary Tai Chi master Chen Zhenglei described it this way: "Concentrating upon the entire body as a system rather than upon any obvious external point, the skilled Taijiquan [Tai Chi] exponent uses complete relaxation to read and respond to the intentions of an attacker."[22]

Interestingly, Daniel Stern—the pioneer in studies of mother-infant attunement that we mentioned before—also realized that the principles of attunement go far beyond the setting of mothers and babies and extend into the arena of skillful martial conflict. Stern carried out a frame-by-frame analysis of a 1966 boxing match of Muhammad Ali and Karl Mildenberger, and realized, in this study, how crucial attunement was to expert boxing. Because the boxers moved so quickly, landing a punch depended on the puncher correctly anticipating the other boxer's trajectory in time and space. Only by the puncher tuning in to his opponent very closely, and being calm enough to accurately predict the opponent's next movements, could his fist arrive at the same time as the opponent's face or body.[23] Similarly, in one of the old texts on Tai Chi, sometimes called the Tai Chi Classics, there is a saying about boxing that "if others don't move, I don't move. If others move slightly, I move first." This means that the good Tai Chi practitioner is so attuned to his opponent that he can sense when his opponent is about to move, and moves first, which gives him the advantage over his opponent or allows him to meet the opponent where he will be.[24]

EXERCISES: MUTUAL RESPONSIVENESS

The goal of the following exercises is to develop the key components of mutual responsiveness: meeting the other person where they are, contingent responsivity, and staying in the flow. These elements of mutual responsiveness have been called the dark matter of social neuroscience, because they are crucially important but have barely begun to be explored or understood by neuroscientists.[25] As challenging as it is to study mutual responsiveness in the lab—because of the spontaneous, quick, and uncontrolled nature of two-person interactions—it is clear that mutual responsiveness can be improved with practice, and scientists are beginning to make inroads into understanding the biology of this learning process.[26] In the conversation, walking, and push hands exercises here, we will add the elements of spontaneity and reciprocity into the mix. By adding them, we can practice employing all the elements of attunement in situations that simulate the unexpected twists and turns of our everyday social interactions. And when we incorporate an unpredictable alternation of leading and following into these exercises, we build mutual responsiveness and nonverbal communication.

RECIPROCAL CONVERSATION*

Try practicing the Understanding in Conversation exercise from Chapter 4, but this time don't choose roles of speaker and listener at the outset. Instead, engage in a more typical, natural conversation where there is back-and-forth, and both people take turns speaking and listening. One person should try to initiate the conversation by "meeting the other person where they are" (i.e., starting on a topic or question that is likely to be of interest to the other person, based on what you know of them). Then, try to focus on the contingent responsivity aspect of conversation in which each person's speech and responses build on something that the other person just said. After a while of this, either person can decide to shift the topic, but try to do so in a way that connects to the other person and builds on what you were just talking about. When one partner shifts the topic, the other partner should try to follow them to the new topic, instead of sticking rigidly to the old topic. Try to stay in the flow of the conversation without drifting off mentally or pursuing a tangent of little interest to your partner. If you do space out, or if you fall out of connection somehow, try to begin again. Avoid monologuing or dominating the conversation—continue to allow a give and take.

---

*Indicates that this is a partner exercise.

SPONTANEOUS WALKING EXERCISE*

Refer to the instructions for the Synchronized Walking exercise in Chapter 3. Decide who will be the leader (pacesetter) and who will be the follower at the outset. The leader will vary the pace as you begin to walk. However, this time, with no spoken warning, the follower will unpredictably start to change the pace. The leader should sense and pick up on that change of pace, and try to align with the pace of the follower. In other words, the two people switch roles (leader becomes follower, and follower becomes leader) spontaneously and with no verbal warning. When one person changes the pace, the other person should try to stay with them. This should be done just by sensing each other's movements and following each other.

PUSH HANDS EXERCISE*

In this exercise, we'll build on the Tai Chi push hands exercise that we learned in Chapter 4. We'll try to develop a greater physical sense of mutual responsiveness, incorporate meeting the other person where they are, practice contingent responsivity, and stay in the flow. We will learn how to initiate push hands by meeting the other person where they are. Try to make your responses contingent on the responses of the other person, and keep them on target and proportional. Each person can change pace or direction spontaneously and without verbal warning, and the other person should try to stay in the flow, follow, and maintain contact. The goal is to keep up the connection, "listen" to each other, and move fluidly together. Remember that "leading" still has a little bit of following in it, because even as you lead you still "listen" to the other person.

For more detailed steps and videos on how to practice push hands in this way, as well as videos and tips on troubleshooting all exercises described here, go to MissingEachOther.com.

CHAPTER SIX

ARTIFICIAL ATTUNEMENT

"All tools can be used for good or ill. . . . The more powerful the tool, the greater the benefit or damage it can cause."

—BRAD SMITH, PRESIDENT OF MICROSOFT[1]

ATTUNEMENT IS PERSONAL, ANIMATE, INTIMATE. It's deeply rooted in each of our own life histories, going back to our earliest relationships as infants with our parents or caretakers, and continuing through the close relationships in our childhood, adolescence, and adult lives. Right now, we're living through a unique moment in history—a technological revolution that is encroaching on attunement as a personal, human-to-human phenomenon. We've entered the age of what we will call artificial attunement (AA) in which machines have the rapidly growing, powerful capability to mimic attunement, and in some cases even exceed human abilities in certain aspects of social information processing. The advent of AA holds a huge variety of potentials, depending on how it is used and

170

regulated. This is true of the growth of any new technology, but the potential for good versus misuse is particularly stark with AA, given how integral attunement is to the essence of ourselves and our relationships. The possibilities range from AA providing breakthrough treatments to boost self-awareness and communication skills for those with disabilities to AA being used as a tool of mass surveillance and, in some ways, displacing our human partners in our most personal interactions.

THE BIRTH OF ARTIFICIAL ATTUNEMENT

Artificial attunement has its roots in the computer science of the 1940s and '50s, when the field of artificial intelligence (AI) was first emerging, with the aim of developing computers that could simulate aspects of human intelligence. In 1950, Alan Turing, a British mathematician and computer scientist, developed a test to assess a computer's ability to generate humanlike responses using language.[2] If a human could not distinguish the text responses of a computer from that of a human, then the machine passed what became known as the Turing test. In 1990, an American inventor, Hugh Loebner, established the Loebner Prize, an annual competition to determine which computer programs can best simulate humans in a Turing test.

Since 1990, there have been breakneck advances in AI and, particularly, machine learning, an application of AI that gives machines the ability to learn and solve problems, such that they continuously and autonomously improve their own abilities beyond what was preprogrammed, and, in some cases, beyond the control of the programmer. AI has already outstripped human abilities in certain frontiers of human intelligence. In 1997, IBM's Deep Blue supercomputer defeated world chess champion Gary Kasparov. In 2016, Google's DeepMind program, AlphaGo, defeated Lee Sedol, the greatest living champion of Go. The game Go is considered to be one of the most complex and intuitive of all board games, which many doubted could ever be within the capacity of a machine to master. In 2019, Lee Sedol decided to retire from the game at the age of thirty-six because of the rise of AlphaGo, which, he said, "cannot be defeated."[3] AlphaGo was not preprogrammed to defeat these champions, but it was capable of learning by repeated practice, and then exceeding the abilities of any living human. In 2017, Google's machine learning program, AlphaZero, in just four hours of self-play practice, exceeded the chess abilities that took humanity hundreds of years to acquire.[4] Google's DeepMind program recently developed an artificial intelligence program that can play as part of a team and defeat the best human professional players at multiplayer team competitions—after repeated trials, the program is able to tailor its behavior to the performance of its teammates.[5] And in 2019, an AI called Pluribus—which had played against copies of itself repeatedly, and gained skill—defeated the best human players at multiplayer poker.[6] However, some human capacities are still difficult for AI to match, such as abstract thinking and applying knowledge flexibly to suit the particular context. In 2019, Microsoft made a $1 billion investment in a company called OpenAI, as part of an ambitious project to build artificial general intelligence (AGI), with the goal to develop a system that could do anything that the human brain could do.[7]

In recent years, the power of AI has been turned to other capabilities that were once considered uniquely human—human communication and attunement. This raises the prospect of machines equaling or surpassing human abilities in some aspects of attunement, and even insinuating themselves into our most intimate relationships. This idea was portrayed in the 2013 science fiction–romantic drama film *Her*, in which the main character, a lonely, depressed man named Theodore, develops a relationship with an AI program with a female voice that he named Samantha. As their relationship grows, Samantha learns and adapts through interaction with Theodore, and they become increasingly close and intimate with each other. Though it was science fiction, the film points to the reality that machines are able to "read" and respond to us with increasing precision and skill, and can sometimes make us feel close to them, like we would with a friend.

AI programs, and the computers and robots that they run, can simulate certain aspects of attunement. But it is a simulation—AIs are not attuned in the same sense that another person could be. For starters, computers have no true awareness. And they don't experience anxiety, tension, or stress, nor do they experience relaxed awareness. They can't because they aren't conscious. But when an AI or a robot responds to you in an uncannily humanlike way, it's easy for them to create the illusion of a conscious entity. AI can simulate listening by gathering information about us from our speech or writing, the patterns of our facial expressions, our tone of voice, or our body language. But this *information gathering* is not *listening* in the sense that a conscious human would listen. AI has no emotions of its own, and it cannot truly resonate with us emotionally in the way that a human with emotional empathy can. AI can simulate understanding. It can identify specific people based on their faces and other characteristics. It can recognize patterns in our speech, facial expressions, and other behaviors that indicate certain emotions or intentions. And AI is becoming increasingly sophisticated in its ability to respond to us in a way that mimics human mutual responsiveness. But its response is based solely on machine algorithms.

ARTIFICIAL UNDERSTANDING

Companies like Microsoft, Apple, Google, Amazon, and Facebook are all developing software that can identify specific people's faces, as well as distinguish among different facial emotions.[8] The technology is incredibly powerful, and it's only continuing to improve in accuracy. As of the time of our writing this, Google's FaceNet system can distinguish one face from a million others.[9] The potential impact of these technologies on our daily lives depends on how they are used. On the one hand, facial recognition software can be useful for any of us in cataloging the photos on our smartphones. On the other hand, the AI can be used—and possibly misused—for more questionable purposes by governments or corporations as facial recognition technology for surveillance and monitoring (e.g., to identify suspected criminals or potential terrorists, and potentially for surveillance of the general population).[10] AI systems have used face images from a variety of sources, including social media sites and dating websites, to train themselves on facial recognition.[11] Many of these facial recognition software services are being sold to police departments and government agencies, resulting in backlash from citizens concerned about potential government surveillance.[12] One company, Clearview AI, has developed an extremely powerful facial recognition app that allows the user to check a photo of a person against a database of more than three billion images that the company scraped from the internet (Facebook, YouTube, and the like). For context, this database of faces is much larger than the FBI's database. This app is now used by hundreds of law enforcement agencies and can be paired with augmented-reality glasses so that users can identify every person they see through the glasses.[13] There is concern that these facial recognition systems are less accurate, hence may make more mistakes, in identifying women, people of color, and other minority groups.[14] Facial recognition technology is being utilized in defense projects, as it can aid in analysis of video footage shot by military drones, meaning that it can potentially be used to recognize targeted people. The emergence of these kinds of projects has led many leaders in the field to call for facial recognition technology to be publicly regulated, pointing out that facial recognition software poses a threat to protections of fundamental human rights like privacy and freedom of expression.[15]

In addition to recognizing faces, AI is able to recognize patterns in what you are saying or writing. Already, machines with abilities to predict what you will say are in common use. The Smart Compose feature in Google's Gmail uses natural language processing AI to predict what you will type next in your emails, and it can finish your sentences for you.[16] A growing number of AI and machine learning systems have been developed that can analyze the emotions expressed in text—a function called sentiment analysis.[17] For example, Facebook is funding research on developing wearable, high tech headband-like devices ("speech decoders") that can determine what you are trying to say in a natural conversation based on the patterns of electrical activity in your brain.[18] The researchers see potential therapeutic applications for these speech decoders in helping individuals who are unable to speak or otherwise communicate due to neurological disorders. Concerns have been raised about the potential of this technology to "read" an individual's thoughts from their brain activity, to some extent. According to a report in *MIT Technology Review*, Facebook wants to develop a headset that can measure brain activity and enable users to control their devices or interact in virtual reality using only their thoughts. Another piece of technology, also patented by Facebook, has the potential to track your emotions through the phone camera as you view content on the app, ultimately paving the way for companies to tailor content placed in your newsfeed.[19] As far-fetched and futuristic as some of this research might sound, we're really not too far from such advanced technology.

A leading researcher in the field of developing AI to recognize emotions is MIT professor Rosalind W. Picard. Her lab has pioneered the field of "affective computing" in which computers are used to decode, simulate, and influence people's emotions, even enabling computers to adjust their behavior based on the emotional state of a person.[20] Her Affective Computing research group at the MIT Media Lab has worked on projects to build computer systems that can automatically detect affect (emotion) in speech, and that can monitor nonverbal expressions of emotion, such as facial expressions, body language, and physiological signs of emotion (like the electrical conductance properties of skin, which change with emotion).[21] Professor Picard, together with Dr. Rana el Kaliouby, started the company Affectiva, which has developed technology to detect complex and nuanced human emotions and cognitive states from face and voice.[22] The company's products enable advertisers to do market research by monitoring the emotional reactions of consumers to digital content; enable apps and devices to sense and adapt to users' facial expressions of emotion; and enable monitoring of emotional reactions during political discussions. Affectiva's website (www.affectiva.com) keeps a running list of its numbers: at the time this was written, over nine million faces have been analyzed and the data has been used by corporate brands.

This strong interest in developing AI to read human emotions has gone well beyond research interest, leading major strategic consulting firms, international think tanks, and large corporations to get together to brainstorm how to utilize this type of information effectively. In September 2019, The International Workshop on Social and Emotion AI for Industry was held in Cambridge, England, and was attended by representatives of well-known entities (e.g., KPMG, McKinsey, World Economic Forum, IBM). A major goal for the workshop was to bring together academic and industrial leaders to think about how to develop future technologies with the ability to deal with people's emotions, attitudes, intentions, and desires. It's data collection at an uncomfortably intimate level.[23]

One of the potentially constructive ways that AI can be put to use is in assisting individuals with disabilities such as autism. People on the autism spectrum commonly miss social cues and misread people's expressions of emotions, especially when people on the spectrum are interacting with neurotypical people. Artificial attunement technologies may be useful as aids to individuals on the autism spectrum, to help them interpret facial expressions and other social cues. At the 2018 International Society for Autism Research (INSAR) meeting in Rotterdam, Netherlands, Professor Picard was a keynote speaker. She emphasized the potential therapeutic uses of affective computing for helping autistic individuals to interpret other people's facial emotions. There have been an increasingly large number of research presentations at recent INSAR meetings about using AI and machine learning, wearable devices, smartphones, and robots as tools for teaching social skills to autistic children, indicating that there is a growing interest in these technologies. The tools being developed and tested for supporting social understanding in autistic individuals include virtual reality (VR), in which the user interacts with a computer-generated, simulated world through a headset. The idea is that individuals on the spectrum can acquire greater understanding of social situations through VR, and may become less anxious about being in these situations with repeated virtual experiences.

ARTIFICIAL RESPONSIVENESS

The ability of AI to respond to us at a basic level is already commonplace. We can talk with virtual assistants on smartphones or other devices, like Apple's Siri, Amazon's Alexa, or Samsung's Bixby. These AI systems can decode our spoken questions and answer us in a human-sounding voice, as they respond to our requests for information. Although they can roughly simulate conversation, the systems are still relatively crude—the machine-generated voices sound somewhat artificial, and the AI makes errors fairly frequently and often misunderstands our questions or requests. Their responses are preprogrammed and limited in flexibility. However, rapid progress is being made in making the experience seem more natural. The result of this increasing sophistication is that the machines can appear to attune to us. For example, Google developed a humanoid bot, called Duplex, that can make phone calls that sound like they are from a human. It uses human-sounding intonation, as well as "mm-hmms" and "umms."[24] Not to be outdone, the company Lyrebird created an AI technology that can synthesize speech, mimicking the sound of a particular person's voice from a one-minute sample recording of their voice.[25] The speech it generates sounds like that real person, and is much more natural-sounding than Siri, Alexa, or Bixby.

To make artificial responsiveness more lifelike and engaging, AI would not just have a more human-sounding voice, but it would ideally be able to adjust its responses based on the behavior of its human conversation partner—to make it's responsiveness contingent on not just what the other person says but on the other person's emotions as well. Professor Picard's lab at MIT has worked on developing software to help a machine interact with people while detecting whether the person was bonding with or trusting the machine, thus enabling the machine to make course corrections to foster the person's ability to trust and bond with the machine.[26] Large tech companies are developing ways of doing this as well. Amazon has patented technology for having Alexa analyze the pitch and volume of people's voices, use that information to recognize emotions in the voice, and then respond according to the person's emotions, possibly with targeted ads. Google has a similar patent for detecting negative emotions, and then offering advice.[27] Imagine asking Alexa to set a therapy appointment in your calendar, after which Alexa decides to play you a soothing mindfulness meditation melody because it "noted" the heavy emotion in your voice.

The growth of artificial responsiveness has reached some of the most personal of our interactions. For people who are lonely and want a friend to confide in, but can't talk to another person for whatever reason, there are now AI programs called care chatbots and friendship chatbots that you can communicate with by text. For those seeking psychological help, AI chatbots are available that can "listen" and respond in a way that simulates a therapist's response. The developers of these therapy bots argue that they address the real limitations of live therapy, such as the difficulties associated with accessing live therapy due to cost or geographic inaccessibility, as well as the reluctance some people have about talking with another person about such personal issues. AI talk therapy chatbots (text-based, online therapy programs) that simulate empathy are already in current use; they include Woebot and SimSensei. A number of mental health professionals decry the replacement of real, human-to-human psychotherapeutic relationships with human-machine interactions. They argue that though it may seem more difficult or embarrassing to talk with a live person, there is something of great therapeutic value in talking with a human therapist—in being seen, heard, and truly understood by a fellow human—something that can't be replaced by a machine that doesn't really hear, empathize, or care, but only appears to.[28]

ARTIFICIAL BODIES

Researchers and companies interested in developing artificial attunement (AA) realize that a disembodied AI voice or texting program can't fully simulate a human-to-human interaction. So much of our feeling of connection to each other has to do with our physical presence—our bodies—and not just our minds and voices. Even without any physical contact, the physical presence of another person can enrich the sense of connection. We pick up on each other's cues and emotions through our physicality. We connect partly through the experience of physical synchrony. During the recent periods of global shelter-in-place orders due to COVID-19, interactions have become primarily mediated through Zoom, Skype, or FaceTime. Even so, many people have been left craving in-person interactions. Even though we see people through video, the interactions feel stilted due to a combination of unreliable Wi-Fi signals, time lags, blurriness, and the way in which eye contact and other physical cues aren't transmitted the same way as they are in person. (Not to mention all the energy expended looking at yourself on each call!) A friend of ours described how stressful it was to feel as though he was missing crucial pieces of social information—like cye contact, subtle body movements, and gestures—by not actually being in the presence of whomever he was videoconferencing with. He noticed that he was feeling exhausted after a series of daily video calls, and was, at first, unsure why. Then he recalled that while video chatting made it mentally seem like he and his conversation partner were together, physically they were not. That cognitive dissonance took a toll on him over time.

The 2013 film *Her* may have been ahead of its time in the way it illustrated our craving for physical presence during social interactions. The AI program, Samantha, can only talk with the human character, Theodore, but Samantha has no physical presence. As Theodore starts to have romantic feelings toward Samantha, she suggests that Theodore can be physically intimate with her through a live human being, Isabella, who could serve as a surrogate for Samantha. In the 2014 film *Ex Machina*, a robot named Ava has a robotic body but a very human-looking face, hands, and feet. Those humanlike physical traits, along with her ability to simulate a human voice, emotions, and responses are enough to make a programmer, Caleb, feel attracted to her, and to try to save her from her owner. Ava seems to reciprocate Caleb's romantic feelings, but in the end, Ava manipulates him so that she can escape without him. At the end of the movie, [spoiler alert!] she covers her mechanical body with artificial skin, dresses in human clothes, and escapes into a crowd in the city, where she is indistinguishable from a live human. These films grapple with this issue of to what degree AI can simulate attunement with a human, and the quest to create an artificial or surrogate body in order to most fully simulate attunement.

This quest is not just science fiction. In reality, artificial attunement is currently growing beyond AI programs with natural sounding voices, all the way to increasingly lifelike robots that can interact with humans in intimate ways. Professor Picard's Affective Computing lab at MIT has worked on developing social robots that can respond to a person's emotional state in real time and promote rapport-building behaviors between the computer and a person.[29] The goal has been to develop a robot with a living presence that can carry on long-term interactions with a person. The AI would enable the robot to use rapport-building responses, giving the human that they interact with a sense of engagement with the robot, shared experiences, and the feeling that they have a relationship. The algorithms for interaction used by these social robots would mimic contingent responsivity of natural, human-to-human interaction. These are not merely academic experiments but are of great interest to corporations around the world. Some robots in production around the world today are virtually as humanlike as Ava at the end of *Ex Machina*. The Hiroshi Ishiguro Laboratories in Japan are producing what they call geminoids, which are androids (humanlike robots) that very closely resemble specific real human beings. These geminoids look, move, and sound like the real men or women that they are modeled after. They even feel like humans, with a lifelike surface "skin." In addition, the company is outfitting them with speech recognition technology, as well as the ability to carry on a conversation flexibly, in a way that fits the context. The Hiroshi Ishiguro Laboratories plan to market these geminoids to individuals who are living alone or are socially isolated for use as conversational robot companions.[30] Hanson Robotics in Hong Kong is also developing a robot, called Sophia, which is extraordinarily humanlike in its appearance. Sophia can use AI protocols called Loving AI that enable the robot to interact with humans in fluid dialogs "that are emotionally sensitive and relationally connective," according to the Loving AI website. Hanson Robotics founder, David Hanson, is known for creating "the world's most humanlike, empathetic robots, endowed with remarkable expressiveness and interactivity."[31]

While the technology behind all these devices is astonishing, it's understandable if you're also feeling somewhat creeped out by the idea of these extremely humanlike robots. You are not alone. Research has shown that people tend to like robots more as they get more humanlike up to a certain degree. But when they get too humanlike, people tend to like them less, which has been called the uncanny valley reaction.[32] But one question is whether this is just a matter of what we're used to. If people become more accustomed to very humanlike robots being part of their daily lives, then it's possible that the aversion to them will fade.

AA ON STEROIDS: BRAIN-MACHINE INTERFACES

AI technology for decoding a person's thoughts and emotions mostly operates at a distance from that person—with video analysis of their facial expression and body language, audio analysis of their voice, or textual analysis of what they write. Sometimes information on physiological signs of emotion, like electrical conductance properties of skin, are integrated with the other information.[33] Although all this information can reveal a lot about people's states of mind, it doesn't get scientists all the way to the ultimate source of thoughts and emotions—brain activity—which in many ways would be the most personal information of all. After all, some people can hide or disguise their thoughts and feelings through a poker face and through restraint in what they do or say. But their innermost thoughts and feelings, as well as their observable actions, are all encoded in some way in their brain activity. AA could evolve into even more powerful tools if developers had access to measures of brain activity, and could better understand relationships between brain circuit activity and thoughts, feelings, and behaviors.

The key technological development that could provide such access to brain activity is brain-machine interfaces. With the goal of pursuing better treatments for neurological and psychiatric disorders, The National Institutes of Health (NIH) BRAIN initiative (Brain Research through Advancing Innovative Neurotechnologies) was launched in 2013 to develop more powerful technologies—including brain-machine interfaces—to measure and manipulate the activity of cells and neural circuits in the human brain. As of

2018, within the first five years of its inception, the NIH BRAIN initiative had funded approximately $1 billion in research grants, and in 2018 the funding was accelerated, increasing by 50 percent relative to the previous year.[34] Similar projects are going on around the world, funded by the European Human Brain Project and the Japanese Brain/MINDS (Mapping Integrated Neurotechnologies for Disease Studies) programs. As these agencies point out, many vital medical applications could potentially come out of this research, including new and more effective ways of diagnosing and treating severe neurological and psychiatric disorders, such as helping people with treatment-resistant depression. In 2017, DARPA (Defense Advanced Research Projects Agency), an agency in the United States Department of Defense, initiated the Neural Engineering System Design Project (NESD), with the goal of developing a "wireless human brain device that can monitor brain activity using 1 million electrodes simultaneously and selectively stimulate up to 100,000 neurons."[35]

The large government investment in this research has spurred new startup companies that are developing brain-machine interface technology. In 2017, Elon Musk launched a new company, Neuralink, to develop ultrahigh bandwidth brain-machine interfaces to connect humans and computers—essentially to enable computers to "read" human brain activity and "write" information into the brain.[36] Around the time that this was written, Neuralink was applying to the FDA for permission to do human experiments to see if a person with electrodes implanted in their brain could input words into a text message or email by thinking them, or could move a cursor and navigate a webpage by thinking alone.[37] Neuralink argues that its technology can lead to breakthroughs in the diagnosis and treatment of brain diseases, and provide breakthroughs in helping and empowering those with physical disabilities, such as helping paralyzed people use computers with their minds only.

Experiments using brain-machine interface technology also promise to greatly advance our fundamental understanding of the brain circuit activity "code" by which the brain processes sensory information and generates thoughts, emotions, decisions, and actions. Ultimately, this research might lead to technology that makes our innermost thoughts and emotions more accessible or readable directly from neural circuitry activity, as well as tools to manipulate the activity of neural circuits that mediate thoughts and emotions. Neuroscientist Rafael Yuste and philosopher Sara Goering write that, "technological developments mean that we are on a path to a world in which it will be possible to decode people's mental processes and directly manipulate the brain mechanisms underlying their intentions, emotions, and decisions; where individuals could communicate with others simply by thinking."[38]

So while the technology promises to generate powerful new diagnostic and therapeutic tools for clinicians who treat patients with neuropsychiatric disorders, the research could also potentially lead to a large leap beyond the current, indirect emotion recognition technologies, such as video analysis of facial expressions. Brain-machine interfaces could directly "read" the brain activity of thought and emotion, virtually reading people's minds. This, in turn, could create a quantum leap in artificial attunement technology that could disrupt typical modes of human communication, which in turn could be exploited by corporations or governments.[39] Given the profound ethical issues that the BRAIN initiative technology could raise, the NIH established a neuroethics program within the BRAIN initiative.[40] A University of Pennsylvania neuroethicist, Jonathan Moreno, argued that the NIH should establish a permanent neuroethics program to regulate the potential impact and implications of these technologies.[41]

ETHICAL DILEMMAS OF AA

As you know by now from reading the previous chapters, we highly value human-to-human connections, and we have respect for each person's sense of selfhood and their rights to privacy and autonomy. Person-to-person attunement is intrinsic to our humanity, and therefore uniquely valuable and worthy of preserving, even in the face of the growing AA technology. It's not to say that we are anti-technology. Technology is a powerful force that can help connect people at great distances who might not have a chance to connect at all, both socially and therapeutically. We've seen technology's power to connect people during the COVID-19 pandemic. And beyond that, by our professional work, we also recognize that there are individuals with neurological or psychiatric conditions who have great difficulty in connecting or communicating with others, and who are in need of better technological tools to improve their ability to communicate.

It is to say, however, that the growth of AA technologies should be met with cautiousness. On the one hand, we sincerely share the hope of the NIH and other medical researchers that these technologies will be put to constructive use to help those with disabilities and brain diseases, to greatly improve the quality of their lives, while showing great respect for the rights of these individuals for informed consent, autonomy, and privacy. Researchers and companies working on AA have emphasized the potential scientific and therapeutic uses of the technology. On the other hand, we know that technologies tend to spread beyond the world of health care, and some causes for concern include the number of ways that these powerful technologies potentially could be used or abused by governments around the world or by corporations to intrude into people's privacy and the domain of our most intimate human relationships, and monitor or manipulate our emotions and our decision making.[42] The effects of these AA tools—whether they can be constructive or destructive—will depend on how they are regulated and used. Developers and researchers alike should continue to highlight the ethical issues raised by these affective computing technologies, and they should call for more research into how the technology can be used for good purposes, and not misused or used without people's consent.[43]

Even as daily users of apps and social media, we still have concerns about the ways that technology now mediates so many people's interactions, and the fact that we have less and less time to cultivate the art of person-to-person, direct communication. Smartphones and social media have been marketed to us as a great way to connect. They are billed as the solution for our sense of alienation, but, when technology chronically dominates our time and our interactions, it doesn't reduce our alienation, but rather it seems to perpetuate and deepen it. With the rapid growth of AA, there is a risk of giving even more preference or priority to interactions with machines over interactions with other humans. The rise of artificial intelligence, virtual reality, and robots has the potential to greatly accelerate our societal atomization. It's been predicted that the line between human and bot will be increasingly blurred, until we won't know, much of the time, if we are interacting with another real human or with a robot. The eeriest part is that we may become increasingly comfortable with that idea.[44] This is a vision akin to that of the movie *Blade Runner*, in which no one is quite sure who is human and who is a synthetic "replicant." This type of world seems to erode something essential about ourselves and our connections.

The growth of brain-machine interfaces poses a new set of ethical dilemmas. In 2017, an international group of scientists, clinicians, ethicists, and engineers, called The Morningside Group, came together to discuss ethical issues raised by the growth of neurotechnologies and AI. They recommended adhering to four ethical principles in pursuing brain-machine interface research and technology: (1) respect people's privacy and consent, (2) protect people's sense of agency and identity (sense of self), (3) set limits on augmentation of brain functions, and (4) prevent bias against groups.[45]

Philosopher Andrea Lavazza has argued that brain-machine interfaces could be used to violate, to a greater extent than was ever possible before, some of our most important and valuable human rights: the integrity of one's one mind and sense of selfhood;

personal autonomy; and the privacy of one's own thoughts, feelings, and "brain data." Lavazza argues that privacy is an essential correlate of autonomy (i.e., one cannot have a sense of agency with freedom of thought and action—which is an important part of true attunement—without being allowed some degree of privacy). It becomes difficult to decide things for oneself and make one's own choices, free of external pressures and conditioning, if one's thoughts are not private.[46]

Views on the rise of AA could not be more varied among influential "thought leaders" today, with some exuberantly embracing the new technology and others who are seriously concerned. In his 2018 *New York Times* editorial "We Are Merging with Robots. That's a Good Thing," University of Edinburgh professor Andy Clark argues that we should welcome and fully embrace the arrival of new AI and AA technologies, not only to help those with disabilities but to enhance members of the general population, so that AI and AA can become the most intimate companion to each of us. "These are the algorithms that talk with us, that watch us, that trade for us, that select dates for us, that suggest what we might buy, sell, or wear," which he believes is all for the good. While he strikes a note of regret that some "have nots" will be left out of the privileged access to these technologies, he mostly sees the rise of these technologies as a moment to savor, as a new age of fluidity that's full of exhilarating freedoms and possibilities. He lauds the arrival of sex and companionship robots; the use of immersive interactive virtual realities; neuroenhancement, including the improvement of our experiences and interactions through brain implants; and the blurring of the boundaries between brain/mind and machine, between human and post-human.[47]

Only two days earlier, another editorial, written by MIT professor Sherry Turkle, took the contrary position that AI and robots cannot, and must not, replace our human-to-human intimacy. She reminds us that the artificial, empathy-like responses displayed by machines are merely a hollow simulation: "we act as though the emotional ties we form with them [robots] will be reciprocal, and real, as though there is a right kind of emotional tie that can be formed with objects that have no emotions at all."[48] Professor Turkle also makes the ethical distinction between the use of artificial intelligence technology to aid those with diseases or disabilities versus the use of AI as an artificial, faux relationship. To deal with the empty feelings of loneliness that so many of us experience in twenty-first-century America, we are being sold companion robots or other forms of AA as a way to fill the void. But Professor Turkle argues that these technologies cannot fill the void, and that in being drawn into the sales pitch, we lose something essential about ourselves, ultimately deepening the void:

> That is the kind of talk that one hears these days. The narrative begins with the idea that companionate robots would be "better than nothing," because there aren't enough people to teach, love and tend to people. But that idea quickly shifts into another: robots would be better than most anything. Unlike people, they would not abandon you or get sick and die. They might not be capable of love, but they won't break your heart.
>
> From better than nothing to better than anything. These are stations on our voyage of forgetting what it means to be human.[49]

The era of artificial attunement is already here, and it's growing at an accelerating pace. There's no stopping the growth of this technology, it seems, even if one wanted to. The growing abilities of machines to identify people, read and evoke emotions, and simulate relationships are particularly powerful in potentially swaying people, and they can have major impacts on our lives. Given this power, the ethical debate about how these technologies are used and regulated is healthy and necessary. How can these technologies help bring humans together and enhance our human-to-human connections, rather than degrading them? That's the big question facing all of us and it deserves our attention.

CHAPTER SEVEN

WHERE DO WE GO FROM HERE?

"We shall not cease from exploration
And the end of all our exploring
Will be to arrive where we started
And know the place for the first time."

—T. S. ELIOT, "LITTLE GIDDING," *Four Quartets*[1]

THE BIG PICTURE: ZOOMING OUT

Writing this book has changed each of us. Before starting on this project, we passed our days in the way that many people do: quintessentially "busy." From the moment we each got out of bed and placed our feet on the ground, the day's conversations and interactions took off and subsequently went by in a blur. We spent much of the day trying to field everything that came at us—the passing interactions, meetings, emails, texts, and social media posts. We weren't always the best listeners. Often, when our buttons were pushed, we would react emotionally rather than responding thoughtfully. And we wouldn't have a chance to think over the nuances of the day's interactions until we were back home, laying our heads down to go to sleep and finally catching a truly mindful moment before drifting off.

But as we worked on our research together and then began writing this book, we started to think more and more about why people seem to miss each other so much of the time, and why they're sometimes—too rarely—able to really connect. People in our field of autism research talk quite a bit about "social skills" as the prime target for improving people's abilities to connect. But we wanted to go beyond a long list of skills and social scripts. We asked ourselves what the key ingredient of human connection is when it's distilled to its essence. The concept of attunement started to take shape in our minds as what makes the difference between connecting and passing each other by. Initially, it was only an academic concept that we had seen used in research on mother-infant bonding, and not one that we thought of in relation to our daily lives. But the more we thought and wrote about it, the more we saw moments of attunement, or misattunement, manifesting everywhere, in virtually all types of interactions and relationships.

As we developed the exercises described in Chapters 2 through 5, we started to practice them ourselves, and we tried to integrate them into our work and personal lives. As we practiced them regularly, they started to become new habits, and we formed what we can best describe as a "muscle memory" for them. For example, now, before walking into a potentially stressful meeting, we instinctively and discretely do a relaxed awareness exercise—head gently suspended from above, shoulders relaxed down, breathing in and feeling our belly expand. Very quickly, within a breath or two, we feel calmer but still aware and alert. We feel more ready to handle anything that might come our way. Before the meeting starts, we remind ourselves to relax, listen, try to understand, and set our ego aside. Rather than getting caught up in worries about the outcome of the encounter, we try to focus on meeting the other person where they are, keeping our responses on target, and staying in the flow. And we've found that focusing on those elements of attunement, rather than potential outcomes, makes the desired result from the meeting more likely. As we developed these new habits, there were increasingly more moments throughout the day in which we felt like we were truly present and could genuinely "make contact" with ourselves and another person, regardless of whether it was a pleasant, neutral, or stressful situation. We're still far from being models of perfection in the art of attunement, but things have moved in a positive direction. We keep working on it, trying to make it a more central part of our lives. There's no final end point or destination. There's no limit to how much you can develop this in yourself. Because we've seen the benefits, attunement has become an important value in our lives, something we will continue to cultivate—and something we want to share with you.

Our hope is that we've described this concept in a way that resonates with you. While attunement can sometimes seem intangible, we want to distill it in a way that is a little bit easier to wrap your head around. While the four components of attunement are interconnected and work together, it's often easier to remember them in sequence. First, strengthen *relaxed awareness*. This is your foundation, a state of mind where you can feel centered and at home, regardless of what's happening around you—what T. S. Eliot called "the still point of the turning world."[2] This fundamental ability allows you to direct attention and nonjudgmental compassion toward your own thoughts and feelings, while also balancing this with awareness of the other person. Only then can we be ready to embark on genuine *listening*, which, in the broadest sense of the term, means being open to perceiving all that the other person is communicating to you through both their words and actions. When you have relaxed awareness, and don't feel so apprehensive about what you might perceive from the other person, then you're ready to receive whatever they are trying to communicate—be it good, bad, or somewhere in between. Attentive listening births deep *understanding*, which often involves more than just understanding the words the other person says. It also includes understanding their point of view and your own, in addition to each of your own personal "filters" through which you communicate and "hear" one another. Relaxed awareness, listening, and understanding lay the groundwork for what actually happens between us—*mutual responsiveness*, the intricacies of which bring fluidity and cohesion to the back-and-forth exchange of conversation. We hope that the exercises we offer you can give you a more concrete sense of what these concepts are like when they are put into action, and we hope that you can take that same kind of "muscle memory" that we described off the yoga mat or couch at home and utilize it during all the ups and downs of your busy days. The more you start to integrate these practices into your routine with consistency, the more moments of connection you will recover per day.

Developing attunement can seem like a process full of paradoxes. We've encouraged you to relax *and* also focus. Listen to yourself in order to listen to the other person better. Meet the other person where they are in order to effectively assert yourself. These dialectical relationships can feel challenging to understand initially. As you learn and practice the elements of attunement, and try to implement them in interacting with others, you may at first feel awkward and self-conscious. It will take you some conscious effort to incorporate specific strategies, like noticing your breath or checking in with your body tension while you're listening to someone speak. But the goal is for you to practice and use them consistently enough so that you reach a place where these skills come naturally and spontaneously, and are seamlessly integrated into the way you interact. They shouldn't seem contrived, overly self-conscious, or strained. You shouldn't seem to your family and friends that you're not quite yourself anymore, or that you are putting on a peculiar act. Real attunement manifests as being your very true, genuine self—you're just more tuned in and connected. And once it does become a part of you, your growing ability to connect will start to feel natural and spontaneous. Although the elements of attunement seem to emphasize relaxation and receptiveness, rather than assertiveness, the counterintuitive fact is that, by really relaxing and tuning in to another person, by listening and understanding them and meeting them where they are, we are actually in a much better position to assert ourselves in that relationship, and be listened to and met by the other person.

The power of attunement is paired with an ethical framework of not dominating, manipulating, or harming, but rather being helpful and beneficial to the other person and yourself. True attunement is reciprocal and mutual, and it includes the thoughts and feelings of both people, and it respects the rights and autonomy of each. Even when used in conflict, attunement can be powerful in minimizing harm to yourself and others.

You, as an individual, have taken initiative by reading this book and by investigating how you can strengthen your connection with others. But attunement is most powerful when it is mutual and balanced between people. There may be days when your resources are exhausted and you're tempted not to even bother with trying to tune in. Or there may be days that, despite your best efforts, the other person either won't or can't meet you where you are. On the days in which you're unable to practice these strategies, show yourself compassion, rest, and try again tomorrow. On the days in which you feel like your efforts won't be reciprocated, remember that there is still a lot of power to attunement even when it's more one-sided, whether it's navigating a conflict or an intimate conversation. We encourage you to develop this ability in yourself, regardless of whether you have an enthusiastic partner, and try taking the initiative. When you reach out your hand by using these techniques, you will be surprised how often the other person may resonate with your courage and respond to you in an unexpected way, even if they can't quite understand why.

WHY DOES IT MATTER?

We've spent quite a bit of time in previous chapters describing what can happen when attunement goes awry in our personal relationships. Children with parents or caregivers who consistently fail to attune to them can go on to have difficulty with relationships as they become adults. Even if we had parents or caregivers who were fairly well attuned to us as children, the ordinary distractions of current adult life can lead us to neglect our interpersonal connections, which adds to the pervasive feelings of loneliness and alienation in our society.[3] We hope that we've given you a sense of how developing attunement can enhance your communications and add new life and depth to your relationships.

Ultimately, if an increasing number of people were to cultivate the skills of attunement, a considerable impact could be made beyond each of our own personal lives that would extend to our larger communities. The challenges facing the global community can feel daunting—climate change, viral pandemics, systemic racism, socioeconomic disparities, social atomization and distrust, political strife, and the proliferation of increasingly destructive weapons, to name just a few. Existential threats like climate change and destructive weaponry are global issues, and resolving them will require humanity to communicate and cooperate as a global community. But instead of this happening effectively, there seems to be a vicious cycle of massive environmental, political, and societal problems, on the one hand, and individual alienation, on the other hand. The worse our environmental threats and social strife become, the more overwhelmed, scared, and alienated we may feel. And the more alienated we feel, the less that we feel capable of working together and doing anything effective about our social and environmental problems. Smartphones, social media, and more recently, artificial intelligence and robotics are being marketed to us as the solution for our alienation, but depending on how they are used, their net effect could perpetuate and deepen our alienation.

Although not a panacea by any means, the skills of attunement have the potential to bolster our power to connect, communicate, and cooperate effectively in order to address these overwhelming problems. For example, developing relaxed awareness is a way of navigating between the extremes of panic and blithe denial. Without panicking, we can face the realities of these problems and cooperate to develop constructive ways of addressing them. This is similar to one of the Dalai Lama's ideas of "world peace through inner peace"—that to address our global problems it's essential for each of us as individuals to develop, as we would express it, our own relaxed awareness, listening, and understanding, which will help us to work together effectively. The Dalai Lama has said, "Change starts with us as individuals. If one individual becomes more compassionate it will influence others and so we will change the world."[4]

A major obstacle to attunement and cooperation is bias and fear based on perceived differences among us. In Chapter 4, we spent time drawing your attention to the way in which we are constantly making attributions about the people and situations around us. These can be exacerbated in the worst way when particular identity groups make sharp distinctions between themselves and other groups. This sort of "othering," whether it be along racial, ethnic, generational, or political party lines, blocks our ability to listen and authentically understand someone. And without that listening and understanding, we're likely to respond to them unskillfully. Active listening and informed dialogue, for example, have become a cornerstone of anti-racism activism that continues to rise to collective awareness as a result of the protests following the killing of George Floyd. Non-Black allies of the Black Lives Matter movement are encouraged to listen, learn, and educate themselves on the Black experience and the way in which systemic racism infiltrates so many aspects of society. Individuals and institutions alike are encouraged to identify racism within themselves and call out racism within others—both of which lead to challenging emotions and awkward conversations. Relaxed awareness gives you the chance to slow down and search for biases and privilege that could be clouding your perspective or that of the other person. It also gives you pause to identify reactivity and defenses, long enough to regulate yourself so you can continue listening. Once you recognize those biases and emotional reactions, you have a greater chance to set them aside as you try to really work toward mutual understanding. If we lead with ego rather than humility, or hatred rather than love, and we shut the door before giving each other a chance, it's nearly impossible to hear the other person with clarity through the barrier.

In order to move forward and make progress as a global community, we'll need to improve our ability to listen and understand each other, even when we have deep differences and disagreements; to be respectful and responsive to each other; to navigate inevitable conflicts skillfully, and with a minimum of destructiveness; and to work cooperatively as a human family to address the threats that we face. This may sound like a lofty, idealistic view of the power of attunement. Certainly attunement alone, without political action and leadership, won't be enough. But it's hard to see how we can address these global, existential problems effectively without an effort to improve our capacity to communicate and cooperate.

A LITTLE BIT (EVERY DAY) GOES A LONG WAY

"Courage is the most important of all virtues
because without courage, you can't practice any
other virtue consistently."

—MAYA ANGELOU[5]

We applaud you for your interest in strengthening attunement in your life. The decision to embark on any self-reflective journey, like this one, takes courage and self-compassion. Not everyone reaches a moment in their life when they take time to invest in their ability to connect and grow relationships. Trying to connect more meaningfully with others can enrich our lives, but this effort can also stir up some of our strongest emotions. It takes deep vulnerability to be willing to sit with these emotions, some of which may be difficult to face. If you consistently practice the exercises that we've laid out, it should get a little easier each time to acknowledge your thoughts and emotions with some distance and perspective—just enough that you can identify how they play a role in your communication style, and ultimately how they impact the way you relate to others.

It won't be easy—which we know is not something most people want to hear when they're trying something new. We recognize that the goals we've set through this practice may seem ambitious and challenging. Learning to attune to others and yourself, to balance the two, and to maintain a state of relaxed awareness through the often stressful twists and turns of interactions can be very difficult—and actually implementing these things may seem unrealistic, or even impossible to ever really master. Developing attunement may seem especially difficult for those who did not have someone—a parent or caregiver—who really tuned in to them when they were a child; or for those whose basic needs for safety and care are not currently being met or were not met as they were growing up; or those who were traumatized; or those who suffer from grief or medical problems; or those who have mental health issues. We acknowledge the reality that these obstacles may seem insurmountable at times. The exercises that we've laid out in this book are no substitute for appropriate medical, psychological, or psychiatric help, and we encourage you to seek that help if or when you need it. However, when you feel ready, we think that working on developing these capacities in yourself—even to a limited extent—can be helpful across many areas of your life. It's not necessary to implement them with perfection—few, if any of us, can. But some degree of effort in developing attunement can go a long way.

As in training any complex skill set, the fundamentals are key. The stronger your fundamentals, the further you'll go—something that any good athlete or musician will tell you. If you want to develop the power of attunement as much as you can, keep returning to practicing the basic elements of it, especially relaxed awareness. You'll make the most progress when you tailor your practice approach to your own pattern of strengths and weaknesses, and to your own level of time, energy, and motivation. We've laid out a general, progressive set of exercises to develop each component of attunement, but you should feel empowered to individualize this program to your particular needs. To get a sense of your needs, take a look at your results from the Attunement Quiz in the Appendix. Did you have lower scores in certain components of attunement, suggesting you need more work on those areas? As you were reading the earlier chapters, did some components of attunement seem like the ones that you could use the most work on? If relaxed awareness is most challenging, focus your practice on those exercises. Or if you're not a natural listener, then you can spend more time on the exercises meant to help you strengthen those skills. If you have physical disabilities or limitations, skip the more physical exercises like the stretching, silk reeling, and push hands, and focus on the sitting meditation and conversation exercises. A practice partner can be anyone you choose—a friend, romantic partner, family member, neighbor—but if one isn't available, it'll still be extremely valuable for you to practice the solo exercises and try to integrate the components of attunement into whatever interactions you have in your daily life.

The exercises that we outline in this book are a good way to develop the fundamentals of attunement. This may be a solid starting place for many of you. However, learning the basics of these skills from this book and the accompanying website may not feel like enough for those who want to take their training further, or for those who have specific issues that they want to address, such as areas of their work lives that could use some development, or personal relationships that could benefit from integrating attunement. In that case, go ahead and take things to the next level. Feel inspired to develop attunement further, either by becoming involved in some activity or discipline that develops attunement (like Tai Chi, music, dance, theater, or sports) or by seeking further consultation or counseling on relationship issues. While we've often emphasized interactions between dyads (pairs of people), the components you've developed can be applied to larger groups as well, be it in your family, among your friends, in a sports team or musical group, or at the workplace.

Taking it to the next level of attunement doesn't mean being continually close to others. We all need some of our own space. And it certainly doesn't mean invading another person's space such that you become overly enmeshed or codependent with the other person, nor does it mean either person losing their own individuality or freedom of thought and action. Never forget to find the space you need for yourself, and to give others the space they need. Try to find a balance between space and closeness. Closeness itself may be more or less challenging for people, particularly for those who generally tend to need a lot of space for themselves, or for those who may have had trauma or who have histories of abuse. If this is the case for you, feel free to focus your attention on certain exercises and pay less attention to those that could involve a greater level of physical closeness that may make you particularly uncomfortable.

We know sometimes it can feel overwhelming to find room for strategies like these in your schedule, especially if you're typically short on time. It can be good to know, though, that most of the time investment you need to make is up front. Once you've been practicing these exercises for a while, they become second nature, and it will gradually take you less time to incorporate them into your interactions with others as you go about your daily life. Soon enough, they'll start to come automatically, effortlessly. Sometimes, all it takes is a moment to remember to relax your shoulders, notice your breath smoothly going in and out, and prioritize listening more carefully.

OUR HOPE FOR YOU

Human-to-human connection has a unique power and value, and it is one we should cherish and reclaim, rather than relinquish. Attunement lies at the core of our humanity and our capacity to reach across the interpersonal divide and connect with each other. The study of attunement can bring together the insights and practices from ancient fields like music and Tai Chi with those of the most current scientific research. While some elements of attunement, like mindfulness and social cognition, have been the focus of accelerating neuroscience and psychology research in recent years, attunement as a whole has not received the research attention that it deserves. We have much left to learn about the science of attunement, and research developments will be exciting to follow in the coming years.

We urge you to refocus on the art of attunement now, and to take steps in your own lives to try to build up these inherently human abilities in the near future. Our hope is that the ideas outlined in this book will generate more recognition of the key importance of attunement in all of our lives, and help to set off a renaissance of interest and research in this area. Our hope for you is that, in the meantime, you start now to put the power of attunement to good use in building a greater understanding of yourself and a deeper connection to the people in your life.

ATTUNEMENT QUIZ

OVERALL ATTUNEMENT

A low score (< 5) in the *Overall Attunement* section may go along with a low score(s) in other section(s), or the *Overall Attunement* score may be lower than that of other sections. Sometimes smaller issues in several components of attunement add up to a bigger effect on attunement overall. It could also be that at this point it's hard to identify where in the chain of attunement you're having difficulties, as nothing stands out. As you read this book, come back to the quiz periodically to adjust your answers to each item as you increase your understanding of each component—do your answers change as a result?

RELAXED AWARENESS

A low score (< 5) in *Relaxed Awareness* may indicate that anxiety, tension, difficulty tolerating strong emotions, and/or difficulty regulating your own emotions may be making attunement more difficult for you.

LISTENING

A low score (< 5) in *Listening* may indicate that difficulty paying close attention to another person over time, difficulty resonating with another person's emotion (being less impacted by other people's emotions at a gut level), and/or difficulty in being aware of your own thoughts and feelings (difficulty "listening" to yourself) are making attunement more difficult for you.

UNDERSTANDING

A low score (< 5) in *Understanding* may indicate that you have difficulties in picking up on another person's cues (e.g., facial expressions, tone of voice, body language, implied meanings), difficulty in appreciating the other person's perspective while still honoring your own, and/or difficulty in staying open to updating your understanding (not jumping to conclusions). Challenges with *understanding* may appear as miscommunication or misinterpretation of conversations that in turn can lead to conflict or difficulty connecting with others.

MUTUAL RESPONSIVENESS

A low score (< 5) in *Mutual Responsiveness* may mean that you have difficulty in "meeting the other person where they are"; difficulty responding to them in a way that is "on target" and proportional (responsive to something they actually said or did, rather than something else you thought of; and responsive in a way that communicates that you actually heard and understood them); or difficulty "staying in the flow" (i.e., keeping up with the pace and flow of the interaction), and being "in sync" with the other person.

Overall Attunement | | | | Score

I'm able to establish a mutual feeling of rapport with another person, to "click" with them.	Never (0)	Sometimes (1)	Often (2)	Almost always (3)	
When I'm talking with someone who I'm not very close with (e.g., someone in a work meeting), the communication between us is effective and goes well.	Never	Sometimes	Often	Almost always	
When I'm having a conversation with a friend or my partner, I feel in sync with them.	Never	Sometimes	Often	Almost always	
I feel emotionally close to my friends, family members, and/or romantic partner.	Never	Sometimes	Often	Almost always	
In my relationships with friends, family members, and/or my romantic partner, I feel like we "get" each other very well.	Never	Sometimes	Often	Almost always	
				Total:	

Relaxed Awareness | | | | Score

I am able to feel alert *and* calm at the same time.	Never (0)	Sometimes (1)	Often (2)	Almost always (3)	
I stay cool under pressure.	Never	Sometimes	Often	Almost always	
I stay calm *and* present when talking or interacting with people.	Never	Sometimes	Often	Almost always	
My connections with other people are good and aren't easily impacted by distraction, strong emotions, stress, or tension.	Never	Sometimes	Often	Almost always	

I enjoy mindfulness and/or taking time alone to recharge and relax.	Never	Sometimes	Often	Almost always	
				Total:	

Listening   **Score**

It's easy for me to pay attention and listen to another person for a sustained period of time, and to stay open to what they are saying.	Never (0)	Sometimes (1)	Often (2)	Almost always (3)	
I can easily direct my attention to people's eyes, tone of voice, and body language as I listen to them.	Never	Sometimes	Often	Almost always	
I resonate emotionally with what another person is saying.	Never	Sometimes	Often	Almost always	
When I listen attentively to another person, I'm still aware of myself, and my own thoughts and feelings, without getting distracted from the conversation.	Never	Sometimes	Often	Almost always	
It's easy for me to coordinate my physical actions with others, or to move in sync with others (for example, when walking with someone, moving or carrying something with someone, dancing with someone, playing sports with someone, driving with other cars around me).	Never	Sometimes	Often	Almost always	
				Total:	

Understanding Score

Question					Score
It's easy for me to understand what other people are communicating, and what they really mean.	Never (0)	Sometimes (1)	Often (2)	Almost always (3)	
It's easy for me to imagine things from another person's perspective.	Never	Sometimes	Often	Almost always	
When empathizing with someone, I don't lose touch with my own perspective and emotions.	Never	Sometimes	Often	Almost always	
Close family members, friends, or romantic partners feel that I understand them well.	Never	Sometimes	Often	Almost always	
I keep my mind open about other people, and I'm open to updating my understanding of them.	Never	Sometimes	Often	Almost always	
				Total:	

Mutual Responsiveness Score

Question					Score
To get a conversation going, I ask about something or bring up a topic that I think might interest the other person, even if that topic is not something foremost on my mind.	Never (0)	Sometimes (1)	Often (2)	Almost always (3)	
When talking with someone, what I say to them is on target (i.e., is responsive to what they just said, builds on what they just said, or is connected in some way to what they just said).	Never	Sometimes	Often	Almost always	

I easily keep pace with another person in conversation. The give-and-take and turn-taking of conversation come naturally to me.	Never	Sometimes	Often	Almost always
If I want to change the direction of a conversation or bring up a new topic, I can do it in a way that makes a smooth transition and brings the other person along (i.e., I don't "lose" the other person).	Never	Sometimes	Often	Almost always
In a conversation, I can "improvise" with another person and go where the conversation takes us.	Never	Sometimes	Often	Almost always

Total:

ACKNOWLEDGMENTS

THE IDEAS IN THIS BOOK emerged from our connection with each other and our connections with many other people who are important to us. We want to acknowledge the people who have loved, nurtured, inspired, mentored, challenged, guided, and encouraged us along the way, too many to list completely here, but all of whom made this book possible. First, we thank our families, who've taught us, and continue to teach us, what unconditional love and connection mean: Jacob, Martha, and Ryan Pallathra; Charlie, Louis, Adele, and Roger Brodkin, and Elizabeth Brauer.

We're indebted to our mentors and colleagues in neuroscience, who sparked our fascination with the social and emotional brain, and supported our growth as researchers: Drs. Eric J. Nestler, Steven E. Hyman, William A. Carlezon, Noboru Hiroi, George Heninger, Lee M. Silver, Ted Abel, Robert T. Schultz, Wade Berrettini, Maja Bucan, Raquel Gur, Ruben Gur, Martha Farah, Adrian Raine, and Joseph Kable. The interactions we've had with our labmates, students, and research colleagues have buoyed us and challenged us to think and communicate as clearly as we can. We're grateful to our psychology and psychiatry mentors and clinical supervisors, who taught us so much about psychotherapy and assessment, and about the centrality of attunement and connection in the therapist-patient relationship and in all of our daily lives: Drs. Sidney J. Blatt, Donald J. Cohen, Christopher J. McDougle, Lawrence H. Price, Anthony Rostain, Richard F. Summers, and Brendan A. Rich. We always carry with us what we learned about emotional attunement early on in our lives from our music teachers and our friends from music groups. Our ideas about attunement and how to develop it have been shaped by studying Tai Chi with amazing Chen Tai Chi practitioners and teachers: Ryan Craig, Michael Rosario-Graycar, Rachel Tomlinson, and the teacher to all of us, Ren Guangyi.

We're grateful to friends and colleagues who encouraged the idea of our writing a book on this topic and gave us invaluable advice along the way: Jody Foster, Scott Sill, Dawn Graham, Michael Haugen, Gabrielle Sellei, Jason Presley, Jay Moses, Pat Croce, and William C. Meyers. We learned a lot about attunement from our conversations with Rachel Kabasakalian McKay, Stephanie Heck, Julia Landis, and The Cohort. We appreciate the assistance that Ryan Craig, Beth Goldberg, and Kyra Levy provided with the exercise sections. We give thanks to Ted Abel for providing feedback on a section of the book. We owe so much to our literary agent, Eric Lupfer, who believed in us and our ideas from the very beginning, helped us to shape our early ideas into a coherent book proposal, and guided us in finding a great editor and publisher. And we give enormous thanks to our outstanding editor, Colleen Lawrie, and her colleagues at PublicAffairs, for recognizing the importance of this topic, for giving us a chance to bring our ideas to the world, and for guiding us so skillfully through the journey of turning our book idea into a reality.

NOTES

INTRODUCTION

[1] E. M. Forster, *Howards End* (York, UK: Empire Books, 2012).

[2] D. H. Strober and G. S. Strober, *His Holiness the Dalai Lama: The Oral Biography* (Hoboken, NJ: John Wiley & Sons, 2005).

[3] Strober and Strober, *His Holiness*.

[4] V. Gallese, "Intentional Attunement: A Neurophysiological Perspective on Social Cognition and Its Disruption in Autism," *Brain Research* 1079 (2006): 15–24.

[5] D. Bolis, J. Balsters, N. Wenderoth, C. Becchio, and L. Schilbach, "Beyond Autism: Introducing the Dialectical Misattunement Hypothesis and a Bayesian Account of Intersubjectivity," *Psychopathology* 50(6) (2017): 355–372.

[6] M. de Guzman, G. Bird, M. J. Banissy, and C. Catmur, "Self-Other Control Processes in Social Cognition: From Imitation to Empathy," *Philosophical Transactions of the Royal Society B* 371 (2016): 20150079.

CHAPTER 1. WHAT IS ATTUNEMENT, AND WHY IS IT IMPORTANT?

[1] H. G. Lerner, *The Dance of Intimacy: A Guide to Courageous Acts of Change in Key Relationships* (New York: HarperCollins Publishers, 1999).

[2] T. Gliga, M. Elsabbagh, A. Andravizou, and M. Johnson, "Faces Attract Infants' Attention in Complex Displays," *Infancy* 14(5) (2009): 550–562.

[3] T. Suddendorf, *The Gap: The Science of What Separates Us from Other Animals* (New York: Basic Books, 2013); B. D. Perry, M. Szalavitz, *Born for Love* (New York: HarperCollins, 2010).

[4] J. Holt-Lunstad, T. B. Smith, M. Baker, T. Harris, and D. Stephenson, "Loneliness and Social Isolation as Risk Factors for Mortality: A Meta-Analytic Review," *Perspectives on Psychological Science* 10(2) (2015): 227–237.

[5] R. F. Baumeister and M. R. Leary, "The Need to Belong: Desire for Interpersonal Attachments as a Fundamental Human Motivation," *Psychological Bulletin* 117(3) (1995): 497–529.

[6] N. Spencer, "Look In to My Eyes: What Attunement Means for Communication," Royal Society for the Encouragement of Arts, Manufactures and Commerce (2013), www.thersa.org/discover/publications-and-articles/rsa-blogs/2013/01/look-in-to-my-eyes-what-attunement-means-for-communication.

[7] R. G. Erskine, "Attunement and Involvement: Therapeutic Responses to Relational Needs," *International Journal of Psychotherapy* 3(3) (1998): 235–244.

[8] L. C. Hibel, D. A. Granger, C. Blair, and E. D. Finegood, "Maternal-Child Adrenocortical Attunement in Early Childhood: Continuity and Change," *Developmental Psychobiology* 57(1) (2015): 83–95; C. Suveg, A. Shaffer, and M. David, "Family Stress Moderates Relations Between Physiological and Behavioral Synchrony and Child Self-Regulation in Mother-Preschooler Dyads," *Developmental Psychobiology* 58 (2016): 83–97; R. V. Palumbo, M. E. Marraccini, L. L. Weyandt, O. Wilder-Smith, H. A. McGee, S. Liu, and M. S. Goodwin, "Interpersonal Autonomic Physiology: A Systematic Review of the Literature," *Personality and Social Psychology Review* 21(2) (2017): 99–141.

[9] K. Whitehead, "'On the Way to Two' Offers a Snapshot of a True Jazz Partnership," Fresh Air / NPR Music Reviews (2015), www.npr.org/2015/11/12/455753907/-on-the-way-to-two-offers-a-snapshot-of-a-true-jazz-partnership.

[10] J. Lewis, Terry Gross interview of Jerry Lewis, NPR Fresh Air, "Jerry Lewis on Dean Martin: 'A Love Story'" (2005), www.npr.org/templates/story/story.php?storyId=4973590.

[11] "The Impact of Social Media Use on Social Skills," New York Behavioral Health, staff writers' blog, https://newyorkbehavioralhealth.com/the-impact-of-social-media-use-on-social-skills.

[12] M. G. Hunt, R. Marx, C. Lipson, and J. Young, "No More FOMO: Limiting Social Media Decreases Loneliness and Depression," *Journal of Social and Clinical Psychology* 37(10) (2018): 751–768.

[13] S. Turkle, *Alone Together: Why We Expect More from Technology and Less from Each Other* (New York: Basic Books, 2011); S. Turkle, *Reclaiming Conversation: The Power of Talk in a Digital Age* (New York: Penguin Books, 2015).

[14] B. A. Primack, A. Shensa, J. E. Sidani, E. O. Whaite, L. Lin, D. Rosen, J. B. Colditz, A. Radovic, and E. Miller, "Social Media Use and Perceived Social Isolation Among Young Adults in the U.S.," *American Journal of Preventive Medicine* 53(1) (2017): 1–8; O. Sacks, "The Machine Stops: The Neurologist on Steam Engines, Smartphones, and Fearing the Future," *The New Yorker* (February 11, 2019).

[15] Sacks, "The Machine Stops."

[16] Turkle, *Reclaiming Conversation*; S. Turkle, "Stop Googling. Let's Talk.," *The New York Times*, Sunday Review, Opinion (September 26, 2015).

[17] Brian Lamb interview of Cornel West, "Cornel West on John Coltrane, American Transcendentalism, Jazz, Radical Politics," *C-SPAN Booknotes* (2000), www.youtube.com/watch?v=FFcKjok4ZZ4.

[18] J. Keller, "Americans Are Staying as Far Away from Each Other as Possible," *Pacific Standard* (June 11, 2015).

[19] M. McPherson, L. Smith-Lovin, and M. E. Brashears, "Social Isolation in America: Changes in Core Discussion Networks over Two Decades," *American Sociological Review* 71(3) (2006): 353–375.

[20] A. Novotney, "Social Isolation: It Could Kill You," *Monitor on Psychology* 50(5) (2019): 33–37.

[21] L. C. Hawkley, M. E. Hughes, L. J. Waite, C. M. Masi, R. A. Thisted, and J. T. Cacioppo, "From Social Structural Factors to Perceptions of Relationship Quality and Loneliness: The Chicago Health, Aging, and Social Relations Study, *Journals of Gerontology. Series B, Psychological Sciences and Social Sciences* 63(6) (2008): S375–384.

[22] J. Olien, "Loneliness Is Deadly: Social Isolation Kills More People than Obesity Does—And It's Just as Stigmatized," *Slate* (August 23, 2013).

[23] C. Bethell, J. Jones, N. Gombojav, J. Linkenbach, and R. Sege, "Positive Childhood Experiences and Adult Mental and Relational Health in a Statewide Sample: Associations Across Adverse Childhood Experiences Levels," *JAMA Pediatrics* (2019): e193007.

[24] N. Way, A. Ali, C. Gilligan, and P. Noguera, eds., *The Crisis of Connection: Roots, Consequences, and Solutions* (New York: New York University Press, 2018); V. H. Murthy, *Together: The Healing Power of Human Connection in a Sometimes Lonely World* (New York: HarperCollins, 2020).

[25] Cigna, *Cigna U.S. Loneliness Index: Survey of 20,000 Americans Examining Behaviors Driving Loneliness in the United States* (2018), www.cigna.com /assets/docs/newsroom/loneliness-survey-2018-full-report.pdf.

[26] D. Gaffney and D. S.-V. Sim, *The Essence of Taijiquan* (CreateSpace Independent Publishing Platform, 2009); C. P. Ong, *Taijiquan: Cultivating Inner Strength* (Bagua Press, 2013).

CHAPTER 2. RELAXED AWARENESS

[1] J. Braza and T. N. Hanh, *The Seeds of Love: Growing Mindful Relationships* (North Clarendon, VT: Tuttle Publishing, 2017).

[2] H. Delehant, "Buddha and the Bulls: An Interview with Phil Jackson," *Tricycle: The Buddhist Review* Vol 3 (Summer 1994): 93–94.

[3] M. Csikszentmihalyi, *Flow: The Psychology of Optimal Experience* (New York: HarperCollins Publishers, 2008).

[4] G. Kolata, "Before Hustling to Finish, Relaxed Is a Good Way to Start," *The New York Times* (October 1, 2008).

[5] B. Stulberg, "The Best Athlete in the World Right Now Is an 18-Year-Old Swimmer, and What She's Doing Is Nuts," *Outside Magazine* (August 11, 2015).

[6] "Who Is Eliud Kipchoge?" INEOS 1:59 Challenge (2019), www.youtube .com/watch?v=u5BgB9_6d6c&feature=youtu.be.

[7] B. Lee, *Tao of Jeet Kune Do* (Valencia, CA: Black Belt Communications, 1975).

[8] A. Wallace, "The Wisdom Podcast," in D. Aitken, ed., Alan Wallace Shamatha Live Interview, Talk, Q&A (2017), www.youtube.com/watch?v=xgtoX6tIXwk &t=506s.

[9] Delehant, "Buddha and the Bulls."

[10] P. H. Wolff, ed., "The Causes, Control, and Organization of Behavior in the Neonate," *Psychological Issues, Monograph Series* No. 5 (1966); H. F. R. Prechtl, *The Neurological Examination of the Full-Term Newborn Infant, 2nd Edition* (Philadelphia: L. B. Lippincott, 1977).

[11] J. Moran, "Infant Behavior, Dyslexia and War Orphans: A Portrait of Peter Wolff, MD," *Boston Children's Hospital Vector* (2017); C. Einspieler, "Heinz F. R. Prechtl (1927–2014)," ICNApedia (2014).

[12] S. J. Rogers and J. H. G. Williams, *Imitation and the Social Mind: Autism and Typical Development* (New York: The Guilford Press, 2006).

[13] B. Beebe, F. Lachmann, and J. Jaffe, "Mother-Infant Interaction Structures and Presymbolic Self- and Object Representations," *Psychoanalytic Dialogues* 7(2) (1997): 133–182; T. B. Brazelton, B. Koslowski, and M. Main, "The Origins of Reciprocity: The Early Mother-Infant Interaction," in M. Lewis and M. Rosenblum, eds., *The Effect of the Infant on Its Caretaker: The Origins of Behavior* (New York: Wiley, 1974), 49–76.

[14] C. H. Zeanah and M. M. Gleason, "Annual Research Review: Attachment Disorders in Early Childhood—Clinical Presentation, Causes, Correlates and Treatment," *Journal of Child Psychology and Psychiatry* 56(3) (2015): 207–222; C. A. Nelson, E. A. Furtado, N. A. Fox, and C. H. Zeanah, "The Deprived Human Brain: Developmental Deficits Among Institutionalized Romanian Children—And Later Improvements—Strengthen the Case for Individualized Care," *American Scientist* 97(3) (2009).

[15] C. Robazza and M. C. Ruiz, "Emotional Self-Regulation in Sport and Performance," *Oxford Research Encyclopedia, Psychology* (2019).

[16] R. Feldman, "Mutual Influences Between Child Emotion Regulation and Parent-Child Reciprocity Support Development Across the First 10 Years of Life: Implications for Developmental Psychopathology," *Development and Psychopathology* 27 (4 Pt 1) (2015): 1007–1023.

[17] R. B. Lopez, B. T. Denny, and C. P. Fagundes, "Neural Mechanisms of Emotion Regulation and Their Role in Endocrine and Immune Functioning: A Review with Implications for Treatment of Affective Disorders," *Neuroscience Biobehavioral Reviews* 95 (2018): 508–514.

[18] C. C. Streeter, P. L. Gerbarg, T. H. Whitfield, L. Owen, J. Johnston, M. M. Silveri, M. Gensler, C. L. Faulkner, C. Mann, M. Wixed, A. M. Hernon, M. B. Nyer, E. R. P. Brown, and J. E. Jensen, "Treatment of Major Depressive Disorder with Iyengar Yoga and Coherent Breathing: A Randomized Controlled Dosing Study," *Journal of Alternative and Complementary Medicine* 23(3) (2017): 201–207.

[19] I. A. Strigo and A. D. Craig, "Interoception, Homeostatic Emotions and Sympathovagal Balance, *Philosophical Transactions of the Royal Society B*. 371 (2016): 20160010.

[20] S. W. Porges, "The Polyvagal Theory: Phylogenetic Substrates of a Social Nervous System," *International Journal of Psychophysiology* 42 (2001): 123–146.

[21] L. Wulsin, J. Herman, and J. F. Thayer, "Stress, Autonomic Imbalance, and the Prediction of Metabolic Risk: A Model and a Proposal for Research," *Neuroscience & Biobehavioral Reviews* 86 (2018): 12–20.

[22] S. W. Porges and S. A. Furman, "The Early Development of the Autonomic Nervous System Provides a Neural Platform for Social Behavior: A Polyvagal Perspective," *Infant and Child Development* 20(1) (2011): 106–118; L. S. Colzato, R. Sellaro, and C. Beste, "Darwin Revisited: The Vagus Nerve Is a Causal Element in Controlling Recognition of Other's Emotions," *Cortex* 92 (2017): 95–102; S. W. Porges, "Vagal Pathways: Portals to Compassion," in E. M. Seppala, E. Simon-Thomas, S. L. Brown, M. C. Worline, C. D. Cameron, and J. R. Doty, eds., *The Oxford Handbook of Compassion Science* (Oxford University Press, 2017), 189–202.

[23] Y. Jiang and M. L. Platt, "Oxytocin and Vasopressin Flatten Dominance Hierarchy and Enhance Behavioral Synchrony in Part via Anterior Cingulate Cortex," *Scientific Reports* 8 (2018): 8201.

[24] G. J. Norman, J. T. Cacioppo, J. S. Morris, W. B. Malarkey, G. G. Bernston, and A. C. DeVries, "Oxytocin Increases Autonomic Cardiac Control: Moderation by Loneliness," *Biological Psychiatry* 86 (2011): 174–180; J. R. Yee, W. M. Kenkel, J. L. Frijling, S. Dodhia, K. G. Onishi, S. Tovar, M. J. Saber, G. F. Lewis, W. Liu, S. W. Porges, and C. S. Carter, "Oxytocin Promotes Functional Coupling Between Paraventricular Nucleus and Both Sympathetic and Parasympathetic Cardioregulatory Nuclei," *Hormones and Behavior* (2016): 82–91.

[25] M. Q. Steinman, N. Duque-Wilckens, and B. C. Trainor, "Complementary Neural Circuits for Divergent Effects of Oxytocin: Social Approach versus Social Anxiety," *Biological Psychiatry* 85 (2019): 792–801.

[26] L. J. Martin, G. Hathaway, K. Isbester, S. Mirali, E. L. Acland, N. Niederstrasser, P. M. Slepian, Z. Trost, J. A. Bartz, R. M. Sapolsky, W. F. Sternberg, D. J. Levitin, and J. S. Mogil, "Reducing Social Stress Elicits Emotional Contagion of Pain in Mouse and Human Strangers," *Current Biology* 25 (2015): 326–332.

[27] R. M. Sapolsky, *Why Zebras Don't Get Ulcers* 3rd ed. (New York: Henry Holt, 2004).

[28] C. Robazza and M. C. Ruiz, "Emotional Self-Regulation in Sport and Performance," in *Oxford Research Encyclopedia, Psychology,* https://ricerca.unich.it/retrieve/handle/11564/694477.11/141173/OREP_Robazza2018.pdf (July 2018) 1–33.

[29] J. Kabat-Zinn, *Wherever You Go There You Are: Mindfulness Meditation in Everyday Life* (New York: Hyperion, 1994).

[30] E. L. Garland, A. W. Hanley, A. K. Baker, and M. O. Howard, "Biobehavioral Mechanisms of Mindfulness as a Treatment for Chronic Stress: An RDoC Perspective," *Chronic Stress (Thousand Oaks)* (2017): 1.

[31] B. K. Holzel, S. W. Lazar, T. Gard, Z. Schuman-Olivier, D. R. Vago, and U. Ott, "How Does Mindfulness Meditation Work? Proposing Mechanisms of Action from a Conceptual and Neural Perspective," *Perspectives on Psychological Science* 6(6) (2011): 537–559.

[32] S. Guendelman, S. Medeiros, and H. Rampes, "Mindfulness and Emotion Regulation: Insights from Neurobiological, Psychological, and Clinical Studies," *Frontiers in Psychology* 8 (2017): Article 220; Y.-Y. Tang, B. K. Holzel, and M. I. Posner, "The Neuroscience of Mindfulness Meditation," *Nature Reviews Neuroscience* 16 (2015): 213–225; A. Raffone, L. MarzettiL, C. Del Gratta, M. G. Perrucci, G. L. Romani, V. Pizzella, "Toward a Brain Theory of Meditation," *Progress in Brain Research* 244 (2019): 207–232.

[33] Raffone et al., "Toward a Brain Theory"; A. Lutz, H. A. Slagter, J. D. Dunne, and R. J. Davidson, "Attention Regulation and Monitoring in Meditation," *Trends in Cognitive Sciences* 12(4) (2008).

[34] D. Gaffney and D. S.-V. Sim, *The Essence of Taijiquan* (CreateSpace Independent Publishing Platform, 2009).

[35] J. F. Christensen, A. Gomila, S. B. Gaigg, N. Sivarajah, and B. Calvo-Merino, "Dance Expertise Modulates Behavioral and Psychophysiological Responses to Affective Body Movement," *Journal of Experimental Psychology: Human Perception and Performance* 42(8) (2016): 1139–1147.

[36] M. Nedeljkovic, B. Ausfeld-Hafter, K. Streitberger, R. Seiler, and P. H. Wirtz, "Taiji Practice Attenuates Psychobiological Stress Reactivity—A Randomized Controlled Trial in Healthy Subjects," *Psychoneuroendocrinology* 37 (2012): 1171–1180; M. C. Pascoe, D. R. Thompson, Z. M. Jenkins, and C. F. Ski, "Mindfulness Mediates the Physiological Markers of Stress: Systematic Review and Meta-Analysis," *Journal of Psychiatric Research* 95 (2017): 156–178.

[37] A. Wong, A. Figueroa, M. A. Sanchez-Gonzalez, W. M. Son, O. Chernykh, and S. Y. Park, "Effectiveness of Tai Chi on Cardiac Autonomic Function and Symptomatology in Women with Fibromyalgia: A Randomized Controlled Trial," *Journal of Aging and Physical Activity* 26 (2018): 214–221.

CHAPTER 3. LISTENING

[1] D. Isay, "Listening as an Act of Love," *On Being with Krista Tippett*, April 17, 2014, https://onbeing.org/programs/david-isay-listening-as-an-act-of-love.

[2] E. Hemingway, *Across the River and Into the Trees* (New York: Charles Scribner's Sons, 1950).

[3] S. J. Kayser, R. A. A. Ince, J. Gross, and C. Kayser, "Irregular Speech Rate Dissociates Auditory Cortical Entrainment, Evoked Responses, and Frontal Alpha," *The Journal of Neuroscience* 35(44) (2015): 14691–14701.

[4] M. de Guzman, G. Bird, M. J. Banissy, and C. Catmur, "Self-Other Control Processes in Social Cognition: From Imitation to Empathy, *Philosophical Transactions of the Royal Society B* 371 (2016): 20150079.

[5] S. R. Covey, *The 7 Habits of Highly Effective People: Powerful Lessons in Personal Change* (New York: Simon and Schuster, 2020).

[6] A. Brahm, "Jhanas—The Bliss of a Mind Released," *Buddhist Society of Western Australia Podcast*, 2018.

[7] N. Sebanz, H. Bekkering, and G. Knoblich, "Joint Action: Bodies and Minds Moving Together," *Trends in Cognitive Sciences* 10(2) (2006): 70–76; B. H. Repp and Y.-H. Su, "Sensorimotor Synchronization: A Review of Recent Research (2006–2012)," *Psychonomic Bulletin & Review* 20 (2013): 403–452; M. M. Louwerse, R. Dale, E. G. Bard, and P. Jeuniaux, "Behavior Matching in Multimodal Communication Is Synchronized," *Cognitive Science* 36 (2012): 1404–1426.

[8] C. Gallois and H. Giles, "Communication Accommodation Theory," *The International Encyclopedia of Language and Social Interaction* (Hoboken, NJ: John Wiley & Sons, 2015), 1–18.

[9] T. Vacharkulksemsuk and B. L. Fredrickson, "Strangers in Sync: Achieving Embodied Rapport Through Shared Movements," *Journal of Experimental Social Psychology* 48(1) (2012): 399–402; D. Lakens and M. Stel, "If They Move in Sync, They Must Feel in Sync: Movement Synchrony Leads to Attributions of Rapport and Entitativity." *Social Cognition* 29(2011): 1–14.

[10] S. Cacioppo, H. Zhou, G. Monteleone, E. A. Majka, K. A. Quinn, A. B. Ball, G. J. Norman, G. R. Semin, and J. T. Cacioppo, "You Are in Sync with Me: Neural Correlates of Interpersonal Synchrony with a Partner," *Neuroscience* 277 (2014): 842–858; T. L. Chartrand and J. A. Bargh, "The Chameleon Effect: The Perception-Behavior Link and Social Interaction," *Journal of Personality and Social Psychology* 76 (1999): 893–910; R. Hari, T. Himberg, L. Nummenmaa, M. Hämäläinen, and L. Parkkonen, "Synchrony of Brains and Bodies During Implicit Interpersonal Interaction," *Trends in Cognitive Sciences* 17(3) (2013): 105–106.

[11] N. Zeliadt, "Autism, Through the Eyes of a Computer," *Spectrum* (September 4, 2019).

[12] G. Volpe, A. D'Ausilio, L. Badino, A. Camurri, and L. Fadiga, "Measuring Social Interaction in Music Ensembles," *Philosophical Transactions of the Royal Society B* 371 (2016): 20150377.

[13] A. Chang, H. E. Kragness, S. R. Livingstone, D. J. Bosnyak, and L. J. Trainor, "Body Sway Reflects Joint Emotional Expression in Music Ensemble Performance," *Scientific Reports* 9 (2019), 205.

[14] P. Keller, "Musical Ensemble Performance: A Theoretical Framework and Empirical Findings on Interpersonal Coordination," in A. Williamson and W. Goebl, eds., *Proceedings of the International Symposium on Performance Science 2013* (Brussels, Belgium: European Association of Conservatories (AEC), 2013), 271–285.

[15] A. Shankar Instagram post, June 28, 2018.

[16] N. Shave, "The Berlin Philharmonic: With a Performance of Beethoven and Mahler Symphonies, the German Orchestra Proved Again Why It's One of the Best in the World," *Proms Diary*, Classical-music.com: The official website of *BBC Music Magazine* (September 6, 2010), www.classical-music.com/blog/proms-diary /berlin-philharmonic.

[17] S. Jones, "Can Newborn Infants Imitate?," *Wiley Interdisciplinary Reviews: Cognitive Science* 8 (2017): e1410; A. N. Meltzoff, "Elements of a Comprehensive Theory of Infant Imitation," *Behavioral and Brain Sciences* 40 (2017): e396.

[18] R. Feldman, R. Magori-Cohen, G. Galili, M. Singer, and Y. Louzoun, "Mother and Infant Coordinate Heart Rhythms Through Episodes of Interaction Synchrony," *Infant Behavior & Development* 34 (2011): 569–577; E. Z. Tronick, "Emotions and Emotional Communication in Infants," *American Psychologist* 44 (1989): 112–126.

[19] A. L. Woodward and S. A. Gerson, "Mirroring and the Development of Action Understanding," *Philosophical Transactions of the Royal Society of Biological Sciences* 369 (2014): 20130181; J. Decety and M. Meyer, "From Emotion Resonance to Empathic Understanding: A Social Developmental Neuroscience Account," *Development and Psychopathology* 20 (2008): 1053–1080.

[20] D. W. Winnicott, *Playing and Reality* (London: Routledge Classics, 1971).

[21] Feldman, "Mother and Infant"; M. Davis, K. West, J. Bilms, D. Morelen, and C. Suveg, "A Systematic Review of Parent-Child Synchrony: It Is More than Skin Deep," *Developmental Psychobiology* 60 (2018): 674–691.

[22] R. Brooks and A. N. Meltzoff, "Gaze Following: A Mechanism for Building Social Connections Between Infants and Adults," in M. Mikulincer and P. R. Shaver, eds., *Mechanisms of Social Connection: From Brain to Group* (Washington, DC: American Psychological Association, 2014), 167–183; P. Mundy, "A Review of Joint Attention and Social-Cognitive Brain Systems in Typical Development and Autism Spectrum Disorder," *European Journal of Neuroscience* 47 (2018): 497–514.

[23] H. Moll and A. N. Meltzoff, "Perspective-Taking and Its Foundation in Joint Attention," in N. Eilan, H. Lerman, and J. Roessler, eds., *Perception, Causation, and Objectivity. Issues in Philosophy and Psychology* (Oxford: Oxford University Press, 2011), 286–304.

[24] S. J. Kayser, R. A. A. Ince, J. Gross, and C. Kayser, "Irregular Speech Rate Dissociates Auditory Cortical Entrainment, Evoked Responses, and Frontal Alpha," *The Journal of Neuroscience* 35(44) (2015): 14691–14701; U. Hasson, A. A. Ghazanfar, B. Galantucci, S. Garrod, and C. Keysers, "Brain-to-Brain Coupling: A Mechanism for Creating and Sharing a Social World," *Trends in Cognitive Sciences* 16(2) (2012): 114–121.

[25] I. Tal, E. W. Large, E. Rabinovitch, Y. Wei, C. El Schroeder, D. Poeppel, and E. Zion Golumbic, "Neural Entrainment to the Beat: The 'Missing-Pulse' Phenomenon," *The Journal of Neuroscience* 37(26) (2017): 6331–6341.

[26] Hari et al., "Synchrony of Brains."

[27] G. Rizzolatti and C. Sinigaglia, "The Mirror Mechanism: A Basic Principle of Brain Function," *Nature Reviews Neuroscience* 17 (2016): 757–765; V. Gallese, "The Manifold Nature of Interpersonal Relations: The Quest for a Common Mechanism," *Philosophical Transactions of the Royal Society of London* 358 (2003): 517–528.

[28] Rizzolatti and Sinigaglia, "The Mirror Mechanism"; M. Sperduti, S. Guionnet, P. Fossati, and J. Nadel, "Mirror Neuron System and Mentalizing System Connect During Online Social Interaction," *Cognitive Processing* 15 (2014): 307–316.

[29] Decety and Meyer, "From Emotion Resonance"; F. Happe, J. L. Cook, and G. Bird, "The Structure of Social Cognition: In(ter)Dependence of Sociocognitive Processes," *Annual Review of Psychology* 68 (2017): 243–267; S. Anders, J. Heinzle, N. Weiskopf, T. Ethofer, and J.-D. Haynes, "Flow of Affective Information Between Communicating Brains," *NeuroImage* 54 (2011): 439–446.

[30] F. B. M. de Waal and S. D. Preston, "Mammalian Empathy: Behavioural Manifestations and Neural Basis," *Nature Reviews Neuroscience* 18 (2017): 498–509.

[31] W. Wei, S. Allsop, K. Tye, and D. Piomelli, "Endocannabinoid Signaling in the Control of Social Behavior," *Trends in Neurosciences* 40(7) (2017): 385–396; B. D. Heifets and R. C. Malenka, "MDMA as a Probe and Treatment for Social Behaviors," *Cell* 166 (2016): 269–272.

[32] Y. Jiang and M. L. Platt, "Oxytocin and Vasopressin Flatten Dominance Hierarchy and Enhance Behavioral Synchrony in Part via Anterior Cingulate Cortex," *Scientific Reports* 8 (2018): 8201; R. Hurlemann, A. Patin, O. A. Onur, M. X. Cohen, T. Baumgartner, S. Metzler, I. Dziobek, J. Gallinat, M. Wagner, W. Maier, and K. M. Kendrick, "Oxytocin Enhances Amygdala-Dependent, Socially Reinforced Learning and Emotional Empathy in Humans," *The Journal of Neuroscience* 30 (2010): 4999–5007; Y. Mu, C. Guo, and S. Han, "Oxytocin Enhances Inter-Brain Synchrony During Social Coordination in Male Adults," *Social Cognitive and Affective Neuroscience* 11 (2016): 1882–1893.

[33] V. Gallese, M. N. Eagle, and P. Migone, "Intentional Attunement: Mirror Neurons and the Neural Underpinnings of Interpersonal Relations," *Journal of the American Psychoanalytic Association* 55(1) (2007): 131–176.

[34] R. J. R. Blair, "Psychopathic Traits from an RDoC Perspective," *Current Opinion in Neurobiology* 30 (2015): 79–84; A. Raine, "The Neuromoral Theory of Antisocial, Violent, and Psychopathic Behavior," *Psychiatry Research* 277(2019): 64–69.

[35] De Guzman et al., "Self-Other Control Processes."

[36] R. Brewer, R. Cook, and G. Bird, "Alexithymia: A General Deficit of Interoception," *Royal Society Open Science* 3 (2016): 150664.

[37] T. N. Hanh, *The Way Out Is In: The Zen Calligraphy of Thich Nhat Hanh* (London: Thames & Hudson, 2001).

[38] Brewer, Cook, and Bird, "Alexithymia"; J. Murphy, C. Catmur, and G. Bird, "Alexithymia Is Associated with a Multidomain, Multidimensional Failure of Interoception: Evidence from Novel Tests," *Journal of Experimental Psychology: General* 147(3) (2018): 398–408.

[39] H. D. Critchley and S. N. Garfinkel, "Interoception and Emotion," *Current Opinion in Psychology* 17 (2017): 7–14.

[40] Brewer, Cook, and Bird, "Alexithymia."

[41] B. Bornemann and T. Singer, "Taking Time to Feel Our Body: Steady Increases in Heartbeat Perception Accuracy and Decreases in Alexithymia over 9 Months of Contemplative Mental Training," *Psychophysiology* 54 (2017): 469–482; C. J. Price and C. Hooven, "Interoceptive Awareness Skills for Emotion Regulation: Theory and Approach of Mindful Awareness in Body-Oriented Therapy (MABT)," *Frontiers in Psychology* 9 (2018): article 798.

[42] Y. N. Harari, "Yurval Harari, Author of *Sapiens*, on AI, Religion, and 6-Day Meditation Retreats," *The Ezra Klein Show* podcast (2017).

[43] J. F. Christensen, S. B. Gaigg, and B. Calvo-Merino, "I Can Feel My Heartbeat: Dancers Have Increased Interoceptive Accuracy," *Psychophysiology* 55 (2018): e13008.

[44] D. Grynberg and O. Pollatos, "Perceiving One's Body Shapes Empathy," *Physiology and Behavior* 140 (2015): 54–60; P. Shah, C. Catmur, and G. Bird, "From Heart to Mind: Linking Interoception, Emotion, and Theory of Mind," *Cortex* 93 (2017): 220–223.

CHAPTER 4. UNDERSTANDING

[1] J. Joyce, *Finnegans Wake* (Hertfordshire, UK: Wordsworth, 2012).

[2] A. A. Pallathra, M. E. Calkins, J. Parish-Morris, B. B. Maddox, L. S. Perez, J. Miller, R. C. Gur, D. S. Mandell, R. T. Schultz, E. S. Brodkin, "Defining Behavioral Components of Social Functioning in Adults with Autism Spectrum Disorder as Targets for Treatment," *Autism Research* 11 (2018): 488–502.

[3] A. E. Pinkham, D. L. Penn, M. F. Green, B. Buck, K. Healey, and P. D. Harvey, "The Social Cognition Psychometric Evaluation Study: Results of the Expert Survey and RAND Panel," *Schizophrenia Bulletin* 40(4) (2014): 813–823.

[4] R. C. Gur, R. E. Gur, "Social Cognition as an RDoC Domain," *American Journal of Medical Genetics Part B, Neuropsychiatric Genetics* 171B (2016): 132–141.

[5] C. Frith, "Social Cognition," *Philosophical Transactions of the Royal Society of London B: Biological Sciences* 363(1499) (2008): 2033–2039.

[6] Frith, "Social Cognition."

[7] D. Goleman, *Emotional Intelligence: Why It Can Matter More Than IQ* (New York: Bantam Books, 2005).

[8] J. LeDoux, "The Amygdala," *Current Biology* 17 (2007): R868–R874; R. P. Spunt and R. Adolphs, "The Neuroscience of Understanding the Emotions of Others," *Neuroscience Letters* 693 (2019): 44–48.

[9] L. S. Colzato, R. Sellaro, and C. Beste, "Darwin Revisited: The Vagus Nerve Is a Causal Element in Controlling Recognition of Other's Emotions," *Cortex* 92 (2017): 95–102.

[10] G. Chronaki, J. A. Hadwin, M. Garner, P. Maurage, and E. J. S. Sonuga-Barke, "The Development of Emotion Recognition from Facial Expressions and Non-Linguistic Vocalizations During Childhood," *British Journal of Developmental Psychology* 33 (2014): 218–236.

[11] M. E. Barrera and D. Maurer, "Recognition of Mother's Photographed Face by the Three-Month-Old Infant," *Child Development* 52 (1981): 714–716.

[12] H. Oster, "'Recognition' of Emotional Expression in Infancy?," in M. E. Lamb and L.R. Sherrod, eds., *Infant Social Cognition: Empirical and Theoretical Considerations* (Hillsdale, NJ: Lawrence Erlbaum, 1981).

[13] Chronaki et al., "Development of Emotion Recognition."

[14] Chronaki et al., "Development of Emotion Recognition"; C. L. Gohm and G. L. Clore, "Four Latent Traits of Emotional Experience and Their Involvement in Well-Being, Coping, and Attributional Style," *Cognition & Emotion* 16 (2002): 495–518.

[15] J. M. Salguero, R. Palomera, and P. Fernández-Berrocal, "Perceived Emotional Intelligence as Predictor of Psychological Adjustment in Adolescents: A 1-Year Prospective Study," *European Journal of Psychology of Education* 27 (2012): 21–34.

[16] Frith, "Social Cognition."

[17] F. Happe, J. L. Cook, and G. Bird, "The Structure of Social Cognition: In-(ter)Dependence of Sociocognitive Processes," *Annual Review of Psychology* 68 (2017): 243–267; C. Schwenck, J. Mergenthaler, K. Keller, J. Zech, S. Salehi, R. Taurines, M. Romanos, M. Schecklmann, W. Schneider, A. Warnke, and C. M. Freitag, "Empathy in Children with Autism and Conduct Disorder: Group-Specific

Profiles and Developmental Aspects," *Journal of Child Psychology and Psychiatry* 53(6) (2011): 651–659.

[18] A. Smith, "The Empathy Imbalance Hypothesis of Autism: A Theoretical Approach to Cognitive and Emotional Empathy in Autistic Development," *The Psychological Record* 59 (2008): 273–294.

[19] J. Decety and M. Meyer, "From Emotion Resonance to Empathic Understanding: A Social Developmental Neuroscience Account," *Development and Psychopathology* 20 (2008): 1053–1080; C. Trevarthan and P. Hubley, "Secondary Intersubjectivity: Confidence, Confiders and Acts of Meaning in the First Year," in A. Lock, ed., *Action, Gesture and Symbol* (New York: Academic Press, 1978); D. Stern, "Chapter 6: The Sense of the Subjective Self: I. Overview," *The Interpersonal World of the Infant* (New York: Basic Books, 2000).

[20] L. A. Winczewski, J. D. Bowen, and N. L. Collins, "Is Empathic Accuracy Enough to Facilitate Responsive Behavior in Dyadic Interaction? Distinguishing Ability from Motivation," *Psychological Science* 27(3) (2016): 394–404.

[21] J. Stietz, E. Jauk, S. Krach, and P. Kanske, "Dissociating Empathy from Perspective-Taking: Evidence from Intra- and Inter-Individual Differences Research," *Frontiers in Psychiatry* 10 (2019): 126.

[22] F. B. M. de Waal and S. D. Preston, "Mammalian Empathy: Behavioural Manifestations and Neural Basis," *Nature Reviews Neuroscience* 18 (2017): 498–509.

[23] Happe, "Structure of Social Cognition"; de Waal and Preston, "Mammalian Empathy."

[24] V. Gallese, M. N. Eagle, and P. Migone, "Intentional Attunement: Mirror Neurons and the Neural Underpinnings of Interpersonal Relations," *Journal of the American Psychoanalytic Association* 55(1) (2007): 131–176.

[25] Happe, Cook, and Bird, "Structure of Social Cognition."

[26] T. F. Heatherton and T. Wheatley, "Social Neuroscience," in R. F. Baumeister and E. J. Finkel, eds., *Advanced Social Psychology: The State of the Science* 1st ed. (New York: Oxford University Press, 2010).

[27] C. C. Peterson, H. M. Wellman, and V. Slaughter, "The Mind Behind the Message: Advancing Theory-of-Mind Scales for Typically Developing Children, and Those with Deafness, Autism, or Asperger Syndrome," *Child Development* 83(2) (2012): 469–485; H. M. Wellman and D. Liu, "Scaling Theory of Mind Tasks," *Child Development* 75 (2004): 759–763.

[28] S. Baron-Cohen, A. M. Leslie, and U. Frith, "Does the Autistic Child Have a 'Theory of Mind'"? *Cognition* 21 (1985): 37–46.

[29] Dogen, "The Point of Zazen," in K. Tanahashi, ed., *Moon in a Dewdrop: Writings of Zen Master Dogen* (New York: North Point Press, 1985), 218–219.

[30] N. Rasheta, "Breaking the Chain of Reactivity," *Secular Buddhism Podcast* (2018), https://secularbuddhism.com.

[31] P. Ekman, "How to Deal with Emotions," *Paul Ekman Group Blog* (2019), https://www.paulekman.com/blog/how-to-deal-with-emotions.

[32] M. de Guzman, G. Bird, M. J. Banissy, and C. Catmur, "Self-Other Control Processes in Social Cognition: From Imitation to Empathy," *Philosophical Transaction of the Royal Society B* 371 (2016): 20150079.

[33] E. Hong, "This Korean Parenting Style Is the Best-Kept Secret to Raising Smart and Successful Kids," *CNBC Make It* (November 15, 2019), https://www.cnbc.com/2019/11/15/how-korean-parents-raise-smart-successful-kids-best-kept-secret.htm; "What is Nun-Chi?," *Catch the Wave / K-Talk with Hyunwoo* (2012), www.youtube.com/watch?v=RomYCZ-IHxc.

[34] J. Y. Yim, "Nunchi, a Korean Value of Social Intelligence, and Its Relationships to Emotional Intelligence, Psychological Functioning, and Interpersonal Problems," A dissertation presented to the faculty of the Rosemead School of Psychology, Biola University, ProQuest Number 10269476.

[35] J. Gottman and J. Declaire, *Raising an Emotionally Intelligent Child: The Heart of Parenting* (New York: Simon & Schuster, 1998).

[36] P. Fonagy, M. Steele, H. Steele, G. Moran, and A. Higgit, "The Capacity for Understanding Mental States: The Reflective Self in Parent and Child and Its Significance for Security of Attachment," *Infant Mental Health Journal* 12(3) (1991): 201–218; J. F. Grienenberger, K. Kelly, and A. Slade, "Maternal Reflective Functioning, Mother-Infant Affective Communication, and Infant Attachment: Exploring the Link Between Mental States and Observed Caregiving Behavior in the Intergenerational Transmission of Attachment," *Attachment and Human Development* 7(3) (2005): 299–311; D. S. Schechter and E. Willheim, "Disturbances of Attachment and Parental Psychopathology in Early Childhood," *Child and Adolescent Psychiatric Clinics of North America* 18(3) (2009): 665–686.

[37] F. Larkin, J. Oostenbroek, Y. Lee, E. Hayward, and E. Meins, "Proof of Concept of a Smartphone App to Support Delivery of an Intervention to Facilitate Mothers' Mind-Mindedness," *PLoS ONE* 14 (2019): e0220948.

[38] N. L. Collins and B. C. Feeney, "Working Models of Attachment Shape Perceptions of Social Support: Evidence from Experimental and Observational Studies," *Journal of Personality and Social Psychology* 87(3) (2004): 363–383.

[39] B. E. Kok and T. Singer, "Effects of Contemplative Dyads on Engagement and Perceived Social Connectedness over 9 Months of Mental Training: A Randomized Clinical Trial," *JAMA Psychiatry* 74(2) (2017): 126–134; A. A. Pallathra, J. Day-Watkins, M. E. Calkins, B. Maddox, J. Miller, J. Parish-Morris, J. Herrington, S. Kangovi, R. Tomlinson, T. Creed, C. Kerns, W. Bilker, F. Handy, J. E. Connell, G. S. Dichter, D. S. Mandell, R. T. Schultz, and E. S. Brodkin, "TUNE In, a Novel Cognitive Behavioral Treatment Program to Improve Social Functioning in Adults with ASD: Pilot Study Results," International Meeting for Autism Research (IMFAR) (2017); C. Campos, S. Santos, E. Gagen, S. Machado, S. Rocha,

M. M. Kurtz, and N. B. Rocha, "Neuroplastic Changes Following Social Cognition Training in Schizophrenia: A Systematic Review," *Neuropsychology Review* 26 (2016): 310–328.

⁴⁰ J.-M. Yang, *Tai Chi Theory and Martial Power: Advanced Yang Style Tai Chi Chuan* (Wolfeboro, NH: YMAA Publication Center, 2015).

⁴¹ J. F. Christensen, A. Gomila, S. B. Gaigg, N. Sivarajah, and B. Calvo-Merino, "Dance Expertise Modulates Behavioral and Psychophysiological Responses to Affective Body Movement," *Journal of Experimental Psychology: Human Perception and Performance* 42(8) (2016): 1139–1147; J. F. Christensen, S. B. Gaigg, B. Calvo-Merino, "I Can Feel My Heartbeat: Dancers Have Increased Interoceptive Accuracy," *Psychophysiology* 55 (2018): e13008; T. Shafir, "Using Movement to Regulate Emotion: Neurophysiological Findings and Their Application to Psychotherapy, *Frontiers in Psychology* 7 (2016): article 1451.

CHAPTER 5. MUTUAL RESPONSIVENESS

¹ N. Fischer, *Everyday Zen* podcast, "Sustaining Compassion—Metta Institute September 2016" (September 30, 2016), http://everydayzen.org/teachings/2013/sustaining-compassion-metta-institute-september-2016.

² D. McKesson, S. Sinyangwe, J. Elzie, and B. Packnett, *Police use of force policy analysis* (2016), Campaign Zero. https://static1.squarespace.com/static/56996151cbced68b170389f4/t/57e1b5cc2994ca4ac1d97700/1474409936835/Police+Use+of+Force+Report.pdf

³ J. Vinoski, "Chobani's Hamdi Ulukaya Throws Down the Gauntlet with His 'Anti-CEO Playbook,'" *Forbes* (June 29, 2019), www.forbes.com/sites/jimvinoski/2019/06/29/chobanis-hamdi-ulukaya-throws-down-the-gauntlet-with-his-anti-ceo-playbook/#27c7bedb44d2.

⁴ P. Jackson, *Sacred Hoops: Spiritual Lessons of a Hardwood Warrior* (New York: Hyperion, 1995).

⁵ Jackson, *Sacred Hoops.*

⁶ M. Gladwell, *Talking to Strangers: What We Should Know About the People We Don't Know* (New York: Little, Brown, 2019).

⁷ *Chen Village,* Empty Mind Films, produced and directed by Jon Braeley (2009).

⁸ C. Catmur and C. Heyes, "Is It What You Do, or When You Do It? The Roles of Contingency and Similarity in Pro-Social Effects of Imitation," *Cognitive Science* 37 (2013): 1541–1552.

⁹ U. Hasson, A. A. Ghazanfar, B. Galantucci, S. Garrod, and C. Keysers, "Brain-to-Brain Coupling: A Mechanism for Creating and Sharing a Social World," *Trends in Cognitive Sciences* 16(2) (2012): 114–121.

¹⁰ E. Redcay, D. Dodell-Feder, M. J. Pearrow, P. L. Mavros, M. Kleiner, J. D. E. Gabrieli, and R. Saxe, "Live Face-to-Face Interaction During fMRI: A New Tool for Social Cognitive Neuroscience," *NeuroImage* 50 (2010): 1639–1647.

[11] D. J. Baker, "2020 Vision," *Opera News* Vol 81 (March 2017), https://yan nicknezetseguin.com/en/pressroom/interviews/detail/2020-vision.

[12] M. Griffin, "Chamber Music as Prep for Med School," *Juilliard Journal* (December 2018–January 2019): 18.

[13] T. Hellstrom, editor, *The Dalai Lama Book of Quotes: A Collection of Speeches, Quotations, Essays and Advice from His Holiness* (Hobart, NY: Hatherleigh Press, 2016).

[14] E. A. Butler and A. K. Randall, "Emotional Coregulation in Close Relationships," *Emotion Review* 5(2) (2013): 202–210.

[15] A. Schultz, "The Space Between Us Is a Creative Possibility," *On Being* blog (October 16, 2017), https://onbeing.org/blog/ali-schultz-the-space-between -us-is-a-creative-possibility.

[16] Schultz, "Space Between Us."

[17] S. Braten and C. Trevarthen, "Prologue: From Infant Intersubjectivity and Participant Movements to Simulation and Conversation in Cultural Common Sense," in S. Braten, ed., *On Being Moved: From Mirror Neurons to Empathy* (Amsterdam, the Netherlands: John Benjamins, 2007), 21–34.

[18] B. Beebe, J. Jaffe, S. Markese, K. Buck, H. Chen, P. Cohen, L. Bahrick, H. Andrews, and S. Feldstein, "The Origins of 12-Month Attachment: A Microanalysis of 4-Month Mother-Infant Interaction," *Attachment & Human Development* 12 (2010): 3–141.

[19] D. Stern, "Chapter 7: The Sense of a Subjective Self: II. Affect Attunement," *The Interpersonal World of the Infant* (New York: Basic Books, 2000).

[20] A. Gianino and E. Z. Tronick, "The Mutual Regulation Model: The Infant's Self and Interaction Regulation and Coping and Defensive Capacities," in T. M. Field, P. M. McCabe, and N. Schneiderman, eds., *Stress and Coping Across Development* (Hillsdale, NJ: Lawrence Erlbaum, 1988), 47–68.

[21] Gianino and Tronick, "Mutual Regulation Model."

[22] D. S.-V. Sim and D. Gaffney, *Chen Taijiquan: Masters and Methods* (Blaine, WA: D&D Publications, 2018).

[23] D. Stern, *The First Relationship: Infant and Mother* (Cambridge, MA: Harvard University Press, 1977).

[24] W. Yu-hsiang, "Expositions of Insights Into the Practice of the Thirteen Postures," in B. P. J. Lo, M. Inn, R. Amacker, and S. Foe, eds., *The Essence of T'ai Chi Ch'uan: The Literary Tradition* (Berkeley, CA: Blue Snake Books, 1979), 41–60.

[25] M. Przyrembel, J. Smallwood, M. Pauen, and T. Singer, "Illuminating the Dark Matter of Social Neuroscience: Considering the Problem of Social Interaction from Philosophical, Psychological, and Neuroscientific Perspectives," *Frontiers in Human Neuroscience* 6 (2012): Article 190.

[26] Redcay et al., "Live Face-to-Face Interaction During fMRI"; G. F. Donnay, S. K. Rankin, M. Lopez-Gonzalez, P. Jiradejvong, and C. J. Limb, "Neural Substrates

of Interactive Musical Improvisation: An fMRI Study of 'Trading Fours' In Jazz," *PLoS One* 9(2) (2014): e88665.

CHAPTER 6. ARTIFICIAL ATTUNEMENT

[1] B. Smith, "Facial Recognition Technology: The Need for Public Regulation and Corporate Responsibility," *Microsoft / Microsoft On the Issues* blog July 13, 2018, https://blogs.microsoft.com/on-the-issues/2018/07/13/facial-recognition-technology-the-need-for-public-regulation-and-corporate-responsibility.

[2] A. M. Turing, "Computing Machinery and Intelligence," *Mind* 49 (1950): 433–460.

[3] "Go Master Quits Because AI 'Cannot Be Defeated,' " *BBC News* (November 27, 2019), www.bbc.com/news/technology-50573071.

[4] H. Kissinger, "How the Enlightenment Ends: Philosophically, Intellectually— In Every Way—Human Society Is Unprepared for the Rise of Artificial Intelligence," *The Atlantic* (June 2018), www.theatlantic.com/magazine/archive/2018/06/henry -kissinger-ai-could-mean-the-end-of-human-history/559124; M. Klein, "Google's AlphaZero Destroys Stockfish in 100-Game Match," Chess.com (updated December 6, 2017), www.chess.com/news/view/google-s-alphazero-destroys-stockfish-in -100-game-match.

[5] C. Metz, "DeepMind Can Now Beat Us at Multiplayer Games, Too," *The New York Times* (May 30, 2019), www.nytimes.com/2019/05/30/science/deep-mind -artificial-intelligence.html?smid=nytcore-ios-share; M. Jaderberg, W. M. Czarnecki, I. Dunning, L. Marris, G. Lever, A. G. Castaneda, C. Beattie, N. C. Rabinowitz, A. S. Morcos, A. Ruderman, N. Sonnerat, T. Green, L. Deason, J. Z. Leibo, D. Silver, D. Hassabis, K. Kavukcuoglu, and T. Graepel, "Human-Level Performance in 3D Multiplayer Games with Population-Based Reinforcement Learning," *Science* 364(6443) (2019): 859–865.

[6] N. Brown and T. Sandholm, "Superhuman AI for Multiplayer Poker," *Science* 365(6456) (2019): 885–890.

[7] C. Metz, "With $1 Billion from Microsoft, an A.I. Lab Wants to Mimic the Brain," *The New York Times* (July 22, 2019), www.nytimes.com/2019/07/22/technology/open-ai-microsoft.html?smid=nytcore-ios-share.

[8] Microsoft Azure, Emotion Recognition software, https://azure.microsoft .com/en-us/services/cognitive-services/face/?v=18.05.

[9] R. Yuste and S. Goering, "Four Ethical Priorities for Neurotechnologies and AI," *Nature* 551 (November 9, 2017): 159–163.

[10] P. Mozur, "Inside China's Dystopian Dreams: A.I., Shame and Lots of Cameras," *The New York Times* (July 8, 2018), www.nytimes.com/2018/07/08 /business/china-surveillance-technology.html.

[11] C. Metz, "Facial Recognition Tech Is Growing Stronger, Thanks to Your Face," *The New York Times* (July 13, 2019), www.nytimes.com/2019/07/13 /technology/databases-faces-facial-recognition-technology.html.

[12] K. Conger "Amazon Workers Demand Jeff Bezos Cancel Face Recognition Contracts with Law Enforcement), *Gizmodo* (June 21, 2018), https://gizmodo.com /amazon-workers-demand-jeff-bezos-cancel-face-recognitio-1827037509.

[13] K. Hill, "The Secretive Company That Might End Privacy as We Know It, *The New York Times* (January 18, 2020), www.nytimes.com/2020/01/18/technol ogy/clearview-privacy-facial-recognition.html?smid=nytcore-ios-share.

[14] N. Nittle, "Amazon's Facial Analysis Tech Often Mistakes Dark-Skinned Women For Men, Study Shows" (January 28, 2019), https://www.vox.com/the -goods/2019/1/28/18201204/amazon-facial-recognition-dark-skinned-women -mit-study.

[15] Smith, "Facial Recognition Technology."

[16] A. McCarthy, "How 'Smart' Email Could Change the Way We Talk," *BBC* (August 12, 2019), www.bbc.com/future/article/20190812-how-ai-powered-pred ictive-text-affects-your-brain.

[17] R. Johnson, "How and Why Companies Will Engineer Your Emotions," *IEEE Spectrum* (October 3, 2019), https://spectrum.ieee.org/the-human-os/bio medical/devices/how-and-why-companies-will-engineer-your-emotions; P. Gunde-cha, "IBM Watson Just Got More Accurate at Detecting Emotions," *IBM Cloud* (October 6, 2016), www.ibm.com/cloud/blog/announcements/watson-has-more -accurate-emotion-detection.

[18] A. Regalado, "Facebook Is Funding Brain Experiments to Create a De-vice That Reads Your Mind, *MIT Technology Review* (July 30, 2019), https:// www.technologyreview.com/2019/07/30/133986/facebook-is-funding-brain -experiments-to-create-a-device-that-reads-your-mind; D. A. Moses, M. K. Leonard, J. G. Makin, and E. F. Chang, "Real-Time Decoding of Question-and-Answer Speech Dialogue Using Human Cortical Activity," *Nature Communications* 10 (2019): 3096.

[19] Regalado, "Facebook Is Funding."

[20] L. Fridman, "Rosalind Picard: Affective Computing, Emotion, Privacy, and Health," *Artificial Intelligence* podcast (2019), www.youtube.com/watch?v =kq0VO1FqE6I; R. W. Picard, *Affective Computing* (Cambridge, MA: The MIT Press, 2000).

[21] R. W. Picard, MIT Media Lab, Affective Computing Lab web page, www .media.mit.edu/groups/affective-computing/overview.

[22] R. el Kaliouby, "This App Knows How You Feel—From the Look on Your Face," TED talk, TedWomen (May 2015), www.ted.com/talks/rana_el_kaliouby _this_app_knows_how_you_feel_from_the_look_on_your_face?language=en.

[23] International Workshop on Social & Emotion AI for Industry SEAIxI (Sep-tember 3, 2019), http://seaixi.neurodatalab.com.

[24] G. Colvin and Editors of *Fortune*, "25 Ideas That Will Shape the 2020s," *Fortune* (December 19, 2019).

[25] B. Gholipour, "New AI Tech Can Mimic Any Voice: Emerging Technologies in Speech Generation Raise Ethics and Security Concerns," *Scientific American*

(May 2, 2017), www.scientificamerican.com/article/new-ai-tech-can-mimic-any -voice.

26 Picard, MIT Media Lab.

27 S. Fussell, "Alexa Wants to Know How You're Feeling Today," *The Atlantic* (October 12, 2018), www.theatlantic.com/technology/archive/2018/10/alexa -emotion-detection-ai-surveillance/572884.

28 T. Essig, "The War for the Future of Psychotherapy," *Forbes* (December 27, 2019), www.forbes.com/sites/toddessig/2019/12/27/the-war-for-the-future-of-psy chotherapy/#7947d3dc759b; T. Essig, S. Turkle, and G. I. Russell, "Sleepwalking Towards Artificial Intimacy: How Psychotherapy Is Failing the Future," *Forbes* (June 7, 2018), www.forbes.com/sites/toddessig/2018/06/07/sleepwalking-towards-arti ficial-intimacy-how-psychotherapy-is-failing-the-future/#5d83b61c4037.

29 Picard, MIT Media Lab.

30 Hiroshi Ishiguro Laboratories, www.geminoid.jp/en/index.html.

31 Loving AI, https://lovingai.org.

32 A. M. Rosenthal-von der Putten, N. C. Kramer, S. Maderwald, M. Brand, and F. Grabenhorst, "Neural Mechanisms for Accepting and Rejecting Artificial Social Partners in the Uncanny Valley," *The Journal of Neuroscience* 39(33) (2019): 6555–6570.

33 Picard, MIT Media Lab.

34 "NIH Greatly Expands Investment in BRAIN Initiative, *National Institutes of Health News Releases* (November 2, 2018), www.nih.gov/news-events/news -releases/nih-greatly-expands-investment-brain-initiative.

35 R. Yuste and S. Goering, "Four Ethical Priorities for Neurotechnologies and AI," *Nature* 551 (November 9, 2017): 159–163.

36 Yuste and Goering, "Four Ethical Priorities."

37 A. Vance, "Elon Musk's Neuralink Says It's Ready for Brain Surgery," *Bloomberg Businessweek* (July 16, 2019), www.bloomberg.com/news/articles /2019-07-17/elon-musk-s-neuralink-says-it-s-ready-to-begin-brain-surgery?srnd =premium.

38 Yuste and Goering, "Four Ethical Priorities."

39 Yuste and Goering, "Four Ethical Priorities."

40 H. T. Greely, C. Grady, K. M. Ramos, W. Chiong, J. Eberwine, N. A. Farahany, L. S. M. Johnson, B. T. Hyman, S. E. Hyman, K. S. Rommelfanger, and E. E. Serrano, "Neuroethics Guiding Principles for the NIH BRAIN Initiative," *Journal of Neuroscience* 38(50) 2018: 10586–10588; K. M. Ramos, C. Grady, H. T. Greely, W. Chiong, J. Eberwine, N. A. Farahany, L. S. M. Johnson, B. T. Hyman, S. E. Hyman, K. S. Rommelfanger, E. E. Serrano, J. D. Churchill, J. A. Gordon, and W. J. Koroshetz, "The NIH BRAIN Initiative: Integrating Neuroethics and Neuroscience," *Neuron* 101(3) (2019): 394–398.

[41] T. Requarth, "This Is Your Brain. This Is Your Brain as a Weapon.," *Foreign Policy* (September 14, 2015), https://foreignpolicy.com/2015/09/14/this-is-your-brain-this-is-your-brain-as-a-weapon-darpa-dual-use-neuroscience.

[42] S. Zuboff, *The Age of Surveillance Capitalism: The Fight for a Human Future at the New Frontier of Power* (New York: Public Affairs, 2019).

[43] Fridman, "Rosalind Picard."

[44] G. Colvin and Editors of *Fortune*, "25 Ideas."

[45] Yuste and Goering, "Four Ethical Priorities."

[46] A. Lavazza, "Freedom of Thought and Mental Integrity: The Moral Requirements for Any Neural Prosthesis," *Frontiers in Neuroscience* 12 (February 2018): Article 82.

[47] A. Clark, "We Are Merging with Robots. That's a Good Thing.," *The New York Times* (August 13, 2018).

[48] S. Turkle, "There Will Never Be an Age of Artificial Intimacy," *The New York Times* (August 11, 2018).

[49] Turkle, "There Will Never Be an Age."

CHAPTER 7. WHERE DO WE GO FROM HERE?

[1] T. S. Eliot, "Little Gidding," *Four Quartets* (New York: Houghton Mifflin Harcourt, 1943).

[2] T. S. Eliot, "Burnt Norton," *Four Quartets* (New York: Houghton Mifflin Harcourt, 1943).

[3] J. Spiegel, S. K. Severino, and N. K. Morrison, "The Role of Attachment Functions in Psychotherapy," *The Journal of Psychotherapy Practice and Research* 9(1) (2000): 25–32; N. Way, A. Ali, C. Gilligan, and P. Noguera, eds., *The Crisis of Connection: Roots, Consequences, and Solutions* (New York: New York University Press, 2018).

[4] Dalai Lama, Twitter, (May 1, 2020).

[5] M. Angelou, Convocation address, Cornell University (May 24, 2008).

INDEX

EDWARD S. ("TED") BRODKIN, MD is associate professor of psychiatry with tenure at the Perelman School of Medicine at the University of Pennsylvania. He is the founder and director of the Adult Autism Spectrum Program at Penn Medicine. He has been honored as one of America's Top Doctors by Castle Connolly Medical for the past thirteen years. He received his AB magna cum laude from Harvard College and his MD from Harvard Medical School. He completed his residency in psychiatry and a fellowship in neuroscience research at the Yale University School of Medicine. His research focuses on social neuroscience and the autism spectrum in adults.

ASHLEY A. PALLATHRA, MA is a clinical researcher and therapist. She completed her bachelor's degree with distinction in neuroscience from the University of Pennsylvania. She has a master's degree in psychology and is currently pursuing her PhD in clinical psychology at The Catholic University of America. She is the author of numerous published research articles and a book chapter in the fields of resilience-based interventions, social-emotional functioning in youth, autism research, and social neuroscience.

Learn more about the authors at MissingEachOther.com.